Leadership For an Age of Higher Consciousness

Administration from a Metaphysical Perspective

SWAMI KRISHNAPADA

HARI-NAMA PRESS

Other works by Swami Krishnapada:

The Beggar
Meditations and Prayers on the Supreme Lord

Spiritual Warrior
Uncovering Spiritual Truths in Psychic Phenomena

Leadership
For an Age of
Higher Consciousness

ISBN: 1885414-02-1
Library of Congress Card Number: 95-81994

Cover design by Protean Gilbril, Logo Loco,
and Media Graphics Associated
Text design by Adam Kenney

Printed in the United States of America

Contents

I offer this book to my mentor,
His Divine Grace A.C. Bhaktivedanta Swami Prabhupada,
celebrating the centennial of his appearance.
Srila Prabhupada wrote over one hundred books,
had them translated into all the major languages of the world
and circled the globe numerous times, frequently explaining how the
real problems of the international community were due to a crisis in
leadership.

I also offer this book in memory of seven faithful staff members
who were assassinated on September 21, 1990 in Monrovia, Liberia
as they performed humanitarian service during the Liberian Civil War.

Acknowledgments

J would like to express my deepest gratitude to Marilyn Wood, who greatly assisted me in preparing this book for publication, and to Dina Sugg, who performed invaluable editorial work on the manuscript. I am also grateful to Karla Billups, a managing editor at the Smithsonian Institution, who gave me many helpful suggestions, and her assistant Roslind Brown. In addition, I sincerely thank Portia Pinkney, who assisted in the initial cursory editing, and Leigh Clements and Norma Clements, who made an important contribution to the chapter on conflict resolution. I extend my warmest appreciation to JoAnn Noble, Olivia Cook, and Lisa Ratcliff for their careful, thorough research; to Gilda Dixon, Eric Akridge and Martin Mensah for their assistance in verifying certain passages; and to Adam Kenney, who so painstakingly did the typesetting and book design. I wish to acknowledge Denise Houston, who transcribed many of the earlier tapes; Paulette Bowles and Jacqueline Rearden, who offered expert legal advice; and Joy Mensah, Courtney Parks and Joslin Morgan, who helped bring everything together for publishing. I also extend great thanks and love to two Godsisters, Marsha Bryant and Hladini Dasi, and to several of my students–Patricia Jackson, Michelle Stanfill, Laurice Stewart, and Robyn Terry–who assisted in typing and proofreading. It is only by the mercy of all of you that this book has been made possible.

Foreword

$\mathcal{A}$ few steps down the hallway from the Pentagon office in Washington, D.C. where I once worked is what I consider to be one of the most important rooms in the building. It is a small, quiet place designated by the Secretary of Defense as a haven for people who want to simply "be" in silence for brief periods throughout the day. In a sense, it is an important center for training U.S. Defense Department personnel to be spiritually conscious leaders. Each day, scores of civilians and men and women in military uniform go there to center themselves, meditating and preparing themselves to "be all they can be."

In a similar way, *Leadership for an Age of Higher Consciousness* provides guidance for anyone who wants to grow and progress toward becoming a spiritually conscious leader. Spiritually conscious leaders are capable of accomplishing much more than most people. The secret for success lies in their commitment to a deep, powerful process, the process of transformation. They know what it takes to remove barriers to their own thinking and actions without hurting others. They are also skillful in empowering others to move beyond their own limitations. The commitment to an ongoing process of personal growth and change reaches higher and higher to ever greater fulfillment and happiness, and ultimately to ecstasy in the service of God and humanity.

But how does anyone become spiritually conscious? An essential first step is to learn to be centered. This requires regular practice in directing the conscious awareness to the center of one's being. The center of being is ultimately God. One useful vehicle that can be used to reach the center is the process of thought.

The spiritually conscious leader is an unusually adept thinker who has awakened to new possibilities. Such a leader has an understanding of the importance of thought and knows how to use it to cause internal personal change, to empower others to change and, yes, even to produce changes in the surrounding environment.

Our consciousness is perhaps the most valuable asset we have to shape our destiny, give direction to our life, and generate the results that will fulfill our highest aspirations. Our mind is a builder. It can be used to build up or to tear down, and to bring peace or war, health or disease, chaos or harmony. Thoughts are in a sense raw materials, building blocks that we use to build the foundations to make our dreams come true. When we are one with God in consciousness, our dreams are part of the Master's plan for a better world.

It boggles the mind to understand that our seemingly insignificant thoughts and feelings can and do affect our own circumstances. Without even knowing it, we are often caught in a condition of mental blindness. Freedom from this condition comes with the realization that thoughts and feelings affect our well-being, our physical bodies, our health, and the welfare of the communities in which we live. Sometimes it is just as mind-boggling for people in positions of authority to understand how they could possibly benefit from surrounding themselves with staff members and other spiritually conscious people who know the most basic principles of transformation. Such people can be powerful supports to leaders who seek to center themselves in higher consciousness.

Since the infinite can not be contained within the finite limits of human thought, only a shift in consciousness can take us beyond the rational domain. It is by entering into the realm of "transcendental" thought that we finally enter the sanctuary of self-realization. Living our lives from this holy of holies, we become ever more attentive to the inspiration of the Spirit of God moving within us, aware of the awesome power of the presence of God, aware also that God moves the physical world by thought. Awakening to this realization is like discovering a buried treasure.

There is indeed a treasure that lies buried within every human being. The educational process for leaders presented in Swami Krishnapada's book starts with this basic premise and seeks systematically to raise it to the surface of conscious awareness. This book offers numerous strategies and helpful guidelines for being a successful leader. Here the reader will find prescriptions for becoming more personally successful, and for guaranteeing a more auspicious future for humankind.

The starting point, then, in learning to be a successful leader, or for that matter in learning to be anything, is first to spend some time each day practicing "being."

"Be all you can be" is more than just a catchy slogan used by the U.S. Army to inspire people to reach for excellence. It implies a regular, disciplined practice of "being." As you turn the pages of this book you will read more about what it takes to be a spiritually conscious leader, one who definitely helps to create a viable future for humanity.

-Edward Winchester
Staff Member (Retired)
Office of the Secretary of Defense
U.S. Pentagon

Introduction

$\mathcal{A}$re you a leader? Is the role of leadership a part of your life? Is it a part of your dreams? If the answer to these questions is "yes," this book has been written for you.

Leaders emerge in every life situation to guide others along a particular path of change and toward a final destination point. Effective leadership is not easy. History has shown that the responsibilities and hazards of leadership are as great as its rewards.

Leadership for an Age of Higher Consciousness was specifically written to help people who choose a role of leadership at this time in history, when mature leadership is most needed. However, anyone can apply the principles discussed in this book, because they encourage each person, family, organization and nation to live in a way that upholds the sanctity and stability of all life on this planet. After all, as a global family we share the collective responsibility for the earth and her well-being.

Humankind is currently taking final examinations. Will we pass or fail? The great negativity manifesting in the world today indicates that we need to rethink our present course. We may ask ourselves: Who are we? Where are we going? And whom or what are we following? Obviously, if we are not happy with our present path, we must change direction.

If you, dear leader, feel a responsibility to make a difference, then please read on. We live in an age of global awareness. Global communication networks span the earth, making information from all over the world available to the ordinary person. In addition, we are in the process of discovering the intimate, universal connections between humanity and all other life forms on this planet and in the universe. With this understanding, the meaning of leadership must expand to include an all-encompassing vision of the whole.

❖❖❖❖❖❖❖❖❖

Leadership for an Age of Higher Consciousness starts with a list of ten essential technologies for empowered management. These technologies, which are useful in a wide variety of situations, can provide valuable points for reflection as you read this book.

The book is divided into three sections. *Part I: Raising Consciousness* lays a general foundation, describing principles of higher consciousness and their relevance to leadership. *Part II: Developing Skills* discusses specific qualities and skills that can be invaluable to leaders in today's world. Finally, *Part III: Taking Action* suggests policy areas in which leaders can take action to alleviate suffering, protect the planet as a whole, and help people lead more productive lives as they grow closer to God.

At the end of each chapter is a list of "Highlights" containing important passages from the text for review. A "Mindsets" section follows, providing meditations, reflections and exercises to help you apply the principles just discussed. Thus, *Leadership for an Age of Higher Consciousness* can serve effectively as a handbook or study guide for daily practice. You might want to read through the entire book first, and then from time to time review specific reflections and exercises in order to evaluate your progress and to gain insight into various areas.

Within the pages of this book, you are being instructed by a loving, unseen coalition. We want you to know that we are your friends who sit with you as you address the United Nations, Congress, Parliament, the Board of Directors, the community, and even your family. We appreciate your great strength and would lend you ours to complement your own. We extend strong encouragement to help you resolve what may seem to you to be impossible problems. We are aware of your good intentions and alert you to the dangers of temptation and deviation. We care for you, we love you and we offer you simple advice for your own well-being. Finally, we are your devoted counselors who urge you to consider the primary importance of one essential ingredient for your progress, success and survival. That ingredient is love.

Overall, *Leadership for an Age of Higher Consciousness* seeks to demonstrate that you as an individual, and especially as a leader, can make a significant difference in creating a viable future for humankind. This book is lovingly offered to you and to all day-to-day managers and leaders, who represent the heartbeat of the world.

–Swami Krishnapada

Ten Essential Technologies for Empowered Management

The metaphysical technologies listed here are simple yet profound tools that you may want to incorporate into your management style. To reap the greatest benefit from these principles, you can include a meditation on these ten essential technologies for empowered management in your daily regimen. Also, as you read each chapter, you can reflect on these ten essential technologies as a way to enhance your understanding. In addition, the first exercise in the "Mindsets" section at the end of each chapter refers back to these technologies as a reminder.

1. What of It? What For? So What?

This meditation is designed to help us realize that many illusions can influence or enslave us. Leo Tolstoy once wrote about a transition in his life when he began to question everything, despite his great success. Following Tolstoy's example, in this meditation envision yourself as possessing great material abundance such as exorbitant wealth, worldwide fame, vast knowledge, or dazzling beauty. Consider each of these areas in turn, and others if you wish, realizing that it cannot be the ultimate goal of life. Ask yourself the questions, "What of it?" "What for?" "So what?"

2. Not This Body

This reflection helps us realize that we are more than just the physical body. Therefore, we should not overreact or be overly attached to material stimuli. The exercise consists of saying attentively: "I have a body–but I am not this body"; "I have a mind–but I am not this mind"; "I have a job–but I am not this job"; or "I have a house–but I am not this house." Insert any problem into this meditation to help yourself release any attachment to temporary phenomena.

3. The Other Person's Point of View

This practice helps us become more sensitive to another person's perception of the situation, particularly during interpersonal conflicts. Choose a conflict that has been troubling you. Write a letter to yourself as if you were the opposing party trying to convince yourself of the opposite point of view. Employ this letter-writing technique for any conflict.

4. Seeing God Everywhere

This contemplation helps us give more of ourselves to others and receive more love from people in general. Practice seeing everyone as an energy of God.

5. Everything Has a Purpose

There are no coincidences. Because the universe is controlling higher agencies, each encounter has come to us for a particular reason. We are subject to a spiritual law similar to a law of physics: every action produces a corresponding reaction. Therefore, we can try to discover the lesson in every occurrence. The exercise is to turn negative events into positive ones and positive events into even better ones. If we learn from all events, then everything that happens can become a positive occurrence because we have become wiser.

6. Accountability

The knowledge that we are monitored by the Supreme and His angelic hosts will encourage us to live more righteously in order to be rewarded rather than punished. The exercise is to imagine that we are always being monitored by God's all-seeing eyes.

7. Call for Love

This practice helps us appreciate the many forms in which a call for help can come and reminds us to always examine ourselves to see how we have helped others. The exercise is to see all interactions as either a giving of love or a call for love.[1]

8. Love in Action

This technology helps us shower everyone and everything in our environment with vibrant love. The exercise is to see ourselves as embodiments of love in action.

9. Near Death

Imagine that your doctor has just informed you that you have a serious case of cancer or AIDS, and that you are going to die in three months. If this were your fate, how would you live each of your last days differently? This reflection helps remind us that we can never be certain how much longer we will remain in this material body. Therefore, we must not procrastinate or have a weak list of priorities. Important things–essential things–must be done now!

10. A Second Chance

We must live each day in readiness to depart if our appointment with death arrives. The exercise is to imagine that you are dying right now, and can see what you are leaving behind and the effect that your death will have on others. What are your last thoughts? What are your regrets? What things have you left undone? You should do these things today.

Part I
Raising Consciousness

As a spiritually conscious leader, you stand in the middle between heaven and earth....In this intermediary position between the spiritual and material worlds, you accept realizations and blessings from the higher dimensions and pass them on to others, at the same time accepting service from your people and rechanneling the results back to the higher realms. In this way, you become an empowered being and a highly effective leader.

1

The Phenomenon of Love

For all human beings, love is a constant preoccupation—a never-ending central theme. Indeed, the ultimate motivation behind interactions among people is often the desire to experience some form of love. The fact that love is so important has major implications for leadership. In particular, the degree to which leaders acknowledge the value of love in their own lives and in the lives of others can determine the success of failure of their undertakings.

Far from being irrelevant or impractical, the intention to express love is fundamental for effective leadership. This is so because in the final analysis, a leader's motivation is communicated to others in countless subtle ways. Leaders whose actions are perceived as self-serving often create disharmony, resentment, and disloyalty. On the other hand, those who base their behavior upon a genuine empathy and concern for others can gain loyalty and support that make the attainment of even difficult goals possible.

Love Versus Lust

Actually, although love occupies such an important place in everyone's thoughts, it is often misunderstood. Love is more than an agreeable feeling or a pleasurable sensation derived from the contact of physical bodies.[2] Frequently, what people call love is either sentimentality or the pursuit of carnal pleasures. This means that for many, what passes for love may actually be nothing other than self-centeredness or lust.

Although human beings are constantly subjected to the pull between these two currents of love and self-gratifying lust, each individual has the freedom to choose between them. The success of any leadership endeavor depends entirely upon how a leader surrenders to the current of unselfish love.

This does not necessarily mean that events proceed gently and smoothly. Activities that manifest mature love are performed in a spirit of truthfulness and knowledge. Although truth can be painful, sometimes the desire to attain a higher good will require leaders to face unpleasant realities and act forcefully. Indeed, love is merely sentimental unless it is based on honesty. Leaders need a high level of knowledge, skill and discernment to express their love appropriately according to the circumstances.

Therefore, although love is sometimes soft, it can also be harsh. At times, a leader may demand difficult sacrifices from others for their own well-being. In either case—whether one's actions appear gentle or brutal—the important factor is always the motivation. A leader whose behavior is inspired by selflessness acts just like a mother who sometimes shows love by punishing her children in order to help them develop properly. Leaders must deliberately choose to maintain a level of consciousness that gives priority to what is best for others regardless of outward appearances.

As a day-to-day meditation, leaders should keep in mind that some of the greatest personalities on earth have been toppled by lust, and many great empires have fallen because their leaders had insufficient control of their carnal senses. Their self-centeredness caused them to succumb to the temptation of exploiting people rather than serving them. In contrast,

leaders today should always remember that leadership is first and foremost an expression of selfless love.

The Divine Nature of Human Beings

One way to develop mature love is to see each person as a part of God,
dear to Him and under His watchful eye. Indeed, a form of God exists in
the heart of every living being and it is possible to reach a level of self-realization that enables you to experience this aspect of God within yourself
and others. Even without such a level of understanding, if you remember
that there is an aspect of God within each person, and that God personally cares for every human being, you can then honor and respect anyone.

The human race is actually spiritual or divine in nature, just like God,
although humans are limited in power while God is unlimited. In other
words, people are the same as God in quality, but different in quantity.
This spiritual aspect is the soul, also called the atma or higher self, which
is the eternal aspect of each individual in which the God-essence abides.
Any thoughts, words, or actions that are directed toward a person's higher self will be far more beneficial and lasting than those that are not.

Actually, each human being is composed of three aspects: the physical
body; the subtle, or etheric body; the astral, or metaphysical body; and
the soul, which is the higher self, the directing God-essence principle.
Since time immemorial, cultures have known that human beings have a
higher essence, so that even when a person meets death, which is simply
the termination of the physical body, the soul goes on. For example, in
ancient Greece, Socrates stated before his execution that although his
body might be destroyed, his soul would continue. Those who appreciate
these different aspects of human experience will not limit themselves
merely to material or psychological understanding, realizing instead the
ultimate importance of the spiritual dimension to which the soul belongs.

You cannot love others if you do not sufficiently love yourself, because
it is impossible to give or share what you do not possess. Often, leadership is difficult because of personality problems or because of
attachments to nationalism, racism, sexism or tribalism. To address such
issues successfully, you can learn to radiate a strong love that comes first

from loving yourself by acknowledging the divinity that resides within you. Love of self does not mean love of the body or of the mind, but of the soul. You do not need to focus on making the body comfortable, stimulating the senses, or pleasing the mind through seeking adulation or financial gain from others. Instead, you can realize that the body, senses and mind are just temporary coverings being used by the soul.

Loving activities are in harmony with the universe. Those who are out of harmony with the universe draw negativity to themselves, whereas those who are in harmony act in constructive and fruitful ways, protected from harm.

Love As a Protective Force

In the course of your duties as a leader, you constantly face pitfalls and dangers. To ensure your success, you can learn to protect yourself against the onslaughts of negative thoughts and actions. Not only is it important for you to think and act in a dynamic, positive way, but you should also be conscious of potentially harmful people and situations in order to avoid their invasive negative energy. Your most powerful shield of protection in these circumstances will come from a strong sense of love and compassion.

Throughout the world at every moment, a struggle is taking place between higher and lower forces. One arena for this struggle can be found in the human mind. People are unwitting receptacles for the thoughts and desires of others, whose energy they often internalize. These thoughts are like electrical currents: a person may not see them, but can feel them and experience their effects.

Such thoughts can affect the quality of your leadership. Because you are in a prominent position, many people will focus their thoughts and energies on you. Some will use you as a scapegoat for their own disturbances, and others will regard you with envy. Still others will simply want to test you. Without sufficient love from within, you will lack the necessary armor to protect yourself from such relentless attacks of negative energy. However, strong inner love will allow you to deflect such harmful energy, or even to transmute it so that it has no destructive effects. Therefore, always remember to put up a shield of love for your protection, keeping in mind that in order to love others, you need to love yourself first.

Love as Relationship

At the same time, you should remember that you are called to love your neighbor as well. All of the major religions of the world emphasize this point:

- *Brahmanism:* Do not do unto others that which would cause you pain if done to yourself.
- *Buddhism:* Hurt not others in ways that you yourself would possibly find hurtful.
- *Christianity:* Do unto others as you would have them do unto you.
- *Islam:* Not one of you is a true believer until he desires for his brother that which he desires for himself.
- *Judaism:* Whatever is hateful to you, do not to your fellow man.
- *Zoroastrianism:* That nature alone is good which refrains from doing unto another anything that is not good for itself.
- *Taoism:* Always regard your neighbor's gain as your gain, and your neighbor's loss as your own loss.

Although the mandate to love one's neighbor as oneself is universal, few people are able to follow it. In fact, it is rare to find anyone who even makes the attempt. However, as a leader you can rise above common moral limitations. Indeed, merely to love your neighbor as yourself is not sufficient. Actually, you can learn to love those for whom you are responsible even more than you love yourself.

In your leadership role, see yourself as the caretaker of those around you rather than the proprietor, acting as you would if entrusted with a precious treasure. This approach encourages you to perceive the God-essence in every person and see yourself as an emissary of the Divine in charge of nurturing the God-essence in others. Serving God in this way is one of the highest possible manifestations of love.

To return to the analogy of mother and child mentioned earlier, the love between them is very deep because it is pure. The mother does more than just love her child as she loves herself. She sees that child as helpless, knowing that were it not for her, the child might go hungry and even die. In other words, the mother thinks: "My child's life depends on me." Therefore, she brings a tremendous degree of care, respect and attention to the relationship. Just as the mother goes more than half way to assure the well-being of the child, you can extend a similar level of love in order to succeed in your mission as a leader. You are a care-taker whose responsibility is to promote the peaceful, harmonious well-being of everyone. In the material world, this level of love is known as maternal or paternal love, and it is one of the highest degrees of love that human beings can express toward God.

Often, people think of God as a Being to hold in awe, fear, and rever-ence. However, this is an elementary perception. There are many other types of possible relationships with God. A person whose love grows deeper recognizes the potential for loving God not only as the Creator but also as a friend or as a child. Although the relationship of friend-ship is very profound because two persons of equal status love each other, the maternal or paternal bond is even greater, because the care-taker acts for the benefit of the other who is more helpless.

In this high level of God-consciousness, a person can actually serve God by playing the role of father or mother, with God as the child. Such love is so deep that one makes the utmost effort to offer protection and care with great attention and dedication. If you seek to invoke the high-est blessings for yourself as a leader, you should learn to appreciate this level of love.

Empowerment as a Representative of God

The function of a leader is to act as a representative of God. In ancient times, some kings had the ability to be a channel for the spiritual realms. As a result, people had great love and reverence for these leaders, whom they rightfully saw as God's representatives on earth.[3]

Your role as a leader calls upon you to open your mind and heart to the possibility of being God's representative in order to become a spiritual channel. A key factor in becoming such a channel is selflessness. When those for whom you are responsible offer you devotion, dedication, and service, your role is to accept their offerings and use them for the well-being of others on a larger scale, remembering constantly to give the fruits of these accomplishments to God.

In other words, a leader can hold no claim to being the doer or the controller. By releasing such claims and attachments, you offer all your actions and possessions to the Supreme, who ultimately will reciprocate by giving even more back to you. As a spiritually conscious leader, you stand in the middle between heaven and earth. Whenever you increase your love, you become more available as an instrument capable of connecting those under your direction with the higher realms. In this intermediary position between the spiritual and material worlds, you accept realizations and blessings from the higher dimensions and pass them on to others, at the same time accepting service from your people and rechanneling the results back to the higher realms. In this way, you become an empowered being and a highly effective leader.

Empowerment is everyone's right. How is it that some people can perform the most amazing, apparently superhuman feats, as if they possessed some special blessing? It is not that the blessing is unique; it is simply that these individuals make themselves available for it. Anyone who does not become a great servant offering love and compassion to all becomes a great hindrance. Therefore, whenever you act, remember that your activities are being monitored from a higher level. As you allow your compassion to grow, you will want to serve more and more.

Willingness to Serve Others

Your willingness to serve brings empowerment and makes your service highly effective. Empowerment from the divine realm comes when you gladly offer all your expertise to help others. Then these divine transcendental connections will reciprocate by awarding you increased responsibilities. There is nothing unusual in this; a similar process occurs with those working in your office, administering your government, or helping you manage your corporation. As you notice those who provide excellent service by giving fully of themselves, you arrange to give them more complicated, difficult duties, promoting and rewarding them because you appreciate their dedication.

Correspondingly, as you use what you have wisely, committing your leadership to the service of others, you will surely benefit. However, the converse is also true. If you do not properly use the resources and position that you have, then even if you temporarily live "well," eventually you will be brought down by those you lead as they realize that you do not have their best interests at heart.

This is an important fact to understand, because inevitably some of your plans may prove ineffective or disappointing to others. Such mistakes become unbearable when people sense that the leader does not have their best interests at heart. However, if people understand that their leader has been attempting to help them in good faith, then such mistakes will not cause serious difficulties and may even increase their loyalty.

One last caution about the simple yet complicated phenomenon of love: you should constantly try to anticipate beforehand and review afterwards how each of your policies increases the love of those whom you lead. Indeed, one of your main functions as a leader is to express love and help others develop their experience of love. If you fail to understand the basic points in this chapter, you stand to lose position, prestige, cooperative association, your good health, your sanity, or perhaps even your life.

Learn to love everyone dearly and allow this love for others to radiate through you. As you let the energy of love vibrate around you, all who align themselves with you will contract this contagious, sublime state, and spread it enthusiastically to others.

Highlights

1. Frequently, what people call love is either sentimentality or the pursuit of carnal pleasures. This means that for many, what passes for love may actually be nothing other than self-centeredness or lust. Although human beings are constantly subjected to the pull between these two currents of love and self-gratifying lust, each individual has the freedom to choose between them.

2. Activities that manifest mature love are performed in a spirit of truthfulness and knowledge. Although truth can be painful, sometimes the desire to attain a higher good will require leaders to face unpleasant realities and speak forcefully. Indeed, love is merely sentimental unless it is based on honesty.

3. The human race is actually spiritual or divine in nature, just like God, although humans are limited in power while God is unlimited. In other words, people are the same as God in quality, but different in quantity.

4. Any thoughts, words, or actions that are directed toward a person's higher self will be far more beneficial and lasting than those that are not.

5. You cannot love others if you do not sufficiently love yourself, because it is impossible to give or share what you do not possess. Often, leadership is difficult because of personality problems or because of attachments to nationalism, racism, sexism or tribalism. To address such issues successfully, you can learn to radiate a strong love that comes first from loving yourself by acknowledging the divinity that resides within you.

6. In your leadership role, see yourself as the caretaker of those around you rather than the proprietor, acting as you would if entrusted with a precious treasure. This approach encourages

you to perceive the God-essence in every person and see yourself as an emissary of the Divine in charge of nurturing the God-essence in others. Serving God in this way is one of the highest possible manifestations of love.

7.   The function of a leader is to act as a representative of God. Your role as a leader calls upon you to open your mind and heart to this possibility of being God's representative, in order to become a spiritual channel. A key factor in becoming such a channel is self-lessness.

8.   As a spiritually conscious leader, you stand in the middle between heaven and earth. Whenever you increase your love, you become more available as an instrument capable of connecting those under your direction with the higher realms. In this intermediary position between the spiritual and material worlds, you accept realizations and blessings from the higher dimensions and pass them on to others, at the same time accepting service from your people and rechanneling the results back to the higher realms. In this way, you become an empowered being and a highly effective leader.

9.   Learn to love everyone dearly and allow this love for others to radiate through you. As you let the energy of love vibrate around you, all who align themselves with you will contract this conta-gious, sublime state, and spread it enthusiastically to others.

10.   Constantly try to anticipate beforehand and review afterwards how each of your policies increases the love of those whom you lead. Indeed, one of your main functions as a leader is to express love and help others develop their experience of love.

Mindsets

1. Refer to the ten essential technologies at the beginning of this book, working with numbers 7 and 8 in particular. Practice being the embodiment of love in all your interactions, and consider the actions of others as either expressions of love or calls for help.

2. Lust and love are two eternal forces, two currents of energy constantly swirling around us. Visualize yourself in the center of an ocean. If you swim to the left you will be carried by a current of lust; if you swim to the right you will enter a current of love. Make your choice. Appreciate how this is analogous to your daily experiences, in which each moment you can choose which current to follow.

3. Although love may be painful when it is experienced in the form of truthfulness and knowledge, remind yourself that you will not deviate from acting with integrity, even if you are misunderstood. This reminder will serve to strengthen your resolve and reinforce the positive energy around you.

4. Imagine scenarios of yourself succumbing to lust, which, you may recall, is misdirected love. Let these images serve as a strong deterrent to prevent yourself from ever behaving in such a manner.

5. As an exercise in loving yourself as a soul, speak to your soul each day. Honor it and thank it because it is a part of God. Remember that if you do not love yourself with proper self-esteem, you cannot love others deeply.

6. You are a warrior. Visualize yourself attacking negative energy with your weapon of knowledge, your shield of compassion and your armor of love. This is especially useful when you are negotiating with those of a different mindset, when you are being

attacked by opponents, or when you feel that your efforts are misunderstood or unappreciated.

7. Keep taking inventory of your thoughts, words, and actions to see if you love your neighbor as yourself or even more than yourself. Be honest. To the extent that your thoughts are misaligned, focus on bringing them into accord with the power of love.

8. Always see yourself as a caretaker of God's property, treating everything in your care with greater respect than you would if it were your own.

9. In ancient times a leader was considered both a representative of God and an administrator whose beneficial actions increased people's love. See yourself as such a leader, and practice constantly to maintain this level of consciousness. In your role as a representative of God, accept everything that is offered, passing everything on to God without claiming proprietorship. Give God the credit for your achievements and express gratitude for your willingness to share your abundance with those in your charge.

10. See yourself as a vehicle for contagious love that spreads to others wherever you go. Everyone around you then becomes a carrier, radiating the same selfless love to still others.

2

The Source of True Happiness

As a leader, you are in a better position than most to understand that life in this world can feel unnatural and unfulfilling. Many of those you are responsible for dream of attaining the goals that have become commonplace to you. They might be amazed to know that, despite the fact that you have accomplished so much, there may still be a sense of unfulfillment in your life–a void within that leaves you with a lingering sense of disappointment and sadness.

Filling the Void Within

Many people believe that happiness is attainable simply by acquiring sufficient money, a fulfilling job, the right life partner, or a home in a desirable neighborhood. Often they become frustrated in pursuit of such goals, experiencing dissatisfaction with themselves, their work, their environment, and the people around them. They tolerate their dissatisfaction, however, thinking, "If only I can achieve this next goal, I will be happy."

For many years, I have acted as a consultant to various world leaders and to international celebrities. During the time I was an advisor and friend to the then-world heavyweight champion, Muhammad Ali, we had a very interesting experience at his home in California. Early one morning, Ali looked at me and said, "Just look at my life! Here it is not even 7:30 a.m., and my house is already full of people who have come mainly to harass me and demand something—just to put pressure on me."

He explained that many years ago, as an extremely poor boy growing up in the South, he lived a simple life but dreamed about possessing great wealth and living in a palatial home. Making a sweeping gesture, Ali said, "Look at my house now. See how wonderful it is! Practically all of my furniture and decor have come from different parts of the world, and it is all very high quality. I have so many servants and guards taking care of my house that I cannot even keep up with them. And, you know, there was a time when I used to think how nice it would be to have a wonderful car. Now I have this gorgeous Rolls Royce. It has all kinds of fancy equipment, and when I pass through streets in my car, people say 'there goes Muhammad Ali!' "

Reminiscing about the past, he remembered wanting to become famous so he could have many women at his beck and call. Ali continued: "Now I can get on the phone and call women from anyplace in the world just for fun. But you know, my friend, instead I remember how wonderful that simple life was—when I didn't have all of these things. Even though all my dreams have become a reality for me, I am miserable because now I am a slave to all of this. If only I could have some peace of mind and a simple life again!"

This kind of thinking is not uncommon among those who have attained fame, wealth, prestige, or power. It is evidenced by the many who constantly visit their psychiatrists because their lives are in such chaos. Extreme examples of this situation are the cases of people who, although they have "everything," become so depressed about life that they commit suicide. Their "everything" is still not enough.

This says something interesting: that while the poor are constantly struggling to acquire some of the possessions that the rich have, the rich are also struggling to get even more or to hold on to what they already own. The wealthy are often bored by the routine that accompanies fame or material success and long for a simpler life. To them, life has become a treadmill upon which they trudge ever onward and upward in search of that elusive "happiness."

Trying to Escape the Pain

Suffering is intense throughout the world. In the West, it is so widespread that people increasingly seek diverting and anesthetizing activities to keep their bodies active and their minds distracted from the emptiness that pervades their lives.

Everyone is trying to escape the pain of being away from our home close to God. Some who do not escape kill themselves. Others resort to seeking altered states of consciousness through artificial means such as drugs. Both legal and illegal drugs have become the "painkillers" of the world, numbing the profound psychological depression experienced by many. The drug culture is gradually spreading around the entire globe because it is an artificial way of stimulating consciousness, anesthetizing the pain, or filling the void.[4]

In reality, a longing for ecstasies, higher pleasures, higher realizations, and higher experiences is natural. There is so much more to life than the experiences gained via the physical senses, and it is normal to want to go deeper, beyond the normal routine of day-to-day existence. What is unnatural is the artificial way in which this is occurring today.

Unless people go deeper and establish a higher connection with the universe, both outside themselves and inside themselves, they will always lament their situation and remain unfulfilled. Their plight is similar to that of a person from a royal family who now must temporarily undergo life as a peasant. Even as the peasant occupies himself with his present existence, he feels dissatisfied because of his previous experiences as royalty. Or, to use the analogy of a fish, if one takes a fish out of the sea and puts it in a beautiful house on shore and makes many pleasant arrangements for it, it will not be satisfied because its natural habitat is the water. It can even die if it is not returned to its natural environment, the one that is suited to the essence of its being.

Material Satisfaction Is Not Enough

Every healthy, sane human being has desires that are highly "antimaterial," meaning desires that are beyond this body and beyond this physical world. For example, hopes for bliss, health, and immortality are antimaterial desires. But where have these desires come from, if in the present environment there is always anxiety, frustration, disease, and death? The fact is that these desires are inherent within everyone. The sufferings caused by anxiety, death and disease are unnatural, opposed to humanity's constitutional position, and part of a world to which human beings do not truly belong.

Regardless of their material accomplishments, human beings may still feel incomplete because this material arena is simply not their real home. They are dissatisfied because they have known something much higher, something sublime and divine. Their souls are aware of this fact, so that at the deepest soul level they "remember" the ecstasy of having once been in the presence of God.

They remember the love that infused and engulfed them, and they recall the peace that surpasses understanding that was available to them in that realm of existence. And because they remember these states, such divine ecstasy becomes the standard by which they judge their experiences in the material world and always find them lacking. *Nothing* in the material world–neither money, position, drugs, nor sex–can produce the ecstasy and satisfaction that humans have already experienced when they were back where they belong–at home with God.

Your Real Home

The ancients knew that humanity was not really of this world, and consistently conveyed that message in their writings. Aristotle and Plato, for instance, spoke of much more satisfying and pleasant worlds than this one, and believed that humans originally came from these higher dimensions. The Bible emphasizes the "kingdom of God," and other great scriptures such as the Koran, the Torah, and the Vedas refer to other realms, using such terms as "Paradise" or the "spiritual world."

In the Bible, the following passage in the first Epistle of John[5] serves as an illustration: "Love not the world, neither the things that are in the world." In addition, I Corinthians[6] says: "There is a natural body, and there is a spiritual body....Flesh and blood cannot inherit the kingdom of God." II Corinthians[7] contains this reminder: "Therefore we are always confident, knowing that whilst we are at home in the body, we are absent from the Lord." And II Corinthians[8] ends the chapter with this statement: "We look not at the things which are seen, but at the things which are not seen, for the things which are seen are temporal; but the things which are not seen are eternal."

These passages from the Bible give scriptural confirmation of two important points: that there are greater realities than those which human beings can see; and that this world is not home. The great teachers such as Jesus, Buddha, Mohammed, and many others, constantly point toward a more elevated existence in the higher realms. Their basic message teaches that, although people are in a "fallen state," it is possible for them to attain perfection–that is, to go back to their original home in the spiritual kingdom by acquiring self-realization. It is no accident that all bona fide prophets repeat this same theme. Motivated by great love and infinite compassion, these prophets appear among human beings to guide them back to the higher realms of reality.[9]

From these great teachers one learns that human beings are all visitors to these material universes, which are schools or reformatories–places to which people must return again and again until they learn, step by step, lifetime by lifetime, how to be perfect in order to regain the association of God. The ease and speed with which they learn these lessons determine their progress through subsequent lifetimes on their journey *home*.

Humans are now away from their real home because they have misused their free will and tried to act independently of God. While still in their spirit states, some beings develop an envious curiosity about what it would be like to be God rather than to *serve* God. The Lord accommodates them by sentencing them temporarily to a situation in which they can explore these desires. They are sent to an arena–the material universe–where they can try to role-play God as much as they like.

How to Get Back Home

However, the soul will always feel incomplete until it is again in its natural habitat of the spiritual kingdom. Eventually, those who become sufficiently disillusioned and frustrated with the material world yearn to go beyond the day-to-day patterns of the God-playing syndrome and satisfy their insatiable hunger for higher experiences and more elevated vibratory connections.

The process of reincarnation is the key to returning *home*. According to the Vedic scriptures, reincarnation occurs because a human being is actually a soul who uses the physical and subtle bodies covering it in each lifetime to experience, learn and grow to perfection.[10] The soul's goal is to attain the perfection of the self-realized state–the point at which the karmic energy of many lifetimes is completely balanced or canceled–and not be required to take material birth again.

The fact that people are in material bodies at all is a sign of the incompleteness of their knowledge and their lack of perfection. However, once they recognize who they really are and release their attachment to the material world, following the laws of God instead, they can free themselves from the cycle of reincarnation and go back to the kingdom of God to exist in their original spiritual form.

The True Identity of Human Beings

A grasp of the process of reincarnation depends upon an understanding of what a person really is, both in and out of the physical body. A person is not the body, but comes and goes many times, in many bodies and throughout many lives. Each individual is a spirit soul who has always existed, and always will, as a son or daughter of the Mother-Father God. Humans are beings who, by their own free choice, are now forced to work their way back *home*.

The discussion of humanity's divine nature in the previous chapter made the distinction between a person's true God-nature and the material manifestation in the form of a physical body. Although the individual soul is a user of the physical body, the actual life force within it is the "I," the soul.

One need only look at the example of an infant to see that a person is more than the physical body. Although the baby's body is constantly changing, becoming over the course of a few years a toddler, a child, a teenager, and then an adult, the life force within the growing body is the same. Parents recognize, for example, that this is still "baby" Mary, even though the body that was once so small is now that of a maturing young woman.

The body is always experiencing change. Science reports that the cells in the physical body are constantly dying, so that every seven years the body is totally renewed.[11] That is, someone 21 years old has technically "reincarnated" three times since birth, because a new body has been regenerated three times during those years. Each minute a person possesses a different body. If people think they are the body, which body are they? The body that was five years old, the body that was 20 years old, or the body that will someday be 70? Each of these bodies is different, being actually nothing more than the outer garment of the individual soul.

The body is not the essence of a human being. It is discarded for another body when it can no longer function sufficiently to allow the life force within it to continue work on the physical plane. A verse in the *Bhagavad-gita* clearly describes this situation:

> As the embodied soul continuously passes, in this body, from boyhood to youth to old age, the soul similarly passes into another body at death. A sober person is not bewildered by such a change.[12]

The soul experiences neither birth nor death. Instead, it is unborn, eternal, and primeval, and is not slain when the body is slain. This verse explains that as the body progresses from infancy through childhood, youth and old age, the soul within is constant. Similarly, at the time of death, the body makes a visible change, a more abrupt transition, but the soul lives on. Death is nothing more than the transformation of the flesh back to its original elements while the soul that occupied the body–its life force–continues.

When the soul leaves the physical body, biological life comes to an end because the body has lost its soul. If something can depart, it must also have entered at some point in the past. The question then becomes: Where does the soul come from and where does it go? Reincarnation, or the science of transmigration, provides an answer.

Balancing Energies Throughout Lifetimes

As noted earlier, reincarnation is the process of taking repeated births in order for the soul to become karma-free, which occurs when all of the energies one has generated in the material universes via thoughts, words and deeds become balanced. This reincarnational process is known as the science of the transmigration of the soul. The purpose of balancing one's energies is to evolve into a perfect, nonenvious being who can rejoin God.

The means for balancing these energies is karma: the just conse-quences of all of one's thoughts, words and deeds. It is the universal law stating that every action produces a corresponding reaction. Karma is the process of equal recompense described by Jesus when he said, "Judge not, that ye be not judged. For with what judgement ye judge, ye shall be judged; and with what measure ye mete, it shall be measured to you again."[13] In other words, people get back whatever they give out.

The Scales of Justice

Representations of the "scales of justice," an ancient symbol, still appear today on many American judicial buildings. The image is well-known: a blindfolded woman holds a set of scales high in her right hand. The woman represents wisdom, and her names are many.[14] The blindfold signifies that Justice is impartial, and the scales symbolize the law of karma. To the extent that these scales are out of balance, some measure is still required to re-establish equilibrium.

What most people fail to notice, however, is that in the woman's left hand is the hilt of a sword. The sword is a sign of protection for the good, and a chastisement to the wicked, representing the consequences of "negative" karma that few are eager to confront. The law demands that she use this sword as necessary to help move the scales into balance. She weighs and strikes without taking into account the conventional differences that human beings have established among themselves.

The law of karma is always in operation.[15] Whether one believes in it or not, it is the law by which human beings are bound to or freed from the material world.[16] Each person's respect for this law can greatly decrease the number of life cycles required to bring the energies of cause and effect into balance.

People cannot be free from repeated material existences until they have balanced their individual scales. The key to balancing these scales is to understand that they are a weighing mechanism for the energies generated via thought, word, and deed throughout *all* of one's lifetimes. Just as the subtle body carries the aggregate of all of each individual's lessons and experiences, karma is cumulative as well.

The Law of Karma

Human beings should perform their day-to-day activities as if they had to present a report at the end of each day to an angelic court. Indeed, this "court" is actually a reality. There are supernatural beings who oversee each person's thoughts and activities, judging and rewarding them accordingly. Individual and collective futures are very much based on the consequences of thoughts and actions occurring now. If people can live each day in the awareness that such an angelic court is evaluating their activities, then they may become more conscientious about what they do.

Therefore, you should monitor your motives and actions carefully. One of the most tempting of negative behaviors for leaders is cheating, because it is all too easy for someone in power to exploit people and take advantage of opportunities for personal gain. However, there is no cheating in the higher realms and, although you may cheat on this material plane, your actions are being observed by the higher order and you will be held accountable. To avoid such temptations, take inventory each day when you arise, determining how to do better than the previous day. Such self-examination will produce more constructive projects, more effective policies and more fruitful interactions with others.

Ancient Teachings and Reincarnation

A few uncut passages in the Bible remain that refer to reincarnation, although most of the ancient teachings regarding reincarnation are no longer present in current editions. Among the early Christians, reincarnation was accepted. According to St. Jerome (347-420AD), for example, reincarnation was an esoteric reality that was communicated to a selected elite.[17] Origen (186-253AD) also wrote on the subject of reincarnation in his book, *On First Principles*.[18]

In the sixth century, however, Emperor Justinian and the second Council of Constantinople declared the principle of reincarnation to be a heretical doctrine.[19] As a result, most of the more obvious references to it were eliminated from the official scriptures. Those who believed in reincarnation had to practice underground, and such knowledge was kept alive in the West mainly by a few Christian sects and other groups who carried on the tradition of the ancient mystery schools.

However, several references to reincarnation still remain in the Bible. For example, when Herod heard about the activities of Jesus, he wanted to know: "Who is this? Is this John the Baptist whom I have beheaded, come back again?"[20] The story of Jacob and Esau reports: "The Lord loved one and hated the other even before they were born."[21] How could such sentiments exist unless they were based on previous lives, when one was pious and the other impious? Another example occurs when Jesus was praying: "And it came to pass, as he was alone praying, his disciples were with him; and he asked them, saying, "Whom say the people that I am?" They answering said, "John the Baptist; but some say Elias, and others say, that one of the old prophets is risen again."[22] Here Jesus and the disciples are discussing reincarnation in a very matter-of-fact way. Apparently it was a valid, undisputed concept to them at the time.

Reincarnation was also acknowledged in the ancient mystery schools of Egypt and Greece, among the Essenes and the Pharisees, and in the Jewish Kabbala. Even today, most people in the world accept the idea of reincarnation. Only a small number of persons (primarily in the modern

Western world) do not. For example, reincarnation is a major tenet of Hinduism, Buddhism, Jainism, Sikhism, Zoroastrianism, African cosmology and Native American religions.

Reincarnation: The Lock and the Key

In America, acceptance of the idea of reincarnation is growing. A 1990 Gallup Poll indicated that reincarnation is considered valid by more than 25 percent of the U.S. population.[23] Many books have been written about life after death, near-death experiences, and life between death and rebirth that shed more light on the subject. It is critically important for leaders to understand this process, because reincarnation is both the lock that keeps everyone imprisoned, and the key to getting back *home*. The lock of reincarnation represents the mandatory return to physical form. The key that opens the lock is the proper use of each lifetime to balance karma and "graduate" from the physical plane in order to move to a higher level in the spiritual hierarchy.

Karmically speaking, justice and balance are one and the same. Without balance, there is no justice, because justice can only be achieved by the equalization of *all* the energies–whether thoughts, words, or deeds–that people generate during all of their lifetimes. It is this cosmic accounting system that is responsible for "bad" things happening to "good" people. Each person has a karmic "scoreboard" that tabulates the record of every lifetime, and the opportunity to pay the karmic debt from one particular existence may occur in another lifetime apparently far removed from the original cause. However unfair it may seem at the moment, this opportunity to balance karma at a later time is a wonderful aspect of karmic law. It allows people to pay some of their karmic debts on the installment plan, spreading them out over many life cycles.

Past and Future Lives

As people move through various lifetimes, attempting to balance their karma and get back *home* to God, they become the aggregate of their experiences. The impressions from these existences are recorded in their subconscious mind, where they influence actions, perceptions, and mindsets in this life. These recorded impressions account for otherwise unexplainable fears, emotional predispositions, attractions, tastes, talents, skills, character traits, knowledge, wisdom and memories. This accumulation of many lessons and experiences sheds light on reasons for the unique differences among people–explaining why Mozart could compose symphonies at such a young age, why Adolph Hitler felt justified in ordering the massacre of millions, and why Jesus of Nazareth or Arjuna (in the *Bhagavad-gita*) were able to serve as examples of humanity's fullest potential, being in each case a God-man whose life was a living road-map of the way back home.

Many people have retained distinct impressions from their previous lifetimes. They experience impressions through such phenomena as déjà vu, when they feel that they have lived through something before even though they know that this is not the case, or the strange sense of familiarity that sometimes occurs when a person meets someone for the first time. Sometimes dreams are also a reflection of experiences from earlier existences.

What lies ahead in future lifetimes will be decided to a large extent by how one has behaved in this life, and particularly by the state of consciousness at the time of death. For example, the Vedic scriptures teach that an individual soul undergoes a judgment based on the quality of consciousness at death and the degree of sin or piety expressed during that lifetime, and that this judgment determines the next existence. The activities and thoughts of a lifetime become important at the moment of death because their cumulative effect will guide the soul in a particular direction.[24]

The process of judgment after death is similar to determining the next class an individual must enter in order to continue learning and eventually "graduate" as a liberated soul. Liberation means that one no longer has to return to the "schools" of the material body and the material universes, although a soul may choose to return to help others.

Transcending the Modes of Nature

The *Bhagavad-gita* describes three modes, or principles, of nature–goodness, passion, and ignorance–that determine the soul's next life.

Each of these principles has certain characteristics. The principle of *goodness* causes an individual to be pious, humanitarian, considerate, and kind. The principle of *passion* makes a person self-centered, egotistic, selfish, and extremely interested in attracting adoration, distinction, and personal profit. The principle of *ignorance* produces someone who is lazy, obnoxious, unclean, and disturbing to others. These three principles, which are like ropes that bind every human being, govern each thought and action and form the environment in the material world.

Becoming karma-free actually means to become free from the influence of these modes. In each person, one mode may be more dominant than the others. The more someone is bound by these modes, the more karma remains to be balanced. The way in which these principles interact with someone's physical and subtle bodies determines the conditions of that person's next life. The ultimate goal is not to be trapped by any of these modes, but to go directly back home to God.

The *Bhagavad-gita* explains that a person who leaves the body under the influence of the mode of goodness can go on to higher planets or be reborn on earth under auspicious circumstances, perhaps in a pious family with good education and great opulence. A person who leaves the body while subject to the mode of passion usually comes back to this planet or to similar material universes to continue with the lessons there. Finally, an individual in the mode of ignorance generally experiences demotion to lower, hellish planets or may return to earth as a human being subject to enhanced material suffering in the form of physical disease or deformity, mental aberrations, extreme poverty, lack of beauty or low intelligence. Indeed, someone heavily influenced by the mode of ignorance may even be reborn into the animal kingdom.

This is the sum and substance of what life is supposed to be about: living not as a physical body, but as a soul using this body to find the way back to God. The role of an effective leader is to create conditions in this material world that make the journey *home* a possibility.

Highlights

1. Many people believe that happiness is attainable simply by acquiring sufficient money, a fulfilling job, the right life partner, or a home in a desirable neighborhood. Often they become frustrated in pursuit of such goals, becoming dissatisfied with themselves, their jobs, their environments, and the people around them. They tolerate their dissatisfaction, however, thinking, "If only I can achieve this next goal, I will be happy."

2. Everyone is trying to escape the pain of being away from home. Some who do not escape kill themselves. Others resort to seeking altered states of consciousness through artificial means such as drugs. Both legal and illegal drugs have become the "painkillers" of the world, numbing the profound psychological depression experienced by many.

3. Unless people go deeper and establish a higher connection with the universe, both outside themselves and inside themselves, they will always lament their situation and remain unfulfilled.

4. Regardless of their material accomplishments, human beings may still feel incomplete because this material arena is simply not their real home. They are dissatisfied because they have known something much higher, something sublime and divine. Their souls are aware of this fact, so that at the deepest soul level they "remember" the ecstasy of having once been in the presence of God.

5. Nothing in the material world–neither money, position, drugs, nor sex–can produce the ecstasy and satisfaction that humans have already experienced when they were back where they belong–at home with God.

6.   From the great teachers one learns that human beings are all vis-
        itors to these material universes, which are schools or
        reformatories–places to which people must return again and
        again until they learn, step by step, lifetime by lifetime, how to be
        perfect in order to regain the association of God.

7.   The process of reincarnation is the key to returning *home*.
        According to the Vedic scriptures, reincarnation occurs because a
        human being is actually a soul who uses the physical and subtle
        bodies covering it in each lifetime to experience, learn and grow to
        perfection. The soul's goal is to attain the perfection of the self-
        realized state.

8.   The means for balancing these energies is karma: the just conse-
        quences of all of one's thoughts, words and deeds. Karma is the
        process of equal recompense. In other words, people get back
        whatever they give out.

9.   The law of karma is *always* in operation. Whether one believes in
        it or not, it is the law by which human beings are bound to or
        freed from the material world. Each person's respect for this law
        can greatly decrease the number of life cycles required to bring
        the energies of cause and effect into balance.

10.   As people move through various lifetimes, attempting to balance
        their karma and get back home to God, they become the aggre-
        gate of their experiences. The impressions from these existences
        are recorded in their subconscious mind, where they influence
        actions, perceptions, and mindsets in this life. These recorded
        impressions account for unexplainable fears, emotional predispo-
        sitions, attractions, tastes, talents, skills, character traits,
        knowledge, wisdom and memories. This accumulation of many
        lessons and experiences sheds light on reasons for the unique dif-
        ferences among human beings.

Mindsets

1. Review the ten essential technologies given at the beginning of this book, concentrating on numbers 2 and 4. Happiness on earth is knowing that as you learn to be in this world but not of *it*–in control of your senses and not overly attached–you will soon be released to return *home*. Be aware throughout your daily activities of your level of attachment, and to what degree you identify with your own body and the bodies of others. Also notice how often you see another person as an energy of God.

2. Do the following exercise with a small child, or even with an adult. Ask the person to point to different body organs and limbs. Then ask, "But where are *you*?" and witness the bewilderment that ensues. Notice how we are so aware of what we use or own but are unaware of our own essence–the spirit soul.

3. Look at pictures of yourself, or of a child of yours, at different ages. Reflect on how your body and personality, or your child's body and personality, have been constantly changing. Remind yourself that, although the body has changed so much and continues to change, the actual person–the soul in the body–remains the same.

4. Many people, especially in Western countries, have never seen a dead human body. Remedy this situation by going to a funeral home just to observe the bodies there. Notice how each body is just an outward shell. As soon as the soul is gone, life ceases. We say the person has "died" when, in reality, the body has been discarded and the soul has left.

5. Sometimes we can perceive immediately that we "reap what we sow," because the karmic reaction is not delayed. Reflect on periods in your life when many things seemed to be going wonderfully. You may notice that at those times you were treating

others very favorably. Such treatment produces reciprocation in kind. Now notice the opposite.

6. Have you ever met someone for the first time whom you felt you already knew? Have you ever visited a place for the first time and come away feeling you had been there before? On some occasions, perhaps you have even been able to describe certain aspects of a place before you physically went there. Be aware that these experiences may be a result of past-life memories.

7. Evaluate your own activities in terms of the three modes of material nature. What modes seem to be governing your life at different times? Which mode generally predominates? Study some of your associates and try to identify which modes they are expressing in different situations.

8. Whenever you feel lonely, forsaken and misunderstood, talk to the Lord in the heart and feel solace in knowing that He cares and is always with you.

9. Recall a time when you had a very high fever, or were otherwise ill, and were not conscious of your body. Or notice upon awakening each morning that when you were asleep you experienced a reality separate from your physical body.

10. Meditate daily on your real home, which is in the kingdom of God where there is full knowledge, eternity and bliss. Know that you will be totally satisfied there, because you will be in full connection with the soul rather than with these cumbersome material bodies.

3

Activating Higher Energies

Human beings live in a cosmic river of flowing energy. Everything is energy. All energy is in motion, whether or not that motion is perceptible to the lower, gross human senses of sight, smell, touch, taste, or hearing. The rate at which the energy moves determines one's ability to perceive it: the slower the movement, the more it is perceptible to the physical senses.

The Nature of Energy

Energy is composed of light–the light that emanates from God. Light is at the heart of matter, residing inside every atom. When modern scientists were finally able to split the atom, what they unleashed was the tremendous power of light. As particles of light, atoms vibrate at different speeds, creating electrical charges that cause them to bind together into molecules. Among these molecules, those moving at slower rates of speed join with one another to form what people perceive as the material world.

For example, the only difference between the soft, flexible human body and a bar of steel is the configuration of the molecules and the speed at which they vibrate. Both the body and the bar of steel are made of atoms. Molecules vibrating slightly more rapidly result in more pliable, less solid matter–such as liquids and gases–and those moving at even higher vibratory rates of speed form energies known as thought, emotion, and spirit.

This energetic composition of reality helps explain how everything is one. For example, the cosmic river of flowing energy is what allows the thoughts of one person to be transmitted to someone in another location. This is what enabled Jesus, at the request of the Roman centurion, simply to "speak the word" to heal a dying man somewhere else.[25] In the *Srimad Bhagavatam*, an ancient Vedic scripture, this river of energy allowed Dhruva Maharaj to affect the atmosphere of the entire universe by gaining control of the energy within his own body.[26] It enables a loving mother to "know" that her child is in danger, even when the two of them are apart.

Because this energy–also known as *prana, mana, chi,* or *ki*–encompasses everything that exists, it is inexhaustible. The very air people breathe is filled with it, and the entire universe can be considered an electrical energy grid that conducts these energies. In this view, a person's energies travel across this grid like sound waves, having an effect on various other energies as they move, and then "bouncing back" in kind.

Types of Energy

The underlying principle of the law of karma, discussed earlier, is that people are responsible for the energy they generate. Much of this energy takes the form of thoughts, words, and deeds. Although people can easily perceive their words and actions and frequently observe their impact, they may be tempted to believe that their thoughts have no effect. However, they would be mistaken. Although invisible to the naked eye, *thoughts are things*. They are individual electrical entities that group themselves with similar energy to form clusters. They are real; they are substantive; and they are a force that everyone can learn to balance and control.

In addition to these fundamental forms of energy, people generate less obvious types of energy that are nonetheless major influences upon the world around them. These include: emotional energy, such as guilt, anger, fear, hate, jealousy or envy; sexual energy, which is so powerful that one must use it extremely carefully; physical energy, including the energies of the etheric or astral body; spiritual energy, the force that enables people "to move mountains;" and love energy which, in its pure and selfless state, is the most powerful force in the universe. Human beings may also be influenced by other energies that many consider to be "concepts," including, for example, truth, justice or compassion. These energies vibrate at extremely high rates because they are derived from divine principles.

As people monitor their own karmic scoreboard, becoming conscious of how they use their individual energies, they will understand why each soul is considered to be a microcosm of the whole. It is because the power contained within each human being is so vast as to be unimaginable in its scope. In a sense, one's opportunities to use it, transmute it, release it, withhold it, monitor it or balance it become the only reason for being in human form.

Characteristics of Energy

If you accept that you are responsible for the energy you generate, in your role as a leader as well as in your personal life, you will certainly want to know how to control such energy properly to help balance your karma. It is important to remember that the energies released by your leadership, and their corresponding effects on those you lead, are generated by you and that their repercussions will be reflected on your personal karmic scoreboard.

Energy has two important characteristics that make it possible for people to direct and control it effectively. First, energy is impartial, nonresistant and totally malleable to individual desires. A person's free will determines how it will be used and at what vibratory level it will operate–a high level for spiritual purposes or a low one for selfish ends. The intent, ultimately known only to the individual and to God, is what determines this vibratory level, rather than the ultimate outcome of one's actions.

Many would like to assume that the laws of God work only for the just and the godly. But this is not the case. No matter what a person's intent may be, the laws governing the universe work for everyone. This is because these laws are based on the science of God and, as with any science, they are universal, predictable and unchanging. For example, the formula 1+1=2 always holds true, whether this information is used to build shelters for the homeless or to embezzle funds. To deny the use of these laws to the unrighteous would be to deny them their God-given free will to choose their own paths back home. Only by learning from their experiences–both good and bad–can people ultimately make the right choices that balance their karma.

A second characteristic of energy is that it cannot be destroyed, only transformed. When a skyscraper burns to the ground, apparently destroyed, in reality the fire has simply returned the building's materials to their original elements–such as carbon or hydrogen–or changed them into newly formed substances called soot and ashes. Any remaining energy has either recombined with energies existing in the surrounding air, water or land, or returned to the universal energy pool as uncombined energy. Energy can also be accumulated, moved, gathered and stored, transmitted, dissipated, shattered, released, transmuted or balanced.

Nothing exists unless it is sustained by thought. Therefore, the easiest way to control and manipulate energies is by thought processes. People can control their words and actions simply by changing the way they think, recognizing that "as a man thinketh, so shall he be."[27] The biblical story of Job is an excellent example of the law of thought in operation. Unfortunately, Job worked the law against himself, not realizing that each calamity he worried about manifested because he had created it in his mind.[28]

Worry is a prayer for something one does not want. To avoid an undesirable outcome, people can learn to control their thoughts, especially when they are under stress and have an emotional investment in a desired outcome. At such times, stress and emotions represent thought energy fueling the creation of the image being held in their minds. Instead of worrying, one can replace the negative thought with a visual image of the desired outcome, and then help that image manifest rather than the unwanted one. As people get into the habit of energizing only the positive, their thoughts, words, and actions will automatically reflect this higher state of mind. They will, in effect, stop creating new negative karma, because they will no longer generate energy that has to be rebalanced, and their positive energy will begin paying off some of the debits on their scoreboard.

Transmuting Energy

The decision to function in a positive mode represents the first step in transmuting energy to a higher level, which means raising its vibratory rate. Energy transmuted in this way attracts even more positive energy, producing a snowball effect that further enhances the benefits of an existing situation or helps speed the creation of a new, more desirable one–whether a housing project or a state of mind.

However, transmutation works in both directions. To transmute simply means "to change or alter in form, appearance or nature," without reference to positive or negative effects. Naturally, this implies that one can degrade the level at which an energy is operating, by transmuting it to a lower vibratory status. Unfortunately, human beings do this often, especially when they speak carelessly or harbor thoughts of envy, anger, hatred, or jealousy. As a leader, you can make sure that those who work with you understand this reality and are committed to transmuting their energies to a higher level. You should make this same commitment yourself. This can make the difference between success and failure.

One of the most obvious, but perhaps least recognized, ways that people handle energy is to accumulate it in their physical bodies instead of releasing it. Stagnant, unreleased emotional energy can eventually have a harmful effect. These energies are dense, vibrating at a level too low to be processed by the highly efficient physical body. As a result, they become blocked and crystallized, manifesting at best as diminished stamina or decreased mobility, and at worst as disease. Such energies can be released through methods such as forgiveness, prayer, or meditation, or through conscious transmutation.

Release and Balance Negative Energy

Modern medicine is slowly coming to accept the reality of "mind over matter," recognizing the power of the mind to influence the functioning of the human body. Therefore, it is in everyone's best interest to learn to release low energy by moving it out of the physical body, the conscious and subconscious mind, the etheric body and the aura. People can accomplish this by dissipating it through a conscious release of old grudges and resentments, or by deliberately shattering it into smaller components in order to make the subsequent release more effortless.

The bigger the energy blockage, the easier it will be to let go if a person first separates it into more manageable elements, just as one might break a boulder into small pieces before trying to dispose of it. For example, a relationship with a long-term rival might consist of an endless series of hurt feelings, nasty actions, and cruel betrayals. The accumulated resentments may be easier to release if the aggrieved individual addresses each of these hurtful situations one at a time.

Those who think that their refusal to forgive in these circumstances hurts the offender eventually discover that they are only hurting themselves. In the long run, the law of karma requires negative energies to be returned to their source, for that is where they originated.

Your effectiveness as a leader frequently depends on your ability to view situations objectively, without distortion. Negative emotions can interfere with this process. To free yourself from the long-term accumulation of resentments, begin to shatter the energy by recalling images, one by one if necessary, of the painful thoughts, words, and deeds that have characterized a particular relationship or situation. Then visualize a bright light–the light of Spirit–engulfing you and the other person or situation, penetrating and transmuting the event and your feelings about it. Silently or out loud, say the person's name, followed by: "I release you [or the situation] into the light of the Supreme." Actually see the situation and your reactions being transmuted to higher levels and watch them being absorbed into the light.

When you no longer react to that particular memory or person, you will know that you have become free. Until then, use this technique as often as necessary to release the energy. If you work with it, you will release it.

In addition, strive to "love your enemies," as Jesus admonishes.[29] Pray for them; such prayer decreases their power to hurt you, and the high energy released in the process will be returned to you in kind.

Finally, it is important to remember that energy can be balanced, and that the ultimate goal of working with energy is to achieve just such a state of equilibrium. Although you may think you are facing overwhelming odds at times, remember that the basic laws of mathematics also apply to balancing energy. As an example, the expression "Only love can conquer hate" can be understood mathematically. Since love and hate are energies at opposite ends of the same spectrum, in order to neutralize a hatred that has, say, a value of -10, you need to generate at least a +10 charge of love. To progress even farther toward the love end of the spectrum, a charge of more than +10 would be required. This is how to balance and counterbalance energies. It is a matter of simple mathematics.

Protecting Yourself During Sleep

Part of your responsibility as a leader is to keep your consciousness as pure as possible at all times, even while you are sleeping. Therefore, in addition to transmuting energy in your waking state, it is important to be able to do so during sleep. Your increased vulnerability during sleep makes you more susceptible to negative energies and influences from lower or "trapped" spirits–subtle disembodied entities who may want to cause some disturbance.

This might happen, for example, if the astral body and the soul of a person who has died suddenly remain in the environment, haunting it. Such a haunting entity may try to make contact with the physical bodies in that environment in order to use them to experience certain physical sensations and pleasures.

In addition, nightmares are a common nighttime affliction. This is why you may want to meditate on spiritual subjects before bedtime and avoid discussions about ghosts or other disembodied entities late in the day. Such discussions may attract them. However, negative entities are repelled by higher vibratory energy.

One means of raising your consciousness before going to sleep is to create a physical environment filled with high spiritual energy. For example, you might place a spiritual painting or image of a great saint at the head of your bed so that the spiritual personality can watch over your body while you are at rest. Another measure is to place spiritual books near your head at night. Also, you can use holy water for protection–water that has been prayed over, used in a worship service, or drawn from a sacred river. (Although water from worship services or sacred rivers is more potent, you can make holy water yourself by repeating any of the names of God over it.) Before going to bed, or if you are awakened during sleep, you can sprinkle such holy water in your sleeping environment.

If you feel the presence of negative beings, you can chant prayers, sing spiritual songs or visualize light clearing the environment. If you feel anything trying to enter your body and are unable to speak, mentally repeat one of the names of God, such as Jehovah, Allah, or Krishna. As soon as you are able, say the name of God out loud vigorously, in order to chase the negativity away from the environment.

Such chanting can also be a great service to these beings. In the mind you can be very loving and say, "I realize that you are in a state of bewilderment. Please come chant with me; let us glorify the Lord together; let us become absorbed in spiritual activity and get properly nourished." In this way, you will benefit such a being by helping to elevate it.

In these situations, you can remember that an evolved soul works to help humanity and serve God under all circumstances. You can be of service to beings who are not in physical bodies, as well as to those who are. Do not be afraid; disembodied beings are often like children. They are usually just being mischievous, without harmful intent, or they are wandering in confusion and need assistance. Actually, even if their intentions are sinister, fear is not useful, because it will attract them even more and cause greater disturbance.

Once again, you can always rest assured that love–a real energy–conquers all. Often these beings just need to be guided and released from their state of imprisonment. By speaking positive, reassuring thoughts and engaging them spiritually, you will help to free them. In addition, your higher, loving energy will neutralize negativity.

Masculine and Feminine Energies

Another aspect of energy concerns its dual nature in the material world. In modern science, the disciplines of psychiatry and neurosurgery make frequent references to "left brain" or "right brain" activity. Research has shown that each side of the brain has its own unique characteristics and corresponding functions within the total being. Although there are exceptions, generally the left hemisphere is responsible for logical, analytical, linear, matter-of-fact behaviors and thoughts, while the right hemisphere handles the intuitive, creative, imaginative, psychic, and spiritual aspects of human experience.

It has become popular to consider those traits originating in the left brain as "masculine" and those based in the right brain as "feminine." Most day-to-day business and survival activities are managed by the left side of the brain, which involves the more active, outer-directed, "masculine" aspects of human thought and behavior. On the other hand, those who have psychic abilities, or engage in such activities as meditation or biofeedback, are calling upon the brain's right hemisphere, which represents the receptive, "feminine" aspect of the mind. Whether in a male or female body, the human brain is androgynous, and both hemispheres must be active in order for a person to achieve balance.

Regardless of whether the body is male or female, mentally and spiritually everyone is androgynous. In a world psychologically programmed to believe that one sex is more important than the other, this statement may provoke some resistance, or perhaps even a violent reaction. However, any opposition to this reality is futile, because such androgyny–like reincarnation and the karmic scoreboard–is a universal reality that cannot be changed by egocentrism or a need to dominate and manipulate.

This planet, the loving Mother of all physical life, is in pain. Suffering from an overdose of misused masculine energy, she needs a massive injection of feminine energy in order to regain her balance and prevent human beings from destroying her–and themselves–in the process. One might wonder, since the planet needs more feminine energy, why women cannot give it to her. Indeed they can, and they are doing so. However, even if all the women on this planet used their entire right brains–and they have been doing a fantastic job for centuries, especially under oppressive circumstances–the result would still be insufficient. The reason is simple: women only control 50 percent of the feminine energy on the planet because they only possess 50 percent of the right brains. Men have the other 50 percent. Therefore, men as well as women need to become more aware of this reality so that they can participate in rebalancing the energy on earth before it is too late.

Left-Brain and Right-Brain Attributes

Listed below are some of the characteristics attributed to each side of the brain. Taken together, these traits indicate a well-rounded, balanced human being. In addition, they are necessary for a well-functioning family, organization, business or nation. Indeed, without the ability to access both sides of the brain, a person or group can become dysfunctional. Once you have recognized the importance of such balance, you can learn to generate energy from the appropriate side of the brain in various circumstances, and can respect the need for such balance in all of your daily activities. In addition, you should monitor the proportion of "left-brain" and "right-brain" energies operating in your family, organization, business or nation.

Everything in this material world is part of a dual polarity. To illustrate this point, the following chart lists several apparently opposite concepts that, when taken together, create wholeness and balance. Each attribute is listed across from its complementary one.

Left Brain (Masculine)	Right Brain (Feminine)
Conscious mind	Subconscious mind
Aggressive/assertive	Passive/receptive
Logical/analytical	Emotional/sensitive
Intellectual	Intuitive
Mental	Psychic
Objective	Subjective
Giving	Receiving
Will	Creation
Force	Power
Knowledge	Wisdom
Voluntary systems	Involuntary systems
Separate/individualized	Inclusive/unifying
Sun	Moon
Yang	Yin

Those who are only using the side of their brain that corresponds to their male or female body are actually out of balance. The ideal is for both sexes to have the flexibility to access the appropriate trait at the proper time, depending on the circumstances. It is important to realize that this discussion is not only a "wake up call" for men. Women also need more balance. They have often failed to accept their masculine energy, and now have an opportunity to learn how to use both sides of their brains as well.

Femininity can become distorted by too much passivity, receptivity, and emotionalism, just as exaggerated masculinity may rely too much on force, aggression, and intellectualization. For example, excessive passivity and receptivity have meant that too many women on this planet, in all societies, have endured mental and physical abuse–and allowed their children to be abused–rather than owning some of their masculine energies by asserting their rights to be without being misused. In such cases, passivity becomes as destructive as aggression.

It is your energy! As you realize the importance of both polarities, then your actions become appropriate to each unique circumstance. Recognize the totality of your being and access masculine and feminine energies as required–being guided by your inner self, not necessarily by the established social norms. This knowledge of yourself can deepen your understanding of effective leadership as you help yourself and others to balance the karmic scales and get back *home.*

The Last Illusion: God the Father

In support of the universality of masculine and feminine energies, the Kybalion, a book based on ancient Egyptian wisdom, states: "Gender is in everything. Everything has its masculine and feminine principles. Gender manifests on all planes."[30] In addition, the ancient Law of Correspondence teaches: "As above, so below; as below, so above."[31]

If everything in the universe is both masculine and feminine, and if the same principles are true on all levels, then it follows that God must also be dual in nature. Or, to put it another way, because humans are mentally and spiritually androgynous beings who are made in the image of God, God is also an androgynous being. People can no longer cling to the illusion of an exclusively male God. Of course there is a Mother God!

The existence of the Mother God is not a new concept by any means. In fact, the opposite is true: throughout most of history, humanity worshiped a female God.[32] It is a relatively new perception to consider the Godhead as only male. Many early societies, for example, gave men a secondary role. Their worship ceremonies honored the Mother, considering the woman as the origin of creation and Mother Earth as the source of their livelihood. The matriarchal system of inheritance was–and in some areas still is–the foundation of the social, cultural, and religious norms of the community.[33]

In more recent times, the Judeo-Christian world has espoused the philosophy that God was a male figure having no equal and opposite feminine counterpart. In many other religions the female partner to the male God is not only assumed, but is considered to be equal to or even more significant than the male—as, for example, in the divine couple Radha and Krishna.

As with so many realities hidden away for centuries by people who wished to subjugate and control others, the existence of the Mother God was camouflaged by some religions for the purpose of exploiting the people, especially women. This denigration of the Mother, for human selfish purposes, was so successful that even religions that had previously acknowledged the feminine factor began to allow their modern societies to promote male domination.

Regardless of how humanity got to this point, it is time to re-enthrone the Mother God. She has never ceased to exist despite the many attempts to degrade Her and eliminate Her role. At the highest level, the Mother represents all of the feminine qualities and powers in the universe. However, human ignorance and lack of respect for Her, coupled with the low regard in which many people hold their own feminine natures, has led to widespread denial of the importance of the feminine. This unimaginable injustice will be judged by God, and many will be found wanting. It is incumbent upon everyone to get to know the Mother God. She is the Mother of all creation. She is the Divine Mother–the overseer of all devotion. Any mature appreciation of the Godhead must include Her.

Highlights

1. Human beings live in a cosmic river of flowing energy. Everything is energy. All energy is in motion, whether or not that motion is perceptible to the lower, gross human senses of sight, smell, touch, taste, or hearing.

2. Energy is composed of light–the light that emanates from God. Light is at the heart of matter, residing inside every atom.

3. This energy–also known as *prana, mana, chi,* or *ki*–encompasses everything that exists; it is inexhaustible. The very air people breathe is filled with it, and the entire universe can be considered an electrical energy grid that conducts these energies. In this view, a person's energies travel across this grid like sound waves, having an effect on various other energies as they move, and then "bouncing back" in kind.

4. Although invisible to the naked eye, *thoughts are things.* They are individual electrical entities that group themselves with similar energy to form clusters. They are real; they are substantive; and they are a force that everyone can learn to balance and control.

5. Energy is impartial, nonresistant and totally malleable to individual desires. A person's free will determines how it will be used and at what vibratory level it will operate–a high level for spiritual purposes or a low one for selfish ends. The *intent,* ultimately known only to the individual and to God, is what determines this vibratory level, rather than the ultimate outcome of one's actions.

6. Worry is a prayer for something one does not want. To avoid an undesirable outcome, people can learn to control their thoughts, especially when they are under stress and have an emotional investment in a desired outcome.

7.   The decision to function in a positive mode represents the first step in transmuting energy to a higher level, which means raising its vibratory rate. Energy transmuted in this way attracts even more positive energy, producing a snowball effect that further enhances the benefits of an existing situation or helps speed the creation of a new, desirable one.

8.   It is important to remember that energy can be balanced, and that the ultimate goal of working with energy is to achieve such a state of equilibrium. Although you may think you are facing overwhelming odds at times, remember that the basic laws of mathematics also apply to balancing energy.

9.   Regardless of whether the body is male or female, mentally and spiritually everyone is androgynous. In a world psychologically programmed to believe that one sex is more important than the other, this statement may provoke some resistance, or perhaps even a violent reaction. However, any opposition to this reality is futile, because such androgyny–like reincarnation and the karmic scoreboard–is a universal reality that cannot be changed by ego-centrism or a need to dominate and manipulate.

10.   It is time to re-enthrone the Mother God. She has never ceased to exist despite the many attempts to degrade Her and eliminate Her role. At the highest level, the Mother represents all of the feminine qualities and powers in the universe.

Mindsets

1. As you review the ten essential technologies mentioned at the beginning of this book, note how each of them can help you remain calm during your daily activities and give you a clearer sense of direction. Pay special attention to number 5, and practice transmuting negative energy into positive energy in all your leadership endeavors.

2. Monitor your thoughts carefully. As you think of someone lovingly, angrily or lustfully, note how that person becomes unconsciously affected by your energies.

3. Read from spiritual texts for half an hour or so before going to bed. Try to reflect on the subject matter as you fall asleep. Also listen to relaxing, spiritually-oriented music. These measures will create a protective climate during the night.

4. If you feel that a place is occupied by negative energy, you can light incense, sing spiritual songs, chant or put on a tape of prayers to God as soon as you enter. You may also use pictures of saints or other divine beings to purify the atmosphere, especially if you are going to sleep there. Since every environment absorbs the energy of those who frequent it, in both gross and subtle forms, take these measures in all new environments. Such purifying activities will also raise the energy in the atmosphere in general.

5. Instead of worrying, replace your worries with a visual image of the outcome you want to create. Help that image manifest, rather than feeding emotional energy into the thought form you fear.

6. As you develop the habit of energizing only positive mental images, your thoughts, words, and deeds will automatically reflect a higher state of being. Notice the changes in your life that occur as a result.

7.   Always use methods such as forgiveness, prayer, meditation, or energy transmutation to release the low vibrations of anger, resentment, or envy. Otherwise, these negative energies will produce serious blockages that can eventually lead to mental or physical illness.

8.   Make the effort to become a more well-rounded and whole person, maintaining a healthy balance between your masculine and feminine energies. In such a state you will uplift consciousness wherever you go.

9.   Spend some time recharging yourself by getting away for self-rejuvenation. Being close to nature and associating with the elements can be very refreshing. It brings out creativity and lets you shed some of the weight you normally carry.

10.   Practice raising the consciousness of those who try to attack you. First, remember there is no attack unless you accept it. See these attacks as calls for help, and review what you will do or say the next time to help your would-be attackers. This will protect you and help them as well.

$$4$$

Expanded Realities for the Mind

The mind, which has great range and power, is capable of extraordinary accomplishments. Your awareness of its vast potential can deepen your appreciation of the mind's contributions to the progress of human civilization, provide you with invaluable guidance in personal and leadership matters, and enhance your ability to serve the highest good in all that you do.

Tapping the Mind's Potential

Almost everyone has heard that people only use about five to ten percent of their brains. What an incredible thought, especially since many individuals seem to be extremely impressed with themselves, believing that the entire universe revolves around them and that they are its only intelligent beings, far superior to other forms of life! What would human beings be capable of if they used the entire brain–all 100 percent of it? If they did so, they would be the gods they were intended to be: microcosms of the macrocosm, self-contained energy units with the power to move mountains. "Whosoever shall say unto this mountain, Be thou removed, and be thou cast into the sea; and shall not doubt in his heart, but shall believe that those things which he saith shall come to pass; he shall have whatsoever he saith,"[34] Jesus said to the disciples–and he was not joking.

If one were to combine the wide range of possible human talents–especially those considered to be supernatural–into one person, the result might approximate a human who was using 70 percent of the brain, still leaving unharnessed the other 30 percent. The potential is vast, and can be developed simply by training unused portions of the brain to work in new ways. You can develop your capabilities by helping your conscious, subconscious and superconscious minds work together. Then you can teach those you lead how to do the same. What is possible for one human being is possible for all.

The mind's power is demonstrated in many ways. Among these are the capacity of thought to influence the physical body, the extrasensory abilities manifested in so-called psychic phenomena, the potential inherent in everyone to learn complicated information quickly and effortlessly, the purported capability of some to perceive extraterrestrial beings, and the rich potential of dreams to provide guidance and knowledge.

The Mind-Body Connection

One demonstration of the mind's great potential can be found in the many ways in which the physical body responds to the mind's influence. For example, psychosomatic illness is a physical ailment generated by mental processes and having no discernible biological cause. Many diseases have direct or indirect psychological correlations, in which the mind causes the physical body to accept its conclusions and the body reacts accordingly. For example, case histories have reported paralysis of a limb with no obvious biological cause. Despite the absence of apparent medical problems, an arm may function as if it were physically paralyzed because of some traumatic memory or fear buried in the individual's unconscious mind.

Further, in phobias such as agoraphobia or claustrophobia, a person may experience levels of fright and dysfunctional behavior that appear unwarranted to others. In some of these cases, with a proper change of consciousness, the subject no longer experiences the symptoms.

Another classic example of the mind's effect upon the body is the placebo effect. In controlled experiments, one group of subjects is given actual medication for a particular problem, while those in another group, told that they are taking medication, in fact simply receive sugar pills of no medicinal value. Improvements frequently occur in the group taking the placebo, a phenomenon that researchers attribute to the subject's expectations—in other words, to the mind's power of suggestion.

Psychoneuroimmunology is the study of the mysterious way in which a person's mind and emotions can influence the immune system. Research in this dynamic, new area of modern science is providing insight into ways of harnessing the power of the mind, including the emotions, to heal the body. This field has provoked interest in the role of emotions in determining whether someone can recover from such infirmities as blindness or terminal cancer. Indeed, it appears that in addition to the thoughts in a person's mind, positive emotions such as hope and love can help speed the healing process. There is little doubt that the mind can be a most powerful healing tool.

Yet another phenomenon encountered in studying the mind-body connection is that of spontaneous remission: a medical "miracle" in which no clear medical explanation exists for the disappearance of a previously degenerative condition. Spontaneous remission has been observed with all types of illnesses, even cancer. Several studies, such as one at the Institute of Noetic Sciences in Palo Alto, California, are exploring this phenomenon in greater depth.[35]

The Mind's Learning Power

Another example of the vast potential of the mind can be found in the learning process called suggestology. Also referred to as superlearning, this is an effortless technique in which specifically selected music is played in the background while the learner, in a deeply relaxed state, listens to lessons, commands or instructions. This approach is not hypnosis or sleep learning, because the student is fully awake and completely in control. The subject learns the material without any exertion or attempt at conscious memorization. Such a technique is said to affect the 90 percent of the brain that is not normally used.

One of the greatest researchers in this area is Dr. Georgi Lozanov of the Institute of Suggestology in Bulgaria, who believes that such a teaching method speeds up learning 50 times. The Bulgarians have thousands of controlled test results to prove the success of their method, which increases retention, requires virtually no effort on the part of the students, reaches the retarded as well as the brilliant, succeeds with young and old alike, and needs no special equipment.[36]

At the Institute of Suggestology, hundreds of people from all levels of society have learned an entire language in as little as 20 days. Some experimental groups are mastering courses in basic mathematics, physics, chemistry, and biology in a matter of weeks.[37]

The Expanded Mind: Psychic Phenomena

The vast power of the mind is also demonstrated by the existence of psychic phenomena. The field of parapsychology, which studies these phenomena, can be viewed as a bridge linking together the humanities, religion, and the arts and sciences into an integrated understanding of how the human mind interacts with the cosmos. This is why some of the most splendid minds in history–such as Madame Curie, Franklin D. Roosevelt, William Butler Yeats, Thomas Edison, Winston Churchill, and Carl Jung–have been interested in psychic matters.

Many individuals demonstrate unusual, or paranormal, abilities that defy current scientific explanation. Some have gifts of precognition, foretelling events before they occur. Others demonstrate clairvoyance or clairaudience, seeing or hearing beyond the range of ordinary physical perception. Certain people can read another's thoughts, or transmit thoughts telepathically into someone else's mind. There are others who are gifted in psychokinesis, using their mental energy to move or bend physical objects, while still others practice psychometry, the ability to obtain information about someone merely from touching an object with which that person has come in contact. And almost everyone has heard of healers who cure illnesses or other disturbances by resorting to the power of thought and prayer.

Many of the earlier pioneers in the field of psychology–including Sigmund Freud, Sandor Ferenczi, Wilhelm Stekel, and Carl Jung–possessed a vital interest in psychic phenomena, magic, and the occult, which they justly regarded as intimately related to the deeper levels of the mind. It is interesting to note that two of the persons who have made the most significant contributions to modern-day psychology, Carl Jung and Sigmund Freud, both had an interest in psychic studies.

In a letter written to the noted psychic researcher Hereward Carrington in 1924, Sigmund Freud stated, "If I had my life to live over again, I should devote myself to psychic research rather than to psychoanalysis."[38] Many of Jung's maternal ancestors had frequent involvement in the supernatural.[39] His grandfather, the Reverend Samuel Preiswerk, had encounters with invisible entities. Jung's mother, Emilie, recorded in her diary how as a young girl she was often obliged to sit beside the Reverend Preiswerk in order to prevent the spirits from disturbing him. The same grandfather was also known to hold weekly seances with the spirit of his first wife. His second wife, Jung's grandmother, was also gifted with unusual clairvoyant abilities. Jung himself, while in his early twenties, began his career as a psychic experimenter.[40]

The Astral Body

Psychic phenomena greatly expand the range of human capabilities and experience. Yet the current scientific paradigm cannot explain them. How are all of these feats possible?

Every psychic phenomenon represents a conduit to another dimension, or another form of energy that is not acknowledged by orthodox belief systems, and demonstrates that humans are more than just physical beings. One of the most outstanding and reliable mediums of the twentieth century, Eileen Garrett, president of the Parapsychological Foundation in New York and a highly successful business executive, writes: "Throughout my whole life I have been aware of the fact that everyone possesses a second body–a double. The double is a distinct fact in Eastern and theological teachings and as such it is said to be an energy body, a magnetic aura associated with the physical human corpse, an area in which the immaterial forces of the cosmos, the solar system, the planet, and one's more immediate environment are normally transformed in the life and belief of the individual."[41]

An understanding of the human aura can help clarify the function of the etheric double, or astral body. In fact, the aura is the energy field radiating outward from this astral body. According to Mrs. Garrett, this etheric double can be used for the expansion of consciousness, and is a medium for telepathic and clairvoyant experiences. Mrs. Garrett and many others believe that the secret of extrasensory perception (ESP) is related to the astral body.

In Russia, parapsychological research into the aura has demonstrated that the human being is more than just a physical entity. Such research indicates that the human astral body vibrates and radiates energy in the form of different signals that reveal information about a person's current mental and physical state, and even about the future health of various organs.[42]

Kirlian photography has played a significant role in helping identify the aura. In some cases, persons whose arm or leg has been amputated have still felt the limb's presence. Certain researchers believe that the limb's etheric double, which represents the perfect pattern around which the physical body is formed, remains intact even after the physical limb has been removed.[43]

Another indication that such an astral body exists is found in accupuncture, a science that makes use of the energy pathways, or meridians, of that etheric double. When there is a blockage of energy along these pathways, the mind and physical body are affected. Acupuncture is a method of releasing the stored energy and freeing the meridians for the improvement of both mental and physical health.

Beyond Time and Space

Another way to explain parapsychological occurrences is by adopting an expanded understanding of time and space. Many psychic events seem to happen outside of one's perceptions of these two dimensions. In his autobiography *Memories, Dreams, Reflections,* Jung wrote that the psyche by its very nature extends into a spaceless and timeless sphere. Extrasensory perceptions, he felt, are natural to the psyche, which operates beyond the realm of physical sensation.

In Jung's words: "We must face the fact that our world, with its time, space, and causality, relates to another order of things lying behind or beneath it, in which neither 'here and there' nor 'earlier and later' are of importance. I have been convinced that at least a part of our psychic existence is characterized by a relativity of space and time. This relativity seems to increase, in proportion to the distance from consciousness, to an absolute condition of timelessness and spacelessness."[44] Jung made similar observations in his description of the collective unconscious, stating that there is an ongoing, universal connection among all ideas, actions, and thoughts to which people can attune and which they can influence.

The Oneness of All Things

Yet another explanation for psychic experiences is that everything is actually God, and therefore all phenomena are simply different aspects of God's energies. The Vedic scriptures explain that the Lord has three different types of energy, or *shakti: bahiranga shakti, tatastha shakti,* and *antaranga shakti. Bahiranga shakti* is the material energy that is perceived as existing separately from the Lord; *tatastha shakti* is the soul or essence that is lodged inside of the physical body of each living being; and *antaranga shakti* is the divine spiritual energy in its most direct and pure expression.[45]

The Vedic philosophers believed that since all things are "one" in the sense that they come from God and are but different aspects of God's energy, this "oneness" is responsible for the interconnections that underlie psychic experiences. In this sense, God is simply knowing, relating, or interacting with different aspects of Himself. Thus, it is easy for God to heal Himself, or to know Himself, because everything comes from God in the first place.

One means of understanding the unity of all things is to consider that everything is sustained through energy vibrations. Just as science is now recognizing that mind underlies matter, it is also beginning to acknowl-

edge that spirit is the source of mind. Given, then, that all matter ultimately is spirit manifesting in different frequencies that influence one
another, the interconnections among phenomena become easier to
understand.

Another interesting perspective on the oneness of all things is found in
the *Bhagavad-gita:* "I am seated in everyone's heart, and from Me come
remembrance, knowledge and forgetfulness. By all the Vedas I am to be
known; indeed I am the compiler of Vedanta, and I am the knower of the
Vedas."[46] Here the speaker, Krishna (God), explains that He is in the heart
of every living being. From this it follows that guidance and knowledge
are also in everyone's heart, because a form of God resides there. Given
that such a form of God is in all life, then each individual aspect of life
should have no difficulty identifying, relating to, or connecting with
another aspect.

Extraterrestrial Life: Fact or Fiction?

Although the possibility of life on other planets is a controversial topic,
the subject has been mentioned frequently enough in books, articles and
other media to merit inclusion here. As a leader, you must keep an open
mind. It just might be possible that reported encounters with extraterrestrial visitors to this planet tap into some unknown capability of the
human mind to transcend everyday, generally accepted perceptions of
time and space.

Discussions about extraterrestrial life have existed since time immemorial. Throughout the ages, there have been reports by many cultures
about unidentified flying objects (UFOs) appearing in various locations.[47]
In such countries as Peru, for instance, UFOs have been investigated for
years because the local people constantly report their presence. Recent
times have witnessed an increase in the reporting of such incidents. A
Gallup poll in the late 1980s reported that 15 million Americans claimed
to have seen UFOs, while more than half of the U.S. population believes
that UFOs are real.[48]

Some American leaders have apparently had encounters of their own.
President Eisenhower reportedly saw UFO visitors at Edwards Air Force
Base in California in 1954.[49] During his campaign for President, Jimmy

Carter promised that if he were elected, he would encourage the Air Force to make public its UFO files. He had apparently sighted a UFO when he was the Governor of Georgia. In addition, there have been many other UFO sightings by reputable people throughout the world.[50]

Whatever one may think about the validity or the meaning of such experiences, these investigations are helping the human race gain more information about the vastness of God's creation and demonstrating that people perceive only a small microcosm of the total reality that can be experienced. Some individuals believe that in the twenty-first century there will be much more knowledge about, understanding of and communication with beings from other universes and other dimensions. For those who want to explore this topic in greater depth, numerous books and reports discuss UFOs, many written by quite respectable scientists commissioned to investigate these phenomena.[51]

Your Subsconsious Arsenal of Power

Another way in which the potential of the human mind becomes actuated is through dreams. Dreams affect a person's life more profoundly than one might expect. One way to appreciate the power of the dream state is to consider that a person's waking activities could be the result of these dream world experiences. In other words, whatever happens to people when they are asleep becomes manifest in some form during the waking state.

When someone is asleep, only the physical body actually takes rest. The astral body, composed of the mind, intelligence and ego, is often more active during sleep than in the waking state.[52] One could even say that people are more asleep when they are awake and more awake while sleeping!

Many great inventors and thinkers have received amazing inspiration from the higher dimensions after "sleeping on" a particular problem. During sleep, the physical body is at rest, but the subtle body is much more active and able to have experiences beyond this three-dimensional world. Considering that one-third of a person's life is spent sleeping, one can appreciate the need to understand the sleep state in order to gain the maximum benefit from it.

Dreams can be of inestimable benefit to you as a leader, providing guidance, inspiration, self-understanding and self-purification. You have many helpers in both your waking and sleeping states–another indication that you are not really alone. Legions of angels and also what are called "demigods" are ready to help you to serve those in your care more effectively.

Many dreams present information from a source of higher knowledge that can help you lead with clarity, decisiveness and integrity. During sleep, when the mind is not subject to the same limitations imposed by waking consciousness, you may discover unexpected, creative solutions to problems and gain useful insights into your motivations and behavior.

Creating the Proper Environment

People need different amounts of sleep, some requiring ten to twelve hours each night and others needing only four or five. However, the amount of sleep is not the only important factor for replenishing the body. The quality, and even the timing, of the sleep must be considered as well. For instance, the most restful hours for the body are from 10:00 p.m. to 12:00 midnight. Those two hours are so important that it is well worth the effort to get to bed by 10:00 p.m. If you go to bed after 10:00, you may need more hours of sleep to compensate. Also, remember that the quality of sleep will suffer if the mind is restless or disturbed, or if the body is feeling discomfort from eating late at night.

As you develop an appreciation of the dream state, you will be able to monitor and "program" your dreams in order to receive maximum benefit from them. One way to accomplish this is to set aside time to become peaceful before going to sleep. For instance, you might listen to pleasant, spiritually-oriented music or read literature of a spiritual and philosophical nature. In addition, for about thirty minutes before going to sleep, monitor your thoughts carefully, because the nature and quality of your thoughts just before sleep can have a powerful effect on your experience during the dream state. You can also request that answers to important questions appear to you in your dreams.

Whenever possible, avoid eating as bedtime approaches. If you eat within three hours of going to sleep, your body will be busy digesting food instead of getting the rest it needs. For example, if you consume a large meal before going to sleep, you will awaken feeling sluggish and tired the next morning, because the body did not fully replenish itself. Eating heavily before bedtime also increases sexual stimulation, creating a heavy abdomen that pushes on the genitals and can provoke sexual dreams.

Dream Interpretation

Interpreting dreams has recently become quite popular. Numerous books and journals discuss dream interpretation, and many people keep journals of their dreams and study the meaning of dream symbolism.[53] However, it is important not to become overly preoccupied with dream interpretation, which is often based on speculation and uncertainty. Dreams do not need your conscious assistance to serve their intended function. If a dream is significant, it will ultimately affect the conscious mind whether you analyze the dream or not. For example, a spiritual dream will make its impression by producing some new awareness during your waking state.[54]

However, there is still value in paying attention to dreams and heeding their messages, without becoming excessively preoccupied with analyzing them. In the process, it is wise not to become attached to a particular interpretation–especially if it appears self-serving–and to remain vigilant at all times about motivations and desires that might distort perceptions.

Here is a simple technique to help you remember your dreams: As soon as you awaken, and before you get out of bed, try to remember everything that happened during the previous night. Do this before moving any parts of your body. Then, if you so desire, you can write down your dreams in a journal in order to appreciate them at a later time. Keep in mind that once your feet touch the floor, you will immediately shock yourself back into the physical waking state and much of the subtle dream experience may fade from your awareness.

Importance of Sleep

The sleep state is one of the most important aspects of life. During this period, individuals have many opportunities to grow: they can meet with loved ones who have transcended to higher planes of life; visit great centers of learning; receive instruction from great spiritual masters; and encounter a variety of other experiences that can contribute to a deeper understanding of the purpose and meaning of life. The soul also has a chance to be in its more natural state, less bound to the gross physical body.

The importance of sleep is easy to understand if one remembers that, in terms of the perennial philosophy upon which all the world's great religions are based, the physical body is only a temple for the soul. If, then, the soul is the essence of a human being, people are closer to this natural soul state when they are dreaming and unaware of the physical body. This raises an essential question: Is it possible that the waking state is actually the dream and that the so-called dream is closer to the true awakened state? Ponder these thoughts. There is more truth in them than you may realize.

Highlights

1. What would human beings be capable of if they used the entire brain–all 100 percent of it? If they did so, they would be the gods they were intended to be: microcosms of the macrocosm, self-contained energy units with the power to move mountains. "Whosoever shall say unto this mountain, Be thou removed, and be thou cast into the sea; and shall not doubt in his heart, but shall believe that those things which he saith shall come to pass; he shall have whatsoever he saith,"[55] Jesus said to the disciples–and he was not joking.

2. Many diseases have direct or indirect psychological correlations, in which the mind causes the physical body to accept its conclusions, and the body reacts accordingly.

3. Psychoneuroimmunology is the study of the mysterious way in which a person's mind and emotions can influence the immune system. It appears that in addition to the thoughts in a person's mind, positive emotions such as hope and love can help speed the healing process. There is little doubt that the mind can be a most powerful healing tool.

4. The vast power of the human mind is also demonstrated by the existence of psychic phenomena. The field of parapsychology, which studies these phenomena, can be viewed as a bridge linking together the humanities, religion, and the arts and sciences into an integrated understanding of how the human mind interacts with the cosmos.

5. Every psychic phenomenon represents a conduit to another dimension, or another form of energy that is not acknowledged by orthodox belief systems, and demonstrates that humans are more than just physical beings.

6.   The Vedic philosophers believed that since all things are "one" in the sense that they come from God and are but different aspects of God's energy, this "oneness" is responsible for the interconnections that underlie psychic experiences. In this sense, God is simply knowing, relating, or interacting with different aspects of Himself. Thus, it is easy for God to heal Himself, or to know Himself, because everything comes from God in the first place.

7.   Whatever one may think about the validity or the meaning of UFO experiences, these investigations are helping the human race gain more information about the vastness of God's creation and demonstrating that people perceive only a small microcosm of the total reality that can be experienced.

8.   Another way in which the potential of the human mind becomes available is through dreams. Dreams affect a person's life more profoundly than one might expect. One way to appreciate the power of the dream state is to consider that a person's waking activities could be the result of these dream world experiences. In other words, whatever happens to people when they are asleep becomes manifest in some form during the waking state.

9.   Before going to sleep, you might listen to pleasant, spiritually-oriented music or read literature of a spiritual and philosophical nature. In addition, for about thirty minutes before going to sleep, monitor your thoughts carefully, because the nature and quality of your thoughts just before sleep can have a powerful effect on your experience during the dream state. You can also request that answers to important questions appear to you in your dreams.

10.   The sleep state is one of the most important aspects of life. During this period, individuals have many opportunities to grow: they can meet with loved ones who have transcended to higher planes of life; visit great centers of learning; receive instruction from great spiritual masters; and encounter a variety of other experi-

ences that can contribute to a deeper understanding of the purpose and meaning of life. The soul also has a chance to be in its more natural state, less bound to the gross physical body.

Mindsets

1.   Meditate on the ten essential technologies listed at the beginning of this book each night before going to sleep. From them, select a theme or question and request a dream to help deepen your understanding and give you guidance.

2.   Be aware of the relationship between your state of mind and your physical condition. Through self-examination, discover negative thoughts and feelings that may be harming your health, and take steps to release or transmute them. Refer to the preceding chapter for suggestions about how to do this.

3.   Try not to go to bed on a full stomach. Eat several hours before sleeping so your food will have time to digest. Observe the effects for yourself. One night, go to sleep immediately after a full meal and notice how you feel in the morning. Another time, wait several hours after eating before you retire. You will probably feel the difference the next day.

4.   If you want to remember your dreams better, keep a tape recorder or notebook at your bedside. Immediately upon awakening, before you begin moving around, reflect on your dream experiences. Then record them.

5.   Assess your attitude toward psychic phenomena. Do you scoff at them or consider them irrelevant to your work? Take some time to consider the importance that paranormal abilities might have to you as a leader, either in your own actions or in understanding the actions of others.

6.   Try rising at 4:00 or 5:00 a.m. to write, reflect, meditate, chant, pray, study or engage in other productive activities. These are the most potent hours of the entire day. If you are not excessively tired from staying up late the previous night, you will notice an

increased quality in your work or spiritual practice. You can also use these hours to make more thoughtful and effective decisions.

7. Explore the potential of suggestology or superlearning to enhance your own ability to absorb large amounts of information quickly, and encourage others to do so.

8. Take some quiet time each day to listen to the voice of your own intuition. In the silence, ask for general or specific guidance and then allow thoughts and images to emerge. You may want to write them down. Trust that they have meaning for you, and heed their messages.

9. Make an effort to get to know individuals who have special healing powers or other paranormal abilities. Speak with them about their work, and learn from them. Find ways to apply your learning in your leadership role.

10. In your daily life, pay attention to hunches, unexplainable feelings, or ideas that seem to come unbidden. Consider that these may be valuable sources of guidance, and do not discount them. At the same time, monitor your motivations and use your common sense to validate these hunches, feelings and ideas to ensure that they are not based on illusion.

Part II
Developing Skills

Human beings are co-creators with God, reflecting the fact that they are made "in the image of God." The thoughts they think and the words they speak today are constantly creating their tomorrows... those who learn to control their thoughts and words will control their future.

5

Patience, Tolerance and Empathy: Keys to Effective Leadership

*E*very leader can benefit from the qualities of mature patience and tolerance. However, there is a great difference between patience and laziness or apathy. Sometimes those who seem to be patient, or who want others to think they are being patient, are actually being apathetic. They are procrastinating about something that needs an immediate response.

Leaders should make special efforts to evaluate their own activities to see if they are displaying true patience and tolerance. They should also observe their patterns of avoidance, apathy or insensitivity, especially at those times when they need to be more involved in productive action.

Consider the Perspective of Others

The virtues of patience and tolerance are too important to be marred by individual character flaws. For example, one way to erode patience and tolerance is by failing to consider the position of another person, recognizing only one's own motivations and desires. Although someone may be able to tolerate another out of a sense of duty or magnanimity, the underlying attitude in such a situation is one of intolerance that considers the other as a nuisance whose opinion has little merit. Oftentimes people have such high regard for their own insights and realizations that they are reluctant or even unwilling to consider another person's perspective.

To behave in this way is to deny another's individuality and humanity, and to minimize that person's contributions. Therefore, instead of thinking, "I will tolerate this situation," it might be more helpful to think, "I will try to understand this situation and respond appropriately, without overreacting or minimizing its significance."

Those who are satisfied with a superficial evaluation of behavior will have difficulty being patient and tolerant in this way. People who lack compassion for others cannot be tolerant, because they do not feel obliged to adjust their world-view to factor-in anyone other than individuals of importance to them personally. This limited perspective also engenders feelings of insecurity and fear. Individuals who are insecure and fearful also tend to be impatient. Afraid of the future, they will try to do everything based on the present.

However, in one sense there is nothing but the future–which actually emerges from the present. At every moment, the past is already gone, the present is leaving, and the future is about to arrive. Therefore, being impatient actually has little meaning, because each desire, aspiration, and affirmation is creating what is to come, which will soon become the present. There is no reason to be worried about the future, because in a sense it is already upon us, manifesting according to what has been requested.

Be a Conscious Creator

As the well-known aphorism states, you must be careful about what you pray for because you may get it. This is a simple phrasing of one of the laws of creation. Human beings are co-creators with God, reflecting the fact that they are made "in the image of God." The thoughts they think and the words they speak today are constantly creating their tomorrows. As explained earlier, thoughts are things. They are composed of the same electrical, spirit-based energy that pervades the rest of the universe. Thoughts have substance and power, and the more emotional energy people give them, the faster they become a manifested reality. The spoken word has this same force and creative energy. Therefore, those who learn to control their thoughts and words will control their future. Since humans are constantly creating, the only issue is whether they are being conscious creators or unconscious ones.

The universe will supply whatever people ask for. Just as someone orders a meal in a restaurant, thoughts and words "order" various situations that are then delivered exactly according to the request. Although the results may not seem to be what was consciously wanted, the outcomes do indeed conform to the original "order." At some point the person made a request–consciously or unconsciously–that created them. Even if an item does not always "taste" as anticipated, the person is responsible for the "dish" because of the original order.

Since you are a co-creator with God, the more you are in tune with Him, the greater your power. So why think on a small scale? Think of plans that can assist the whole of humanity. Raise your level of consciousness! To understand that you are a co-creator is to be in pure harmony with the universe, acting as a servant of and co-worker with the divine. If you fail to appreciate this reality, you become destructive and are responsible for causing even more chaos in society. The choice is yours and so are the consequences.

Remember Who is Ultimately in Control

People who think in terms of being co-workers with God, but refuse to recognize His supremacy in all things, assume the unfortunate position of trying to control everything themselves. Anyone who acts and thinks in this irresponsible way eventually becomes an instrument of chaos.

It is difficult to be patient while idly waiting for something to happen. Patience comes more easily when one can channel energies into important projects. Such projects can be as valuable, or even more so, than whatever was being awaited in the first place. When people are actively involved in creating dynamic events around themselves, they are more able to balance their energies and to be less frantic and impatient.

While giving your very best at all times, as a leader you should also remain detached and not overly preoccupied with the outcome of your actions. Spiritually conscious people know that ultimately they are not in charge. They can only give their best, realizing that the result will accrue according to what has been consciously–or unconsciously–ordered.

On the other hand, leaders who consider themselves proprietors and controllers can be impatient and intolerant, viewing themselves as centers around which all things revolve for their personal pleasure. Others, who envy God and want to be the Godhead themselves, may work hard to acquire mystical abilities and other powers. Such people tend to be ruthless and will interfere with the health and welfare of others instead of helping them.[56]

Whenever you are tempted to succumb to a desire for power and control, reflect once again on the discussion about love in the first chapter. Remember that as your consciousness is directed by love, your impatience will recede, and any difficulties you encounter will become more smoothly resolved.

Laugh at those situations that cause you anxiety. Sometimes you only need to look objectively at yourself, especially at your mind, to become amused by the absurd dictates it produces. If you allow yourself to identify with such ridiculous thoughts, you will increase your anxiety and have greater difficulty serving others.

The Decline of Patience and Tolerance

In the future, the highly mechanized impersonal structure of modern society is likely to engender even more impatience and intolerance than exist today. Automation is changing the lives of millions of people. For example, in the coming decade, companies will increasingly turn to robotics and other forms of automation. In the next 20 years, a great number of the factory workers in the industrialized countries may be replaced by robots.[57]

Not only do people risk becoming impersonal, insensitive, and intolerant in such circumstances, but they are also endangering one of the most important aspects of a strong society: the opportunity for its citizens to perform gratifying work. Although widespread automation produces a greater number of commodities in a shorter time, it does so at tremendous human cost. Leaders should weigh the long-range consequences, and support processes that enhance human well-being by making decisions that are people-oriented rather than just profitable.

Another effect of modern technology is its ability to have a widespread impact very quickly. For example, modern weapons can wipe out entire cities in a matter of minutes, a plane crash can end hundreds of lives in a flash, or a small problem in an electrical grid can instantly cause power failure for millions. Computers linking businesses, banking systems, government agencies and a host of other organizations can crash, causing instantaneous problems for those dependent upon them. With such tools at everyone's disposal, the importance of patience and tolerance cannot be overestimated.

Even eating habits seriously interfere with patience and tolerance toward others. As people eat more "fast" foods, the general pace of life becomes more rapid. A vast number of foodstuffs are available to many within a few minutes, and rapid transportation brings delicacies halfway around the world in a few hours. Such speed affects the psyche and causes people to act like children seeking instant gratification.

The way people farm and treat animals also directly affects the general level of patience and tolerance. Many animals are now being raised just for slaughter. Kept under extremely artificial conditions, they are injected with different drugs to speed their growth and to make them ready for our eager consumption. In many places around the world, farms are large enterprises geared towards massive production.

However, this approach damages the planet's ecology and puts small farmers out of business, eliminating the opportunity for many to live close to nature and make a meaningful contribution to society. Many small farmers, who are in direct contact with the earth's rhythm in their daily work, have learned the importance of adapting themselves to the natural order. They have more opportunities to practice patience than those who have lost touch with the natural world.

Worst of all is the way people treat their own bodies. Numbers of people die every year from hypertension and ulcers, aggravated by an atmosphere of impatience and intolerance. In addition, modern medicine can replace almost any limb or reconstruct almost any type of body that someone might want. Instead of accepting what they have and appreciating natural body changes, those who can afford it may seek to alter bodily features to suit an idealized image. In addition to plastic surgery, cosmetics are available to change appearances temporarily. All of these adjustments add to the general intolerance and impatience with the way things are.

Developing Patience and Tolerance

One way to increase your patience and tolerance is to monitor this highly mechanized and cosmetic world carefully in order to offset its negative effects. As mentioned earlier, you can be in this world but not of it or, as the first Epistle of John puts it: "Love not the world, neither the things that are in the world. If any man love the world, the love of the Father is not in him."[58] This does not mean to be impractical. Rather, it means not to be unnecessarily attached to this world of limitations and its transitory activities. Instead, while doing what is required in the material world, you can make sure that you connect with the higher realms and their more divine activities and relationships.

Everything has its natural rhythm. In some cases people can interfere with this scheme and get rather good immediate results. However, negative reactions will occur at some point in the future. Much of the chaos in the world today can be traced to the failure to look holistically at the long-term effects of human actions. Unbridled material growth has caused many societies to become orgies of competing sovereign interests in which individuals seek their ends by any means available. As a result, the whole cosmic body suffers more every day from the poisonous diseases that the human race is spreading throughout its system.

Consider the case of a pregnant woman. If all needs have been carefully met, in time she will be the mother of a healthy child. When this woman first learned of her pregnancy, she would have been foolish to say to her doctor, "Now that I'm pregnant, where is the baby?" A natural course of maturation is required before the child is ready to appear outside of the womb.

In the same way, people who recognize their role in creation and allow everything to unfold in its natural rhythm will enhance the quality of life for themselves and for others. But if human beings continue to act in an unconscious and erratic manner, they will produce frivolous, superficial or destructive results. By being more in harmony with nature instead of interfering and creating unnecessary confusion, people can improve themselves and benefit the world.

Patience and tolerance are essential factors of true leadership, because they are signs of strength and power. It is easy to produce useless or harmful results, but it takes great strength to create beneficial outcomes in the right way at the right time.

Pitfalls of Leadership

Leadership has many pitfalls. One serious problem is the temptation for leaders to become autocratic or to act solely on the basis of their own desires, aspirations and perceptions. Instead, leaders can view their role as one of coordinating the activities of those for whom they are responsible. To do so properly requires the constant awareness of being a servant to others. Being a servant entails keeping abreast of the people's problems, needs and goals, in order to be in a position to stimulate growth and develop useful projects that enhance the quality of life.

A second pitfall for leaders is the tendency to take the benefits of leadership for granted, forgetting that most people do not share in the blessings and privileges inherent in such a position. One way to counteract this complacent attitude is to visit, from time to time, the various institutions for the less fortunate. For example, no matter what your level of leadership, you might make periodic visits to hospitals, mental institutions, prisons or orphanages. Seeing such suffering can greatly increase your desire to help others. Further, by helping the most unfortunate, you will be helping yourself as well, because an organization, a society or a nation is only as strong as its weakest link.

International statistics concerning the misery of the less fortunate are quite disturbing. Throughout the world, hunger and poverty are a fact of life. Half a billion adults and children are in a constant state of hunger. Another half billion–20 percent of the world's population–are too poor to obtain an adequate diet for a productive work life.[59]

Although hunger is a serious issue, the entire range of basic human needs is unfulfilled in the lives of many of the world's people. For example, millions of children die every year in the Third World from common childhood diseases that inexpensive vaccinations could prevent.[60] Basic education, safe drinking water and even freedom from political persecution and torture are rights that many of us take for granted. However, these blessings are only dreams to many people on this planet. The degree of human suffering, already staggering, is increasing every day.[61]

A third pitfall associated with leadership is the temptation to be bored, unenthusiastic, and even depressed at times. Those who feel this way can lose perspective of their situation, forgetting the extent to which their lives are being guided, controlled and assisted by the Lord, whether they know it or not. Although some may not accept the existence of a God, it is a fact that higher forces do act upon every person's life. Leaders can overcome some of these negative feelings by reflecting on the many wonderful situations God has arranged for them, in contrast to the experiences of the average person. Such thoughts can bring immediate relief, or even exhilaration, as these many blessings become apparent.

The temptations to be autocratic, to take the benefits of leadership for granted, or to become bored or depressed are just a few of the hazards of leadership. There are of course many others. By maintaining a strong connection with divine guidance, and by determined practice, leaders can refuse to give them power and eventually overcome them.

Loneliness: Reality or Illusion?

Another important issue for many leaders is the tendency to suffer from a sense of loneliness and isolation. Although feeling alone often puts people in a state of depression, for a leader, loneliness is an everyday reality. Far from being an unpleasant experience, solitude as a means of self-care can often be rejuvenating and inspiring. If leaders do not take time away from their usual responsibilities and renew themselves, their service can suffer. Although they probably get more work done when constantly surrounded by others who assist them, without regular periods of introspection and silent contemplation they may not be able to maintain their pace.

Spiritual life can offer an antidote to the feelings of loneliness that may be part of your experience as a leader. This is so because there is a presence of God in your heart that is always monitoring your activities. Such a presence can be a source of great solace, and it is increasingly available as you learn to control your passions. Then, even if your psychic space is bombarded constantly, or if you feel agonizingly alone, your contact with the higher self–that aspect of God residing within you–allows you to be guided and protected by higher forces.

Because all souls have emanated from one God, no one need feel lonely or separate. When you realize that all souls are the same and that only bodies, as garments, are different, you may feel refreshed, realizing that everyone is part of a great family sharing the same spiritual inheritance. Daily meditation on this awareness can help you become free from loneliness. How can you be lonely and depressed knowing that you are under the loving care of the Divine Supreme Personality who sends you individualized assistance?

Moving Beyond Loneliness

Periods of great desperation or difficulty are excellent times to cry out to the Supreme. Is it not a fact that people often learn most through their problems? If you are confused, sometimes it is best to do nothing at first. Instead of acting right away, listen to your sources of guidance, feeding the problem to that presence of God within you called the Supersoul or the higher self. Then you can release the problem to divine authority, understanding that a difficult situation is the perfect classroom in which to learn your lesson. When you allow yourself to be guided in this way, you are in harmony with the universe, which ensures that every possible source of assistance will be made available to you.

Of course, it is not easy to experience the Lord in the heart. Those who succeed want self-realization very desperately, as much as a drowning person who rises to the water's surface desperately gasps for air. The intensity of your desire will create a strong bond with your higher self, opening your "communication lines" and eradicating your confusion. When your determination becomes this strong, all kinds of channels will open to help you gain higher levels of awareness.

When you are feeling lonely and confused, review your previous achievements and activities. Did you make use of the help available to you from higher levels, or instead did you try to do everything alone? Although you may already have been successful in many of your previous undertakings, remember that a limitless supply of guidance is available from the universe–from God–to assist in future endeavors. This may help you feel enthusiastic and inspired by what has happened in the past and by what can happen even more successfully in the future.

This technique of positive thinking allows you to build on past achievements, thereby proceeding further than you would by becoming preoccupied with fears and doubts. Always remember that what you hold in your consciousness manifests outwardly in your body and your affairs. If you think and act in accordance with spirit, you will recognize that you are not alone and that you are constantly being monitored and supported.

Avoiding an Elitist Mentality

A leader's responsibility is to keep the interests of the people always as a number one priority. Therefore, in your leadership role, you should be careful not to give any instructions that you would not follow yourself. Put yourself in the other's position as you plan projects and give instructions. Be careful of elitism, which is a "disease" that can render your efforts irrelevant.

If you are not careful, you may be tempted to consider your present subculture as the entire world. Unfortunately, this can cause you to give inappropriate guidance and instructions or to formulate useless plans that are not based on the day-to-day realities of those you represent. On the other hand, when you consciously practice relating to the positions of others, you minimize the risk of becoming irrelevant, and your plans for those in your care will be more effective.

To avoid the elitist syndrome, you can regularly mingle with those who experience financial hardship, and even perform a simple job as if it provided your sustenance. Such work not only benefits your psyche; it also increases the love of those you supervise, because they see your willingness to put yourself in a position of servitude. When you take such a job, try to feel the daily yearnings and tremendous obstacles that most people experience. Then you can understand how little control many feel over their own lives.

When you are the apparent controller–which, as a leader, you generally are–any small decision may seem insignificant to you. But the people affected by that decision may experience extreme anxiety, especially if they perceive that their survival is being threatened.

To develop empathy and appreciation, try meditating on a simple person in society who has little or nothing, yet still seems to get by. You might also notice that certain spiritual people with few material possessions seem to have a great wealth of inner happiness, peace and love. In contrast, as you look at your surroundings, notice how many superfluous commodities have become a part of your daily environment. Indeed, any confusion, tension, or disappointment you experience may result from having overly complicated your life.

When people are attached to unhealthy, temporary situations, such situations can become stagnating and repressive factors in their lives. Everyone wants to be a free spirit, able to enjoy the finest that life has to offer, but the finest that life has to offer is not material. Instead, it is so transcendental that it makes the basic material pleasures seem bland, and even painful, in contrast to the sublime sentiments, realizations, and sensations obtained from higher spiritual contact.

When you think about the many difficulties faced by those trying to eke out a living, pause a moment to reflect upon the insignificance of your problems in comparison to what others around the world experience every day.

Conquering Envy

The opposites of empathy are intolerance, apathy, and envy.[62] These negative attitudes keep people from empathizing with the less fortunate, or from being of use to anyone at all. Like impatience, envy is a great destroyer of natural compassion, and those who are genuinely trying to be their brother's keepers would do well to exercise vigilance in order to avoid it.

People will often encounter others with admirable attributes who perform better than they do, or who receive credit that they feel belongs to them. Envy is ultimately one of the greatest offenses against God, because it emerges from interactions with aspects of God's creation–fellow human beings. Envy is the major factor that keeps people separated from their natural God-consciousness.

Envy cannot easily be changed, because everyone is subconsciously envious of God, and therefore has a certain tendency to envy any authority. In fact, all difficulties in this material existence can be attributed primarily to the fact that human beings are innately envious of God. This is so because the degree of envy represents the degree to which people break the laws of God, and the extent to which people break the laws of God indicates the extent to which they bring misfortune upon themselves. Fortunately, as human beings become more self-realized, they find that their envy of God decreases, and as it decreases toward God, it also decreases toward other human beings.[63]

Because you are a leader, some people will always be envious of you. Envy can create a drain on your consciousness and interfere with your ability to serve effectively. This situation can test your love and tempt you to react negatively. Be careful not to allow this to happen. Instead just accept the circumstances, recognize them, and refuse to be destroyed by them. Whenever you experience envious people around you, you can also try to uplift them by projecting loving, selfless and caring thoughts.

In the face of your own envy, remember that when you are able to enjoy the achievements, happiness, and successes of others, you become empowered to be a carrier of high spiritual potential. Your productivity will increase and your outlook on life will be far more positive than if you view others with a sense of rivalry. Empathizing and sympathizing with others are not useless exercises. They are great ways to guide, instruct, and assist people, because one learns to have a deeper appreciation of who these individuals are, how they feel, and what their ultimate desires and needs are. In addition, empathy is essential for social and organizational stability. Anyone who has not learned to feel the pulse of other people is sitting on a time bomb that can explode when least expected.

As you practice being less disturbed by the envy of others in all your leadership functions, and as you overcome your own internal envy, you will automatically be transformed into a more loving being. The resulting empowerment will assist you in fulfilling your leadership responsibilities with confidence, compassion and integrity. Try to remember the power of envy every day, not so that it becomes a fixation, but so that you work in a way that reduces the envy of others. When such envy is minimized, you can more easily mobilize people to action.

Highlights

1.   Leaders should make special efforts to evaluate their own activities to see if they are displaying true patience and tolerance. They should also observe their patterns of avoidance, apathy or insensitivity, especially at those times when they need to be more involved in productive action.

2.   Those who are satisfied with a superficial evaluation of behavior will have difficulty being patient and tolerant. People who lack compassion for others cannot be tolerant, because they do not feel obliged to adjust their world-view to factor in anyone other than individuals of importance to them personally.

3.   Thoughts are things! They are composed of the same electrical, spirit-based energy that pervades the rest of the universe. Thoughts have substance and power, and the more emotional energy people give them, the faster they become a manifested reality.

4.   While giving your very best at all times, you should also remain detached and not overly preoccupied with the outcome of your actions. Spiritually conscious people know that ultimately they are not in charge.

5.   Whenever you are tempted to succumb to a desire for power and control, reflect once again on the discussion about love in the first chapter. Remember that as your consciousness is directed by love, your impatience will recede, and any area of difficulty will go more smoothly for you.

6.   Everything has its natural rhythm. In some cases people can interfere with this scheme and get rather good immediate results. However, negative reactions will occur at some point in the future.

Much of the chaos in the world today can be traced to the failure to look holistically at the long-term effects of human actions.

7. Leaders can view their role as one of coordinating the activities of those for whom they are responsible. To do so properly requires the constant awareness of being a servant to others. Being a servant entails keeping abreast of the people's problems, needs and goals, in order to be in a position to stimulate growth and develop useful projects that enhance the quality of life.

8. When people are attached to unhealthy, temporary situations, such situations can become stagnating and repressive factors in their lives. Everyone wants to be a free spirit, able to enjoy the finest that life has to offer, but the finest that life has to offer is not material. Instead, it is so transcendental that it makes the basic material pleasures seem bland, and even painful, in contrast to the sublime sentiments, realizations, and sensations obtained from higher spiritual contact.

9. Because all souls have emanated from one God, no one need feel lonely or separate. When you realize that all souls are the same and that only bodies, as garments, are different, you may feel refreshed, realizing that everyone is part of a great family sharing the same spiritual inheritance. Daily meditation on this awareness can help you become free from loneliness.

10. Whenever you experience envious people around you, you can try to uplift them by projecting loving, selfless and caring thoughts. In the face of your own envy, remember that when you are able to enjoy the achievements, happiness, and successes of others, you become empowered to be a carrier of high spiritual potential.

Mindsets

1. Read over the ten essential technologies at the beginning of this book, concentrating on numbers 1, 3, 4 and 7. Practice applying these in everyday life. Whenever you are disturbed, try to put the situation in perspective by reminding yourself about the ultimate goal of life. In the midst of a conflict, remember to see your would-be opponent as an energy of God, and to consider the problem from that person's point of view. Keep in mind that disruptive behavior is actually a call for love.

2. Patience does not mean tolerating someone from a superior vantage point, considering the other as an inferior or foolish person. Instead, patience means extending yourself and trying to understand the other's position. Once again, remember that each action is either a gift of love or a call for love.

3. See yourself as a co-creator with the Supreme Lord, and be careful what you create or draw to you.

4. Try to have several important projects so that you will not become too impatient with any particular one that may not be progressing at your desired speed.

5. Do your best, but do not be overly attached to the results of any endeavor. The ultimate outcome is up to the Creator. If you think you are the sole controller, you will become a serious failure in the long run.

6. Practice laughing at situations that are causing you anxiety, realizing that the problem is temporary and that you have the power to make a change. In particular, learn to laugh at negative dictates from your mind. Establish that you are different from your mind and that you have the ability to accept or reject its offerings.

7,   Be in the world but not of it. The present highly mechanized impersonal structure of modern society encourages impatience, intolerance and erratic behavior.

8.   Practice being unaffected by the envy of others. You will gradually learn to be concerned about their welfare but undisturbed by their behavior. Bless those who wish you misfortune. This blessing reduces their ability to harm you, because your positive energy counteracts their negative energy. Remember to apply the science of love in all circumstances.

9.   Check your thoughts and actions constantly to ensure that you are not exploiting or abusing others. Remember that a leader is a servant and not a special person who deserves privileges unavailable to most people.

10.   Make a report to God every night about your day's performance. Note those areas that need improvement and make commitments to make specific changes.

6

Exercising Careful Scrutiny

Today everyone lives in an extremely interdependent world. Because of advances in communications and the massive scale of technological development, effects from events in one part of the globe can often be instantaneously felt in another. Also, because modern society is so complex, the causes of a particular situation may not be readily apparent, despite the fact that the effects are easily noticed.[64]

Determining the Underlying Causes

Leaders who seek positive, lasting goals should endeavor to eliminate superficiality in all their interactions, addressing each problem at its roots. Those who rely primarily on facades ultimately encounter serious difficulty. To avoid such pitfalls, you should exercise careful scrutiny, probing beneath the surface to discover the true cause of each effect. If you are accustomed to dealing with situations quickly and decisively, this approach may go against the grain. However, a "quick fix" without the proper understanding can allow original symptoms to recur or new, unexpected disturbances to develop.[65]

In your leadership role, take care not to become too complacent in any situation, even when everything seems to be going well. Any deep underlying conflict–whether in programs or in people–will eventually produce symptoms that require corrective action. The practice of careful scrutiny will encourage you to examine all facets of a particular circumstance, taking into consideration the tensions, problems, and motivations that may not be immediately apparent. Such a perspective allows you to recognize when appearances do not tell the whole story–as, for example, when the successes reported to you by a subordinate are deliberately distorted to create a false sense of achievement.

Your plans for the future will be more successful if you are aware of the underlying realities of the present. After all, everything external has developed from an idea–an internal experience–that later becomes manifested in the physical world. Careful planning involves breaking issues down into their most elementary components in order to identify their essence. Only then is it possible to build on a solid foundation. Those who bypass this essential step may end up wasting their efforts, creating complex structures that unfortunately rest on quicksand and so are destined for a disastrous collapse.

Identifying the Universal Principles

One useful way to become more perceptive about underlying causes, and therefore more effective in all endeavors, is to identify the common denominators and universal principles in each situation. Universal principles are those basic, nonsectarian truths that exist independently of relative human perceptions, and that always operate for the benefit of the whole.

The beauty of universal principles is that they connect many variables with one another and make smooth interrelationships possible among widely divergent people, projects and plans. They enable one to exercise leadership beyond the relative or transitory level. Universal principles create a common ground that engenders a greater chance of success in any interaction–person-to-person or nation-to-nation.

Each Person as an Energy of God

Several of these universal principles can be of particular benefit to you as a leader. One such principle is: *Each individual is an energy of God.* As you interact with people in the performance of your leadership duties, view each of them with concern and affection, remaining undisturbed by any abrasive personality traits. Instead of viewing your adversaries as sources of anxiety and irritation, remind yourself to see them as part of the energy of God. Despite outward appearances, the essence of each person–the life force inside–is in fact divine. Therefore, although you may hate a particular offense, you do not need to hate the offender.

This attitude allows you to maintain a high level of love and equanimity in all situations, whether friendly or threatening. Indeed, whenever you allow an opponent to upset you, you are in fact weakening your own position, because your disturbance may cause you to overreact, underreact, or do harm to yourself in other ways. Also, it is important to remember that anger and frustration produce distorted or diminished perceptions and, on the physical level, even hypertension, neurosis, or ulcers. Instead, if you see everyone as an energy of God, you can make steady progress in all your leadership endeavors, performing necessary actions without being distracted by anyone–friend or foe. This way of thinking takes you beyond the facade, allowing you to deepen your understanding of yourself, of other people, and of life itself.

The Life Force in All Creation

Another universal principle is: *The life force in each person is connected with the life force present in all creation.* When you grasp this idea, you understand that the way to influence the *collective life* force is by channeling and controlling your *own* life force. Your ability to do so allows you to affect the activities of the entire world. Once again, this principle takes you beyond superficial appearances, where everything may seem separate, to discover the deep connections that link you, and those you lead, with all life.

These connections between your own life force and the universal one also mean that unlimited achievements are possible, because you are always in contact with the common reservoir of power, intelligence and love. What is true for you as a leader is also true for those in your charge. When you forget this reality, you minimize your potential for higher achievements and you ignore the same potential in others. Therefore, whether you are sleeping, dreaming, or awake, try to see deeply into each person or circumstance to appreciate the power of the life force at work. Ask yourself: "What is the deepest truth of this situation? How is it related to other phenomena? What is my relationship to this? How can a higher good result from this?"

One way to deepen your awareness is to ponder the intrinsic nature of a situation as if you were meditating with your eyes open. Then you will be viewing phenomena in your environment in a contemplative state, reflecting on how to gain the maximum appreciation from each circumstance. As you reflect deeply on each encounter, you can begin to improve the quality of your leadership and to gain more control over your life.

The Source of All Beauty

Another important universal principle is: *Recognize the source of all beauty.* The sight of something beautiful can help you appreciate the beauty of its origins. For example, when you see a beautiful painting, you may think: "What a clever person to produce this!" At first, you may see only the surface manifestation, but as you contemplate this work of art, you might reflect further about what stimulated the artist to produce such an interesting masterpiece. For example, you might think: "What does the artist want to express through this?" The external situation is just a way of producing more introspection, and that introspection allows you to discover a greater number of internal truths and appreciations that add to the quality of your leadership and your life.

One of the biggest issues in leadership is the need to become more expert at controlling the senses, especially when they are focused on the opposite sex. The mind is very childish, always running madly after different types of gratification. The following technique can be useful: When you see an attractive person of the opposite sex, instead of becoming bewildered, confused, and losing your equilibrium, control yourself by meditating on the source of this attractiveness. Marvel at the fact that in this single individual resides such captivating beauty or handsomeness, and reflect on how wonderful and sublime the Creator is to have produced such a being, whose pleasing appearance is actually a manifestation of divine energy and creativity.

When you recognize the true source of beauty in this way, you can become even more appreciative of an attractive person. As a leader, you are required to maintain your equilibrium at all times, going beyond the temptations of the senses that desire objects of gratification in the material world. Your task is to seek deeper experiences and higher connections that are attainable through proper regulation and control of the senses.

Pleasure-Seeking

This issue of sense gratification is related to one of the most important universal principles underlying all phenomena: *People are always involved in pleasure-seeking.* Pleasure-seeking is behind all of humanity's multifaceted activities. All sane people have this interest in common. Indeed, human beings pursue specific goals and maintain particular lifestyles mainly because these bring pleasure.

The fact that humans are pleasure-seeking beings is consistent with the Freudian view that people are constantly motivated by sex. However, sex in this context does not just mean the physical act. Instead, the word has a more general sense, referring to all forms of pleasurable experiences.[66]

In every endeavor, people are either attempting to avoid something negative or moving toward that which is positive. In other words, in addition to seeking pleasure, everyone is trying to avoid pain. This behavior, because it is so universal, serves as a unifying aspect of civilization, transcending all divergent interests or sectarian distinctions.

On the brink of the twenty-first century, many individuals are suffering intensely despite the fact that pleasure-seeking occupies much of their mental energy. Despair and suicide are increasing everywhere. People numb themselves with drugs, sex, sports, and other types of stimuli to minimize their hurt. It is as if they were trying to arrange their lives to allow themselves to suffer more peacefully. However, no matter what they do, they will ultimately be in pain if they do not penetrate deeper levels of consciousness and seek higher levels of experience.

The desire for higher pleasures and the longing to go beyond the mundane are inherent in everyone. People have the choice of either expanding their awareness to attain a genuine experience of such pleasures, or of using artificial means such as drugs, alcohol or other props to avoid the issue. As a leader, you can help create an atmosphere in which people begin to experience the higher pleasures.

God in the Heart

Another important universal principle is: *God is present in everyone's heart*, an idea that was discussed at the beginning of this book. God, the presence behind all things, is guiding and monitoring each person at all times. Therefore, there are no accidents. God runs a very orderly universe—so orderly that one can set a watch or calendar by its movements. As people exercise their free will, they create the *appearance* of accidents, forgetting that each action produces an effect in accordance with immutable laws. Everything occurs according to the will of God. Eventually, human beings learn to understand that nothing happens by chance.

Regardless of how someone perceives a situation, a greater master plan is unfolding. From this perspective, even so-called "evil" or "bad" events can be considered as part of a higher strategy to correct those who are violating divine law. The Lord expresses love in different ways, and sometimes it is through the chastisement—in the form of inevitable consequences—that karmic law imposes on those who stray from the path. Such chastisement functions as a means to develop the proper character and behavior. Therefore, seemingly negative situations have their role in the total scheme of creation, offering the potential to be ultimately beneficial.

This does not mean that God wills negative events upon people. Instead, these events are the consequences of one's own actions, with which even God will not interfere. Such experiences provide learning opportunities that give individuals the opportunity to rebalance their karmic energies and eventually return *home*. If you grasp this reality, you can recognize each occurrence–whether a success or a setback–as another occasion to make a wise choice that can ultimately create balance and harmony, advancing you and those around you one more step along the path back to God.

The Value of Universal Principles

Many disturbances in the world are caused by a failure to seek unity with those who seem different. In your role as a leader, the more you can identify common ground with others, the less you will be subject to conflicts caused by superficial differences. Universal principles can help you discover the common foundation shared with others by reminding you that everyone originates from the same source and is seeking to return to the same *home* with God.

In your day-to-day practice of leadership, you have many opportunities to examine each encounter and each decision carefully. In so doing, you can bypass the superficial aspects of the situation–which are often simply symptoms of the real underlying issue–and discover the universal truths that will direct you to genuinely constructive action.

No matter what capabilities you possess as a leader, your duty is to determine how to get the most effective use from what the Lord has provided. One way to accomplish this is to practice delving more deeply into the universal principles and to develop the habit of looking beneath the surface in all situations. With regular practice, this process can help you gain a greater experience of God in any circumstance and can demonstrate that divine love is totally available whenever you are willing to accept it. Every experience then becomes elevating and beneficial, because you understand that there is nothing but God, whose mercy is everywhere. This level of awareness brings happiness and joy.

Highlights

1. Leaders who seek positive, lasting goals should endeavor to eliminate superficiality in all their interactions, addressing each
problem at its roots. Those who rely primarily on facades may
ultimately encounter serious difficulty. To avoid such pitfalls, you
must exercise careful scrutiny, probing beneath the surface to
discover the true cause of each effect.

2. The practice of careful scrutiny will encourage you to examine all
facets of a particular circumstance, taking into consideration the
tensions, problems, and motivations that may not be immediately
apparent. Such a perspective allows you to recognize when
appearances do not tell the whole story.

3. Everything external has developed from an idea–an internal experience–that later becomes manifested in the physical world.
Careful planning involves breaking issues down into their most
elementary components in order to identify their essence. Only
then is it possible to build on a solid foundation.

4. One useful way to become more perceptive about underlying
causes, and therefore more effective in all endeavors, is to identify
the common denominators and universal principles in each situation. Universal principles are those basic, nonsectarian truths
that exist independently of relative human perceptions, and that
always operate for the benefit of the whole.

5. One universal principle is: *Each individual is an energy of God.* As
you interact with people in the performance of your leadership
duties, view each of them with concern and affection, remaining
undisturbed by any abrasive personality traits.

6. Another universal principle is: *The life force in each person is con-nected with the life force present in all creation.* When you grasp this idea, you understand that the way to influence the collective life force is by channeling and controlling your own life force.

7. Another important universal principle is: *Recognize the source of all beauty.* The sight of something beautiful can help you appreci-ate the beauty of its origins.

8. One of the most important universal principles underlying all phenomena is: *People are always involved in pleasure-seeking.* Pleasure-seeking is behind all of humanity's multifaceted activi-ties.

9. The desire for higher pleasures and the longing to go beyond the mundane are inherent in everyone. People have the choice of either expanding their awareness to attain a genuine experience of such pleasures, or of using artificial means such as drugs, alcohol or other props to avoid the issue. As a leader, you can help create an atmosphere in which people begin to experience the higher pleasures.

10. Another important universal principle is: *God is present in every-one's heart.* God, the presence behind all things, is guiding and monitoring each person at all times. Therefore, there are no acci-dents. God runs a very orderly universe–so orderly that one can set a watch or calendar by its movements.

Mindsets

1.   Refer to the ten essential technologies listed at the beginning of this book, focusing especially on numbers 1 and 5. Remember to examine each situation carefully to discover the truth beneath any appearances that may exist on the surface. Also, because there are no coincidences, seek the positive lessons inherent in apparently negative events.

2.   Try to appreciate the essence, or intimate nature, of situations. Look for the universal principles to help you establish bridges, develop better communications, and build genuine unity.

3.   As you seek the common denominator, look for how a higher good can come out of each situation, and take steps to make it happen.

4.   Continue your practice of seeing everyone as an energy of God, and appreciate how we are all lovingly connected. Use this approach even with your so-called enemies. Everyone will benefit.

5.   Visualize the connection between your life force and the life force throughout the universe. Since you have access to universal reservoirs of power, intelligence, and love, do not think small. Instead, as you purify yourself, think of yourself as also purifying the world, positively affecting the collective world consciousness. Everything is available to you if you connect properly.

6.   Reflect in a way that keeps you in a constant state of meditation even with your eyes open. Always examine each situation carefully in order to gain the maximum benefit from each interaction.

7.   As you observe beauty in the world, consider how exquisite the source of all beauty must be. Allow this awareness to increase

your interest in contacting the Godhead itself, the Creator and Reservoir of beauty and pleasure.

8.   Remember that the ideal is neither to let your senses run wild through superficial attractions nor to suppress your desires. Instead, you can learn to replace lower desires with higher ones.

9.   By nature, human beings are seekers of altered states of consciousness. However, using drugs, alcohol, or other artificial means to experience deeper states of consciousness will ultimately do nothing but increase frustration. Such temporary stimulation can be replaced with ecstasy from natural consciousness-raising activities.

10.   Because there is nothing but God, practice seeing everything as alive–inanimate objects as well as animate beings. This attitude will help you to approach everything in a more open and respectful way.

7

Resolving Conflict for the Benefit of All

One of the most remarkable paradoxes of modern times involves communication. The capacity to communicate large amounts of information rapidly around the planet has never been greater.[67] Yet the ability of everyone to communicate clearly and lovingly with others has declined, causing much pain, suffering and conflict. As global citizens, human beings are being called upon each day to discover and apply new ways of communicating in order to settle differences effectively and bring an end to suffering. To this end, an important function of any leader is to create an atmosphere in which people have the opportunity to address conflicts honestly and to resolve them fairly.

The Traditional View

In the traditional view, conflicts are negative experiences to be avoided, if possible. One side "wins" and the other "loses"–and no one wants to lose. People who perceive conflicts within this win-lose frame of reference frequently tend to ignore, minimize, or override many underlying differences. Parties in a dispute may attempt to smooth over diverging viewpoints in an effort to avoid feeling the powerlessness of loss, or in a determined effort to win.

In recent decades, it has become apparent that this approach has not worked. A new understanding of conflict is emerging, one that does not view differences as necessarily negative. Instead, it looks beneath the superficial issues to the fundamental needs and values being expressed, and considers the possibility of win-win solutions.

Frequently, conflicts subjected to a win-lose approach flare up again later, because the underlying issues have not been addressed. The warfare in Bosnia is an extreme case in point, being fueled by deep-seated, unresolved antagonisms and hurts. Conflict *management*, which seeks the short-term benefit of containing conflict by addressing its symptoms or by designating winners and losers, is not enough to ensure lasting peace. Conflict *resolution*, which probes more deeply to discover the heart of a problem, is required to implement enduring changes.

Universal Human Needs

In the late twentieth century, humanity occupies a shared global village, and the inherent needs of human beings are intrinsically similar across all cultures and forms of government. Whereas conflicts over material interests tend to lead to a win-lose outcome, conflicts over universal human needs such as identity, love, respect or security do not fit this paradigm. Because the supply of these is unlimited, such needs can be met without depriving others.

Effective conflict resolution addresses this level of essential human needs, which are shared by all. The world today could greatly benefit from learning how to identify the fundamental emotional, psychological and spiritual needs of each culture, going beyond the obvious superficial conflicts to discover the more hidden factors. Such an approach might point out the common elements among cultures and help groups with widely diverging points of view develop a greater appreciation for one another.

If conflict between persons or nations is ultimately caused by a desire to fulfill fundamental human aspirations rather than by wishes for material gain, then many of the methods societies have developed to manage differences are doomed to failure. Indeed, to the extent that they frustrate the pursuit of human, nonmaterial goals, they can actually intensify conflict. Traditional methods of dispute resolution have generally involved the determination of each party's material goals and interests and the subsequent imposition of a solution upon both sides, as in a court of law or before an arbitration panel. An alternative has often been to force a resolution through warfare.

However, disputes that involve intense feelings, values and needs are deep-rooted and cannot be settled easily by an order from an outside authority. The losing party is frequently left with bitter resentment and a sense of impotence that does not go away. Many conflicts cannot be settled by any external arrangement that fails to consider the basic human needs of each participant, independently of the material situation. A less materialistic, more spiritual view of human nature is a necessary prerequisite to the effective resolution of differences in today's world. This makes a deep-rooted, more integrated approach to conflict resolution possible.

Integrated Approach to Conflict Resolution

The integrated approach to conflict resolution does not accept an outcome that is the result of an incomplete or superficial understanding of the situation. Instead, the solution derives from a proper analysis of all the circumstances, including the hidden complexities related to the basic, intrinsic human needs of each party. Such needs cannot be dictated or adjudicated, and they cannot be bargained away. If these fundamental needs are ignored, or if they become subject to negotiation, then the parties involved will have difficulty resolving the conflict. Even if they do appear to reach accord, the solution will not last, because basic human needs are as fundamental as the need for air, food and water: people cannot live long without them.

Every human being in this world is motivated by the desire for great knowledge, eternal existence, and unlimited pleasure, and wants to be valued, respected and loved. Those who help resolve conflicts must always remember that each party in a dispute is pursuing these inherent universal needs. Conflict resolution then becomes a process of finding ways to meet these needs without inflicting serious loss on either side. To attain a lasting, mutually acceptable end to a conflict, mediators and facilitators–and even the disputants themselves–can ask the following questions: "What kinds of needs are manifesting in this conflict? Which of these needs are basic human needs that cannot be compromised? Which of these needs are more superficial and therefore subject to negotiation?"

The Importance of Self-Knowledge

Leaders who understand themselves and their own deepest motivations will be far more effective at resolving conflicts than those not given to self-knowledge. In any particular situation, difficulties are inevitable as long as human beings remain ignorant about who they really are and what would genuinely make them happy. By rediscovering the totality of themselves and the path of their greatest good, and by communicating that understanding in a clear and loving manner, people can learn to solve conflicts. For every leader, just as for every individual, this process of self-discovery involves acknowledging and resolving personal conflicts, and then helping others to do the same in a way that fosters unity and growth, not division and stagnation. To ensure a secure and stable future, individually and collectively, people can begin by committing to solve problems through new partnerships based on cooperation, love and trust.

In every society, the leaders of the future will be those who are willing to resolve conflicts in a creative spirit of collaboration and compassion. New, constructive ways of problem-solving can support the personal development of individuals and the collective evolution of all humanity. As the end of the century approaches, current events indicate an urgent and ongoing need for a form of conflict resolution that helps all parties discover ways to solve problems and grow without resorting to violence.

In America, the 1993 siege of the Branch Davidian compound and the 1995 bombing of the government facility in Oklahoma serve as reminders that violent and destructive methods of addressing conflict leave more suffering than healing in their wake, more questions than answers.[68] These events, along with the continuing strife throughout the world in places like the former Yugoslavia, Africa and the Middle East, indicate that large segments of the earth's population still believe that violence, war and devastation are effective means for resolving problems.

The evolutionary growth of humanity fundamentally involves a change in the conscious understanding of what human beings are, what their purpose is, and how to fulfill this purpose. This change begins with a commitment to a personal self-discovery process. Out of a desire to grow and learn the true meaning of life, one begins to inquire: "Why am I here? Why am I suffering? Who am I? What is the goal of my life?" Conflicts can provide opportunities for conscious growth and self-discovery that involve a willing commitment to change and revolutionize personal lives. Such an approach to conflict resolution is initially inner-directed. Eventually, however, the process moves outward, affecting others. In this way, people committed to inner growth and development of a higher consciousness radiate positive spiritual energy that helps bring more order and balance into the world. All life benefits from such a profound shift.

An Ancient Model

Because conflicts begin within the individual, each human being can learn to look within to uncover inner struggles and discover identity and purpose. A model of this type of conflict resolution exists in the ancient time-honored science of self-realization as revealed in the *Bhagavad-gita*, which records the dialogue between Lord Krishna and the great warrior Arjuna that took place just prior to an important battle 5000 years ago in India. This dialogue offers humanity complete and eternal knowledge of how to resolve the deepest human conflicts and lead a life of happiness and success.

The conflict occurred between cousins over who would rule their kingdom. Arjuna and his four brothers, the Pandavas, were the rightful heirs to the throne. Their cousins, the Kauravas, had cheated Arjuna and his brothers out of their kingdom and set themselves up as rulers of the land. As Arjuna looked out over the battlefield, he realized that many of his relatives, friends and teachers were ready to fight and sacrifice their lives. Despite the fact that he was the greatest warrior of his time, Arjuna was overcome with grief over the potential loss of loved ones. He laid down his bow and collapsed on the ground, refusing to fight.

His personal decision not to fight was at odds with his duty as a warrior, which was to protect and safeguard society from aggression. To fight, and even to die, in a holy war for a righteous cause would fulfill Arjuna's life purpose and mission. Although he tried to justify his decision not to fight by using scriptures, he was unable to end his conflict and grief. Only when Arjuna realized that he could not resolve the conflict himself did he turn to a higher authority for answers. In his willingness to turn to Lord Krishna, Arjuna modeled for himself and future generations the complete process of conflict resolution. Succinctly stated, the process is to turn to God for help.

To assist Arjuna, Lord Krishna explained to him the difference between the body and the soul. He emphasized that the real person is a spirit soul, whose primary needs are maximum pleasure, eternality and knowledge gained in relationship with God. The body, with its demands, is a temporary vehicle through which the spirit soul acts energetically. When Arjuna behaves with a "me-first" attitude, trying to satisfy his senses above all else, he experiences a kind of spiritual amnesia, forgetting who he really is and from where he came. This forgetfulness of his higher nature and of his relationship to God is the cause of all suffering.

Lord Krishna helped Arjuna shift his identity from the body to the soul and from the soul to God. Arjuna came to understand that he was part and parcel of God, and that true happiness can be found in serving God. Arjuna was then able to distinguish between the permanent pleasure that comes from satisfying God and the temporary pleasure derived from trying to satisfy the urges of the body, mind and senses. Once Arjuna recognized the universal needs of the participants in the battle, he acted in accord with the will of God, and he found satisfaction.

What enabled Arjuna to relinquish his personal wish to avoid the battle was the deeper satisfaction he gained by putting God's desires before his own. When people are situated in the knowledge of their eternal relationship with God, the desire to do things their own way becomes secondary. This is the true art of conflict resolution: realizing that people can be satisfied regardless of temporary gain or loss, because their relationship to God meets all universal needs in all circumstances. To resolve the conflict, then, is to take action in accordance with God's design. Having realized this complete vision of life given to him by Lord Krishna, Arjuna resolved his internal conflict and fulfilled his duty to God by engaging his cousins in battle and defeating them. Although it may seem paradoxical to resolve an inner conflict by engaging in an outer war, the battle was in fact not a conflict in itself because it was a situation decreed by the will of God.

Three Features of Conflict Resolution

Taking Arjuna's experience in the *Bhagavad-gita* as a model, conflict resolution can then become a process of aligning personal will with divine will. Approaching conflict in these terms requires an understanding of the following three features: knowledge, the process of knowledge, and the goal of knowledge.

Whenever people attempt to resolve conflict, they require basic *knowledge* of who they are, where they are going, how to get there and what to expect on the journey. The *Bhagavad-gita* explains such fundamentals, teaching that each person is an individualized, eternal spirit soul whose fundamental mission in life is to rediscover this eternal self and to understand the human position as a servant of God.

The *process of knowledge* and conflict resolution involves understanding the cause of personal suffering and learning how to overcome it. According to the *Bhagavad-gita*, the cause of all conflict and suffering is identifying the mind and body as the only reality. This limited identification with the body and mind leads people to pursue desires that are only related to the body, such as the wish for sense pleasure, prestige, profit or power. These desires can be called *secondary needs*, to distinguish them from the universal, primary needs of the spirit soul. Many human beings persist in behaving as if fulfillment of these secondary desires will bring eternal happiness, despite the fact that the satisfaction derived is short-lived. Although people try to fulfill the same desires again and again, permanent contentment continues to elude them.

The belief that one can never be permanently satisfied in life, coupled with the recurrent efforts to achieve satisfaction by material means, is at the core of all conflicts. All too often, people may recognize that they are trapped and frustrated, but go no further. If they do not move to a deeper level, they will remain imprisoned in suffering. The *Bhagavad-gita* shows a way out of this prison, teaching that human beings cannot find permanent happiness in the material world by chasing material desires. Instead, they can only find happiness by fulfilling their universal needs for spiritual knowledge, bliss and eternal life. The *Gita* invites people to remember that by acting to please God, they can release themselves from the material prison of unhappiness and find permanent satisfaction.

The *goal of knowledge* is to love the Supreme and to go back *home.* Such divine love is the force that dissolves all conflicts and eliminates all suffering. Therefore, the aim of conflict resolution is to work with oneself and others in such a way as to understand and ultimately act from this platform of experience. Ancient wisdom states that everyone must come to know perfectly both God and the temporary material world side by side. By knowing the material situation alone, people cannot resolve conflicts. Conflict resolution comes through awakening God-consciousness.

The Process of Conflict Resolution

In many situations, the settlement of conflicts is enhanced by the presence of a facilitator, who ensures the safety of the process and carefully guides the participants in discovering their common ground and mutual interests. The function of a facilitator is not to decree outcomes, but rather to help all parties communicate effectively to get to the root of the conflict and resolve it. Besides skill, the intention and commitment of a facilitator are important factors in bringing disputants to a mutually effective solution.

Facilitators who are grounded in a deep understanding of universal human needs, willing to open to and communicate divine love, can remain in balance even when confusion and strong emotions surface. A facilitator is then prepared to relate with compassion to all parties in a conflict, keeping in mind that love of God and alignment with divine will are the only goals that will bring true satisfaction to all parties involved. To move all parties toward these outcomes is the primary role of the facilitator in this method of conflict resolution.

Six Elements of Conflict Resolution

The actual process of conflict resolution, according to this model, includes six fundamental elements: starting with a centering process, maintaining a service perspective, clarifying the needs of all parties, understanding all viewpoints, moving toward cooperative problem-solving, and expressing divine love and will. Depending on the circumstances, you may wish to serve as a facilitator yourself or invite others to play this role.

Start with a centering process: Facilitators may begin each session with a period of silence that allows for centering prayer, meditation, or reflection, and sets the tone for the exchanges that are to follow. Facilitators take this time themselves to dedicate the process and its outcome to the highest good of all concerned, and to ask for divine help and guidance throughout the meeting. In addition, they ask to be reminded of the Lord's presence if they forget it at any time.

Maintain a service perspective: Effective conflict resolution requires a shift in perspective. This shift involves understanding and activating one's role as a servant. In other words, the facilitator's role is to serve everyone participating in the conflict and ultimately to serve God. A facilitator need not be a *spiritual leader* to apply this concept of service. Leaders from every field of human endeavor have the potential of helping resolve conflicts as they arise. Problem-solving potential exists in everyone and can be activated by a shift in perspective.

This shift can occur whenever someone consciously invokes the idea of being a servant to all life, and not the controller or master of it. One way facilitators can accomplish this is to remind themselves of their proper role, using these words internally: *I am here to serve, and your well-being is my concern.* Such an attitude helps dissolve barriers and creates feelings of cooperation that in turn are helpful in reducing tensions and resolving difficult issues.

Clarify needs: One role of a facilitator is to determine what underlying issues are manifesting in the conflict. Therefore, in order to achieve an agreement that satisfies all sides, a facilitator begins by determining the needs of each party–the subtle as well as the obvious ones. Obvious needs are the concrete things people say they want, such as sums of money, or specific terms and conditions. These are usually secondary needs, as described earlier. Subtle needs are the deeply rooted, intangible motivations–appearing as desires, fears, concerns and aspirations–that lead participants to take the positions they do. These subtle needs are generally universal, primary ones. To clarify the issues, a facilitator can ask clear and direct questions to identify the desires and motivations of all involved parties, delving beneath the surface to discover the deeper truth. Good questions might be: "What do you want from this situation? Why do you want that? What is the basic problem you are trying to solve?"

Understand all viewpoints: In order to uncover the intangible motivations of disputants, a facilitator can cultivate the ability to understand the situation as they experience it. One way to accomplish this is to perform the simple exercise of imagining from their point of view what they care about. The purpose of identifying the interests and motivations of each party is to help the facilitator devise creative options that take these into account. While it may not be possible to satisfy every concrete need of the participants, it is often possible to reach a solution that fulfills their subtle, or primary, needs. The fact that a facilitator has probed beneath the surface to uncover these deeper, less apparent longings means that a greater range of options has become accessible for resolving the conflict.

Move toward cooperative problem solving: Effective facilitators see all individuals as parts of the same God. As such, disputants share similar primary needs. Facilitators committed to this idea can easily find ways to demonstrate to all parties that not only are they actually asking for the same thing–using different expressions–but that as each is helped, the others will also benefit. The turning point in conflict resolution often occurs here, when the participants discover common ground and can then move from opposing positions to shared problem solving.

Express divine love and will: As mentioned earlier in this book, every interaction can be viewed as either an act of extending love or as a call for love. A facilitator can try to view each conflict from this perspective, examining whether disputants are offering love or requesting it. Ultimately, all conflicts are derived from feelings of lack and dissatisfaction, which in turn find their source in the belief that one is separated from God. True satisfaction comes from pleasing the Supreme and experiencing a spiritual connection. Once the facilitator has established areas of agreement and disagreement between disputants, the next step is often to ask them what would be the highest good that could emerge from the situation, or what God would have each one think and do to attain that highest good.

Not a Material Process

The success or failure of the conflict resolution process ultimately depends upon the effectiveness of the facilitator. When a facilitator approaches conflict resolution and problem solving from a limited perspective, only limited results are possible. Someone who relates to problem solving from a solely material viewpoint is not capable of the same type of comprehensive thinking demonstrated by a God-conscious person, because the material approach ignores the deeper, more eternal values of life.

Clearly, it is a mistake to believe that material problems can only be solved by material means. Frequently, problems need to be resolved from a higher–or deeper–level than the one at which they initially appear, particularly those that appear intractable. As mentioned earlier, material solutions cannot comprehensively meet all the given needs in a situation, because ultimately an important element of each problem is spiritual. When spiritual needs are ignored, suffering is the result. Therefore, every conflict is an opportunity for those involved to unravel selfish desires, invoking the highest good for all and placing God's will ahead of their own.

How human beings approach conflict at this time in history will determine the future of this planet. You can make the constructive choice to work with conflict as a means of conscious evolution, facing differences with courage, honesty, compassion and firm resolve. Conflicts that remain hidden can fester and become negative forces, causing even greater problems later on. On the other hand, when they are confronted, understood and resolved, the same conflicts can become powerful sources of creativity and growth. No matter what your responsibilities are as a leader, you can learn not to fear conflicts, instead welcoming the rich learning that they contain for anyone who is willing to dig enough to unearth the treasure. Conflict then becomes a means of clearing away obstacles on the way back *home* to God.

Highlights

1.   In the traditional view, conflicts are negative experiences to be avoided, if possible. One side "wins" and the other "loses"–and no one wants to lose. People who perceive conflicts within this win-lose frame of reference frequently tend to ignore, minimize, or override many underlying differences. Parties in a dispute may attempt to smooth over diverging viewpoints in an effort to avoid feeling the powerlessness of loss, or in a determined effort to win.

2.   Conflict *management*, which seeks the short-term benefit of containing conflict by addressing its symptoms or by designating winners and losers, is not enough to ensure lasting peace. Conflict *resolution*, which probes more deeply to discover the heart of a problem, is required to implement enduring changes.

3.   In the late twentieth century, humanity occupies a shared global village, and the inherent needs of human beings are intrinsically similar across all cultures and forms of government. Whereas conflicts over material interests tend to lead to a win-lose outcome, conflicts over universal human needs such as identity, love, respect or security do not fit this paradigm. Because the supply of these is unlimited, such needs can be met without depriving others.

4.   Disputes that involve intense feelings, values and needs are deep-rooted and cannot be settled easily by an order from an outside authority. The losing party is frequently left with bitter resentment and a sense of impotence that does not go away. Many conflicts cannot be settled by any external arrangement that fails to consider the basic human needs of each participant, independently of the material situation. A less materialistic, more spiritual view of human nature is a necessary prerequisite to the effective resolution of differences in today's world.

5.   The integrated approach to conflict resolution does not accept an outcome that is the result of an incomplete or superficial understanding of the situation. Instead, the solution derives from a proper analysis of all the circumstances, including the hidden complexities related to the basic human needs of each party. Such needs cannot be dictated or adjudicated, and they cannot be bargained away.

6.   To attain a lasting, mutually acceptable end to a conflict, arbitrators or mediators of disputes need to ask themselves the following questions: "What kinds of needs are manifesting in this conflict? Which of these needs are basic human needs that cannot be compromised? Which of these needs are more superficial and therefore subject to negotiation?"

7.   Leaders who understand themselves and their own deepest motivations will be far more effective at resolving conflicts than those not given to self-knowledge.

8.   The belief that one can never be permanently satisfied in life, coupled with the recurrent efforts to achieve satisfaction by material means, is at the core of all conflicts. All too often, people may recognize that they are trapped and frustrated, but go no further. If they do not move to a deeper level, they will remain imprisoned in suffering.

9.   In many situations, the settlement of conflicts is enhanced by the presence of a facilitator, who ensures the safety of the process and carefully guides the participants in discovering their common ground and mutual interests. The function of a facilitator is not to decree outcomes, but rather to help all parties communicate effectively to get to the root of the conflict and resolve it. Besides skill, the intention and commitment of a facilitator are important factors in bringing disputants to a mutually effective solution.

10.   It is a mistake to believe that material problems can only be solved by material means. Frequently, problems need to be resolved from a higher–or deeper–level than the one at which they initially appear, particularly those that appear intractable. Material solutions cannot comprehensively meet all the given needs in a situation, because ultimately an important element of each problem is spiritual.

Mindsets

1. Review the ten essential technologies at the beginning of this book, all of which are directly relevant to conflict resolution. Select two or three that strike you the most, and consider how they can help you resolve your own conflicts and facilitate others to resolve theirs.

2. Reflect upon the conflicts in your life. For each one, list your secondary needs as defined in this chapter. Now, go more deeply into each situation and discover your primary needs. Write them down as well. Based upon your primary needs, can you find alternative ways of getting what you want?

3. Whenever you experience conflict with another person, consider how that person may be reflecting back to you traits that you do not want to acknowledge in yourself. Probe beneath the surface to identify the essence of those characteristics you have in common, which may not be readily apparent. For example, perhaps someone constantly interrupts you, a behavior in which you do not engage. Yet, are there other ways that you interfere with people, do not listen, seek to dominate, or are impatient?

4. Examine some of your inner conflicts. In a spirit of honest self-inquiry, seek to discover the types of material attachments that are causing the difficulty. With compassion for yourself, practice letting these attachments go. Monitor other areas of your life where the same attachments may be creating problems.

5. Practice addressing the conflicts among those you lead with honesty, firmness and compassion. Create a safe, impartial environment in which the parties can communicate their concerns openly and directly, with the confidence that their differences can

be fairly resolved. Remember that unacknowledged or unresolved conflicts create a negative atmosphere and sap energy.

6.   As you perform your duties, notice how every word you hear and every action you witness is either an expression of love or a call for love. Remember to respond to the calls for love with love, regardless of whatever outer action is necessary. Practice being a loving presence for everyone, and observe any changes that occur.

7.   Be careful to consider cultural factors when helping to resolve conflicts, and notice other superficial differences that may give rise to disputes. Help the parties discover their commonalities beneath these differences.

8.   Find ways to demonstrate to all parties in a conflict that not only are they actually requesting the same thing, using different expressions, but that as one party is helped, the other benefits. Help them be creative in seeking solutions that are productive to everyone involved. Encourage them to view the conflict as an opportunity for mutual problem solving.

9.   Remember that universal, primary human needs cannot be compromised. Therefore, any room for negotiation will exist in the area of secondary needs, which provide a number of alternative ways to fulfill these universal, primary needs.

10.   Practice preventive maintenance. Create opportunities for those you lead to communicate with you and with one another on a regular basis, in an environment that promotes honest, friendly, supportive airing of concerns. Encourage everyone to engage in mutual creative problem solving at an early stage to prevent small problems from developing into larger, more complex conflicts later on.

8

Managing Time in Relationship to Reality

Why is it important to be concerned about time? Time is life.[69] The way people manage time reveals much about their personalities, their perceptions of themselves, their relationships to their fellow creatures, and their connections to the cosmos.

Time: A Matter of Perception

Time is treated differently in various cultures. The world-view of people from different nations, races, and tribes is intimately related to how they perceive time. Fewer interpersonal difficulties occur between people who share a similar perception of time. In India and Africa, for example, two people who make an appointment will not be disturbed if one of them arrives an hour or so late, whereas in the West, such behavior would be considered irresponsible and inconsiderate.

Western countries usually have a more dependable infrastructure in place to support punctuality. Technological advances in transportation and communications systems make interruptions in services more infrequent. Westerners are therefore held more accountable for being on time. In much of the Third World, however, events do not always proceed so smoothly. The systems can break down unpredictably, and therefore lateness is not considered a serious offense.

Time is relative even within the same culture. For instance, time passes very quickly for an individual who is experiencing pleasure. However, for someone who is uncomfortable or in pain, a few seconds may seem like hours. When people are enjoying themselves with friends, the hours fly by, whereas when they are forced to associate with someone they dislike, a few moments will seem like an eternity. Time is relative to how the senses experience it.

Space and Time

Space is inseparable from time and plays an equally important role in shaping a particular world-view. Like time, space is relative among and within cultures, and distance is often defined by personal experience rather than by physical measures. For example, someone from a rural area may consider a five-mile walk to be very short, because walking such distances is an everyday experience and not an imposition. However, a city dweller, lacking such experience, might perceive those five miles on foot as an extraordinary distance.

Space and time are perceived in relationship to the body. For a small insect, the distance from one side of the house to the other is vast, whereas a human being simply walks the distance in a matter of seconds. Some insects and other life forms are born, reproduce, and die within 24 hours, which is a lifetime to them. For human beings, however, 24 hours seem insignificant in the totality of a lifespan. According to how the body interacts with its environment, and according to the speed at which the body deteriorates, each person develops a unique perception of time and space.

These various perceptions of time and space can be important to your interactions as a leader on local, national, and international levels. With such variations in mind, you can be alert to the other party's perception of time and be considerate of the other person's world-view. Such sensitivity will help you establish a positive, receptive environment within which cooperative relationships, agreements and negotiations can flourish.

Time Belongs to God

Contrary to popular perception, time is not anyone's personal possession. Time belongs to God, and each person is its caretaker. Those who view time in this way will be even more careful with it than if it were their own. Given that time ultimately is God's, every individual can remember to treat it with love and respect, not wanting to disappoint God. People can take care to be meticulous in all their activities so as not to disappoint One who is so powerful and dear to them.

Correspondingly, as you fulfill your leadership responsibilities, consider that time belongs not to you, but to all those you represent. Then any time you waste is not only your personal time but their time as well. If a leader of a group of 10 million people engages in irresponsible, illicit, or corrupt activities, those activities are multiplied by 10 million. You can then begin to see how serious an affair this is. Not just one individual's time is being wasted in such a situation. The leader is in effect attacking millions of people, devaluing their time by failing to use it productively for the benefit of all. This factor alone should serve as a reminder to be sensitive and mindful of your role as a caretaker of others and as a representative of God.

Detachment from the Effects of Time

Practically everything in day-to-day existence deteriorates. Human lives and bodies are temporary, constantly undergoing different states of change. Every aspect of the material world follows the same pattern: it is created or produced; it remains for a while; it begins to dwindle, fade away, or deteriorate; and eventually it is completely destroyed. This happens to one's house, one's car, one's body, one's beauty, one's family, and one's intelligence. Every second, people are literally losing everything that they cling to and consider important. The time that human beings try to "manage" in their daily activities is the same time that will gradually take away their bodies and all their material possessions.

Considering that all things are transient, people can learn to perceive events just as if they were the changing seasons. At certain moments, one may become depressed by some misfortune, and at other times feel exhilarated by some agreeable event or by the anticipation of something pleasant. As the karmic pendulum swings, a person will experience both happiness and sadness. This is the underlying duality of the material world. A wise individual tries to keep a certain equilibrium, not becoming overly attached to happiness or concerned by distress, knowing that all situations are relative and will eventually change. Such a person is said to be in a state of "equipoise," and this state is a symptom of one who is nearing self-realization. Such a human being does not identify fully with the three-dimensional world, but rather with the higher dimensions.

Much of the confusion about higher dimensions results from a narrow-minded concept of time and an extreme attachment to the temporary pleasures of the material senses. In the *Bhagavad-gita*, Krishna stresses that one who is dear to Him is unaffected by happiness or distress.[70] Speaking to his great disciple Arjuna, Krishna explains that anyone who is powerful, effective, and genuinely noble will not be disturbed by victory or defeat. Such a person will act with a sense of maturity and balance.

Someone who becomes greatly exhilarated in good times can become equally disturbed when events take a turn for the worse. But "middle-of-the-roaders" are less affected by the twists and turns of fate. If you dwell on your successes and failures, you may become too preoccupied to carry out your responsibilities effectively. Instead, you must learn to "regroup" very quickly and to remain unconcerned with temporary ups and downs. Any upset of yours can affect all the people who are taking shelter under your leadership. This fact alone can provide you with a good reason to maintain your balance.

Time Is Temporary Yet Unyielding

Most people view time management as a vehicle for accomplishing more within a shorter time. In terms of efficiency, this approach is valid. However, time management also means focusing on quality rather than quantity. For those in positions of leadership, it is not efficient to waste time in foolish or counterproductive ways. In many cases, taking no action at all is preferable to acting without appropriate planning. Often, thinking things over is a better use of time than behaving extemporaneously and risking unexpected chaos or great conflict.

It is a given that no human being will be here on earth forever. Without becoming paranoid about death, you should be mindful of completing your daily work as if each day were your last, approaching each task as if it were the final act of your life. Naturally, you want to conclude your existence in some meaningful way. You can be more assured of attaining this goal if you are careful not to leave your affairs in disarray and if you take measures that will enable others to easily take up where you left off.

Endeavor to perform your leadership tasks with tremendous clarity, keeping in mind a definite end result. When you give your full attention to the immediate task, then even if today is your last, your legacy will live on through your work. This frame of mind allows you to do your best to offer the highest quality and the greatest quantity of service, without procrastinating or diminishing the quality of your work.

To make the best use of your time, you can develop short-term and long-term goals that you evaluate each day. Short-term goals demonstrate very quickly what you have or have not accomplished. Long-term goals can help you determine, from a broader perspective, if you are moving in the right direction. Having goals, and making pledges or vows about accomplishing them, will naturally push you toward a desired conclusion. If you do not push yourself, you may become lethargic.

Making Better Use of Time

Those who have difficulty with time management often fail to appreciate transitional time. Sometimes, people who are intensely involved in a particular activity can become disoriented when they change their focus to something else. One way to improve your effectiveness as a leader is to become as fully absorbed in the transitional periods between activities as during the activities themselves. In this way, you can avoid being inactive, unaware, or distracted while moving from one project to another, one meeting to another, or one location to another.

You can determine to do something significant during these unstructured transitional periods. One way is to keep a notepad handy on which to write down your ideas and realizations. Another way to use time more effectively is to develop alternative plans, especially in Third World countries where events do not always go as intended. Then, if plan A does not succeed, you can turn to plan B or even plan C. Such advance planning prevents any serious loss of time, because another option is always available.

Still another useful strategy is to make a list each day of tasks to complete, reviewing it periodically to note accomplishments and assess what remains to be done. With such reminders close at hand, you can spend your time more productively, devoting your energies to the most important aspects of your mission, avoiding duplications of effort, and eliminating any unessential activities.

One of the most frequently repeated statements people make is, "There are so many things I would like to do, but I just cannot find the time." This statement is usually not well-founded. By the age of 70, an average American may have spent 10 years working, 23 years sleeping, 6 years in reading and studies, 11 years eating and grooming, 13 years in leisure activities and 7 years on other odds & ends. A person who saves 20 minutes a day from any of these activities will have received a whole extra year by the age of 70. In other words, people cannot really say that they do not *have* time. It is just a matter of how they *use* it.

Utilizing "Sleep Time"

One way to make better use of time is to improve the quality of your sleep, so that you can minimize the number of hours you need each night. On the average, people spend as much as one-third of their lives asleep. If you can use this time to enhance your learning, you will be much more effective and productive as a leader. One way to increase your learning, as discussed earlier, is to recollect your dreams first thing in the morning and write down any insights or answers to questions that may have come during the night. You can also use sleep time for memorization. In the morning, you can see how much you have retained. Some people like to use auto-reverse tape recorders to listen to music or dictations while they are sleeping so that these enter into their subconscious. Numerous books and tapes are available to help you make productive use of your sleep time.

As you learn to appreciate the value of sleep time, you can take better advantage of it to achieve beneficial results for mind, body, and soul. Ultimately, these results can help you render better service to your family, to your particular organization, to society, to the world, and to God.

Time Savers

Alan Lakein, one of the world's greatest time management consultants, has an excellent 61-point checklist describing how he manages his own time. The list, which appears below as a conclusion to this chapter, is excellent and can be of benefit to every leader.[71]

1. I count all my time as "on-time" and try to get satisfaction (not necessarily accomplishment) out of every minute.
2. I try to enjoy whatever I am doing.
3. I'm a perennial optimist.
4. I build on successes.
5. I don't waste time regretting my failures.
6. I don't waste my time feeling guilty about what I don't do.

7.   I remind myself: "There is always enough time for the important things." If it's important, I'll take the time to do it.

8.   I try to find a new technique each day that I can use to help gain time.

9.   I get up at 5 a.m. during the week (and go to bed early).

10. I have a light lunch so I don't get sleepy in the afternoon.

11. I don't read newspapers or magazines (except occasionally).

12. I skim books quickly looking for ideas.

13. I don't own a television set. (My family and I went to a motel to watch the moon walks and we rented a set for the political conventions).

14. I have my office close enough to my home to be able to walk to work. But when I'm lazy or in a hurry, I drive.

15. I examine old habits for possible elimination or streamlining.

16. I've given up forever all "waiting time." If I have to wait I consider it a "gift of time" to relax, plan, or do something I would not otherwise have done.

17. I keep my watch three minutes fast, to get a head start on the day.

18. I carry blank 3"x 5" index cards in my pocket to jot down notes and ideas.

19   I revise my lifetime goals list once a month.

20. I review my lifetime goals list every day and identify activities to do each day to further my goals.

21. I put signs in my office reminding me of my goals.

22. I keep my long-term goals in mind even while doing the smallest task.

23. I always plan first thing in the morning and set priorities for the day.

24   I keep a list of specific items to be done each day, arrange them in priority order, and then do my best to get the important ones done as soon as possible.

25. I schedule my time months in advance in such a way that each month offers variety and balance as well as "open time" reserved for "hot" projects.

26. I give myself time off and special rewards when I've done the important things.
27. I do first things first.
28. I work smarter rather than harder.
29 I try to do only A's, never B's and C's.
30. I have confidence in my judgment of priorities and stick to them in spite of difficulties.
31. I ask myself, "Would anything terrible happen if I didn't do this item?" If the answer is no, I don't do it.
32. If I seem to procrastinate, I ask myself: "What am I avoiding?" and then I try to confront that thing head-on.
33. I always use the 80/20 rule.[72]
34. I start with the most profitable parts of large projects and often find it is not necessary to do the rest.
35. I cut off nonproductive activities as quickly as possible.
36 I give myself enough time to concentrate on high-priority items.
37. I have developed the ability to concentrate well for long stretches of time.
38. I concentrate on one thing at a time.
39. I focus my efforts on items that will have the best long-term benefits.
40. I keep pushing and am persistent when I sense I have a winner.
41. I have trained myself to go down my "To Do List" without skipping over difficult items.
42. I do much of my thinking on paper.
43. I work alone creatively in the morning and use the afternoons for meetings, if necessary.
44. I set deadlines for myself and others.
45. I try to listen actively in every discussion.
46. I try not to waste other people's time (unless it's something that really matters to me).
47. I delegate everything I possibly can to others.
48. I make use of specialists to help me with special problems.

49. I have someone screen my mail and phone calls and handle all routine matters.
50. I generate as little paperwork as possible and throw away anything I possibly can.
51. I handle each piece of paper only once.
52. I write replies to most letters right on the letter itself.
53. I keep my desk top cleared for action, and put the most important things in the center desk.
54. I have a place for everything (so I waste as little time as possible looking for things).
55. I save up all trivia for a three-hour session once a month.
56. I try not to think of work on weekends.
57. I relax and "do nothing" rather frequently.
58. I recognize that inevitably some of my time will be spent on activities outside my control and don't fret about it.
59. I keep small talk to a minimum during work hours.
60. I look for action steps to be taken now to further my goals.
61. I'm continually asking myself: "What is the best use of my time right now?"

Highlights

1. Time is life. The way people manage time reveals much about their personalities, their perceptions of themselves, their relationships to their fellow creatures, and their connections to the cosmos.

2. Time is treated differently in various cultures. The world-view of people from different nations, races, and tribes is intimately related to how they perceive time. Fewer interpersonal difficulties occur between people who share a similar perception of time.

3. Time is relative even within the same culture. For instance, time passes very quickly for an individual who is experiencing pleasure. However, for someone who is uncomfortable or in pain, a few seconds may seem like hours.

4. Space is inseparable from time and plays an equally important role in shaping a particular world-view. Like time, space is relative among and within cultures, and distance is often defined by personal experience rather than by physical measures.

5. Contrary to popular perception, time is not anyone's personal possession. Time belongs to God, and each person is its caretaker. When people view time in this way, they will be even more careful with it than if it were their own.

6. Practically everything in day-to-day existence deteriorates. Human lives and bodies are temporary, constantly undergoing different states of change. Every aspect of the material world follows the same pattern: it is created or produced; it remains for a while; it begins to dwindle, fade away, or deteriorate; and eventually it is completely destroyed.

7.   As the karmic pendulum swings, a person will experience both happiness and sadness. This is the underlying duality of the material world. A wise individual tries to keep a certain equilibrium, not becoming overly attached to happiness or concerned by distress, knowing that all situations are relative and will eventually change. Such a person is said to be in a state of "equipoise," and this state is a symptom of one who is nearing self-realization.

8.   Most people view time management as a vehicle for accomplishing more within a shorter time. In terms of efficiency, this approach is valid. However, time management also means focusing on quality rather than quantity.

9.   To make the best use of your time, you can develop short-term and long-term goals that you evaluate each day. Short-term goals demonstrate very quickly what you have or have not accomplished. Long-term goals can help you determine, from a broader perspective, if you are moving in the right direction.

10.   Those who have difficulty with time management often fail to appreciate transitional time. Sometimes, people who are intensely involved in a particular activity can become disoriented when they change their focus to something else. One way to improve your effectiveness is to become as fully absorbed in the transitional periods between activities as during the activities themselves.

Mindsets

1. Reread the ten essential technologies at the beginning of this book, paying special attention to numbers 9 and 10. Use these reflections as reminders not to procrastinate, but to complete important priorities now. Also, examine your current priorities and reorganize them if necessary.

2. Work more efficiently, with emphasis on improving quality over quantity in all of your endeavors.

3. Each day, reflect on your short-term and long-term goals.

4. View your time not as your own but as belonging to those you lead and to God. If you have one hour, multiply it by the number of people for whom you are responsible. For example, if you have 200 people under your management–or 200 million–and you waste one hour, then you will waste 200–or 200 million–hours of their valuable time.

5. Be clever with transitional time. Always keep a small pad with you to write down ideas, information, and realizations. Do not have periods in your day when you are doing nothing; it is God's time.

6. If you work with people of different cultures, pay attention to their perceptions of time and space. This awareness will establish more harmonious communications. Especially in the Third World, create alternate plans, always considering that the original plan may not work out.

7. Practice maintaining a state of equipoise, not being overly affected by happiness or distress. When something apparently bad happens to you, study it closely to see what you can learn from it. Also, take the attitude that you deserved worse. Consider that God in His mercy gave you only a token of what you deserved, and this only for your personal growth. When something good hap-

pens to you, practice seeing yourself as unworthy but blessed by the mercy of the Supreme.

8.   Get a better quality of sleep and sleep less. Also feed questions to your higher self and spiritual helpers before going to sleep so that you receive guidance to assist you in your waking state.

9.   Avoid small talk or gossip; such activity not only wastes time but also depletes your energy and increases sexual agitation.

10.   Do things right the first time. Mistakes weaken everyone's morale and waste valuable time that cannot ever be recovered.

$$9$$

Reducing Stress for Greater Health and Productivity

M any people consider stress to be a pathological human response to psychological, social, occupational or environmental pressures. However, stress experts view this as only a partial truth. Contrary to widespread belief, stress is more than nervous tension or the aftereffects of trauma, and it is not necessarily something to avoid. The World Health Organization has adopted the following definition of stress: "Stress is the nonspecific response of the organism to any demand made of it."[73]

Stress and Its Effects

According to the above definition, then, stress is not always negative. Stress can be beneficial, motivating people to take action and even to improve their performance. Many differing approaches to stress exist. One approach, considering stress to be a reaction rather than a causative factor, interprets it as the state of a physical body that has been subjected to pressure close to, or beyond, its level of tolerance, as when a piece of metal becomes stressed. Others define stress as the cause that produces these pressures in the first place. In addition, stress can be a subjective experience, associated with psychological and emotional conditions.

Recent studies demonstrate that stress is a natural part of life. Like seasonings used in cooking, people need to have just the right proportions. Too little or too much produces a disagreeable taste. Each person needs exactly the proper amount of stress in order to use it in a positive and healthy way. Indeed, complete freedom from stress is death!

Although stress is an integral part of life, excessive stress is costly. Reports indicate that the United States economy loses billions of dollars a year from stress-related problems.[74] Stress causes people to retire earlier than necessary, provokes accidents on the job, and creates a host of psychological and physiological complications.

In the human body, stress influences the immune system, contributing to infections, allergies, and serious illnesses. Stress also affects the digestive system and related organs, creating conditions favorable to ulcers, colitis, constipation, and diabetes. In the musculoskeletal system, stress can cause backaches, tension, headaches, and arthritis, all of which can also make a person accident-prone. Further, stress affects the cardiovascular system, contributing to heart attacks, hypertension, and migraine headaches.

Fight-or-Flight Response

Many experts believe that stress results from any situation that requires an individual to make psychological and behavioral adjustments. These situations range from petty daily annoyances to such events as a major illness, the death of a loved one, or a divorce. In such circumstances, the person's reaction to perceived stress includes specific, measurable physiological reactions such as a faster heart rate, higher blood pressure, hyperventilation, perspiration and a marked increase of blood flow to the muscles. These changes frequently occur in an integrated, coordinated pattern called the "fight-or-flight response," in which the organism prepares to resolve a threatening situation by either fighting or running away.[75]

Many agree that this response has made the long-term survival of human beings possible. Indeed, in daily life the fight-or-flight response is often associated with increased performance. Before an athletic event, competitors unconsciously invoke this response, as do students before an examination. Similarly, in today's business environment, the fight-or-flight response is often considered essential to survival–and to success.

However, this same response can have undesirable effects. In earlier times, a person confronted with a threatening situation might either have fought or run away. For example, the proverbial caveman probably did not suppress or internalize his reactions when faced with an attacking wildcat. In contrast, many contemporary threats are much more diffuse and abstract, presenting nothing obvious to fight or flee. As a result, human beings today often lack an immediate, direct outlet for their reactions, which become repressed and internalized.

If the fight-or-flight response occurs repeatedly in a person who cannot fight or run–that is, cope in some appropriate way–the resulting chronic stress can invite illness. In physical terms, this repressed stress can damage the circulatory system, the digestive tract, the lungs, the muscles, and the joints. It even hastens the general process of aging. In such circumstances, if the threat is not ultimately addressed and resolved, stress can wear the mind and body out without protecting them in the least.[76]

Manipulative Behavior and Stress

In present-day society, widespread duplicity and dishonesty contribute to the general level of stress. People say things they do not believe and do things they do not wish to do. Manipulating one another cleverly in a variety of ways, many appear more interested in cosmetic appearances than in the essential aspects of life.

This dishonesty encompasses almost all areas of activity. Many leaders around the world say one thing and do another, cheating the very groups they were entrusted to represent. Such an atmosphere is naturally stressful, because everyone relates to everyone else superficially and with suspicion. Instead of relying on natural open expression, people attempt to exploit and control each other and the various organizations to which they belong. If modern society is to develop a stress-free lifestyle, then honesty, straightforwardness, and simplicity–missing ingredients in contemporary life–must become norms of human interaction.

Present-day society is a "take" society. A "take" society has a hungry mood characterized by meanness and jealousy. Enough is never enough. People may be aware that something is missing–and rightly so. However, the way they usually try to fill the void is by acquiring ever greater quantities of material goods–bigger cars, taller office buildings, flashier clothes, more elaborately equipped hotels, more opulent shopping centers, and more complex or perverted forms of entertainment.

True human needs include being able to give, to coexist with nature, and to live simply. To fulfill these needs, people can learn to adopt a "win-win" approach to life, in which one person's gain is not another's loss, and in which personal victories are not used as a means to deny or weaken the advantages of others.

Stress-Producing Technologies

In the modern world, excessive stress is often the product of an environment of rapid technological and economic growth that pushes people to acquire vast amounts of unnecessary commodities. Contemporary society requires its members to work hard, earn sufficient income, and exercise constant vigilance just to maintain the status quo. Such demands, which appear threatening for many, can give rise to fear, insecurity, and loneliness–all contributing factors to unhealthy levels of stress. In order to become divinely empowered, people must become free from such pressures so that they can make rich, healthy contributions to society rather than resorting to–or defending themselves against–abuse, misuse, and manipulation.

A simple lifestyle can provide important health benefits. Physical inactivity contributes to stress. As a rule, members of less industrialized societies are more physically active and so more easily convert stress into constructive energy. In contrast, the automated Western way of life actually produces harmful stress because people spend too much time in such sedentary activities as riding in automobiles or watching television, even going so far as to press a button on the remote control to change the channels. In the workplace, computers allow an executive to manage a group of corporations without having to leave the office. Enslaved by houses, cars, and appliances, people in the Western world have become so addicted to comforts that they are amusing, enjoying, and relaxing themselves to death.

This highly industrialized society causes its members to become increasingly impersonal and to feel less connection with life itself. In earlier times, people lived closer to the land, were more skilled at crafts and had greater hands-on experience in all areas of life. Today, a wide range of technologies allow everyone to accomplish tasks very quickly without much relationship to the surrounding environment. Further, because of the scope and interdependence of these technologies, even a small disruption can have far-reaching consequences and produce tremendous chaos. To be a decision-maker in such circumstances is naturally very stressful. Feelings of uncertainty, regret, and remorse are understandable consequences of such complex, interdependent, impersonal technologies.

Effects of Stress

Modern-day acquisitive society emphasizes industrial development and rapid growth at any cost. One of these costs appears to be human health and well-being. The incidence of heart disease provides a case in point. Since the early twentieth century, heart attacks have become a major problem around the globe, particularly in the West. Yet in many less "developed" areas of the world, such widespread heart disease does not exist. In these societies, which are more humane and genuinely communal, people see themselves as their brother's keepers and consequently experience less isolation and stress.

The incidence of heart disease seems to rise with the increase in the gross national product. In other words, so-called material advancement apparently provides increasing possibilities for heart failure. A World Health Organization report of a 1991 meeting in Geneva regarding cardio-vascular disease states:

> [The Assistant Director-General] pointed out that cardiovascular diseases were already the leading cause of morbidity and premature mortality in industrialized countries, and that their emergence as a public health problem in developing countries had been recognized by the World Health Assembly as early as 1976. He also emphasized the extremely high human and economic costs of the problem....Cardiovascular disease is becoming an increasingly prominent problem in developing countries: rheumatic heart disease, hypertension and cardiomyopathy are already prevalent, and coronary heart disease is assuming growing significance.[77]

Obviously, industrial or material growth and development are not harmful in themselves. However, ignorance of the impact of technological advancement can produce turmoil, and when development is not humanly oriented, it does the opposite of what was intended. Instead of making life appreciably better, it puts everyone in a more diseased condition.

Paradoxically, while seeking ways to enjoy the conveniences of life, modern society has instead increased stress and its complications. Had people initially been aware of the impact of many technologies, they might have rejected them out of hand. For example, in the early twentieth century few people considered the automobile to be one of the most dangerous and devastating inventions of our culture. Yet, as many would agree, despite the fact that automobile travel has enhanced the quality of life in some ways, it has also caused serious problems.

Long-Term Emotional Stress

In some situations, stress can literally be a matter of life and death. In the book, *Stress and Disease*, edited by Stewart Wolf, a study by Dr. Harold G. Wolff compares American soldiers imprisoned in Germany during World War II to those imprisoned in Japanese camps.[78] Conditions in the Japanese camps were far more demoralizing, filled with terror and humiliation for the prisoners. The resulting stress produced distinct differences between the survival rate of captives held by the Japanese and Germans.

This study found that fewer than one percent of American servicemen imprisoned in Europe died before release, while the mortality rate for those in Japanese camps was one in three–despite similar levels of nutrition and medical care. It also found that the average prisoner in Asia was held much longer–40 months, compared with 10 months in the European camps. But the discrepancy in the camp deaths was so large that the author began seeking other factors. He discovered that the major difference was simply the degree of emotional stress.

What happened when the war ended and the survivors went home? According to the report, the death rate for those who survived the Japanese prisons was three times that of those released from the German camps. Further, the causes of death included many diseases not directly related to confinement or starvation. For example, there was twice the normally expected incidence of heart disease, twice the number of cancer cases, more than four times the usual occurrence of gastrointestinal diseases, and nine times the expected number of cases of pulmonary tuberculosis. It became apparent that the greater stress experienced by those imprisoned in the Japanese camps was the determining factor between living and dying for many.

Managerial Stress

Stress occurs in many environments in Western society. A classic example of stress is that experienced by the business executive. In one sense, this situation is ironic, because the attainment of a management position is a sign of success. However, the stress that accompanies such success may sometimes bring complications that ultimately result in unhappiness, sickness, and even death.

In *Executive Families Under Stress*, author Cary L. Cooper summarizes the symptoms of different types of stress experienced by managers. He divides these into three categories: physical symptoms, emotional symptoms, and behavioral symptoms. According to Cooper, physical symptoms include such problems as palpitations, tightness in the chest, indigestion, impotence, tingling in the arms and legs, headaches, rashes, double vision, or muscle tension in the neck or lower back. On the emotional level, symptoms can consist of mood swings, excessive worry, inability to feel empathy, excessive concern about health, withdrawal, fatigue, lack of concentration, and increased irritability. Behavioral symptoms can involve indecision, excessive complaining, absenteeism, becoming accident-prone, producing poor work, increased smoking and alcohol consumption, drug dependency, overeating or loss of appetite, or difficulty in sleeping.[79] The length of this list makes it apparent that stress has wide-ranging deleterious consequences for managers.

Male and Female Managers

Stress patterns appear to be different for male and female managers. Some of the stress-producing difficulties experienced by male executives include: lack of job security, lack of trust throughout the organization, and pressures of too much or too little work. Sometimes additional stress ensues from a lack of effective communication with superiors or from denied promotions. In addition, a dual-career marriage can be stressful.

In the late twentieth century, when more companies are becoming multinational, issues of relocation to another country may arise. In any move to a new environment, the male manager may doubt his ability to master a new job, worry about the effects of job changes on his wife and children, fret about his new mortgage, and in general, be concerned about his family's ability to adapt to a new situation.

The stresses that affect the female manager are often more complicated. These include confronting others' expectations of her role, dealing with patronizing male bosses, addressing the perceived threat to her male colleagues who were usually raised in a chauvinistic environment, and worrying constantly about her promotions being blocked. One extremely difficult experience for the female manager is the threat of sexual harassment. And for many women, the most challenging, stressful problem of all is that of juggling work and family.

The female executive who happens to be married to a male manager has a unique set of difficulties. For example, if relocation becomes an issue, the wife must confront several problems, such as a reluctance to leave her own established career, worries about her children's ability to cope, and the feelings that her husband does not appreciate the depths of the upheaval involved. Sometimes, jealousy of her husband's freedom may trouble her. She may feel lonely and isolated, and in some cases she may feel guilty about abandoning her parents or other family members. In addition, she may be concerned about the new neighborhood and the challenge of making new friends.

As the twenty-first century approaches, around the world everyone is experiencing increasing amounts of stress. Therefore, as a leader, you can make a contribution by seeking ways to lessen, control, and eliminate stress in its various forms, both in your personal life and in the lives of those you lead. Some possibilities are listed in the following sections. In addition, you can exercise your leadership to change stressful situations that force people to make painful, "no-win" choices, such as choices between work and family, or between the needs for personal integrity and for job security.

The Corporate Approach

Corporate America has been forced to accept the fact that healthy, stress-free employees are a valuable asset. The cost of stress to companies in health benefits, lost time for sick leave, and inefficiency is staggering. Leaders are beginning to recognize the importance of reducing these losses through programs that reduce stress and increase health.[80]

Several companies have instituted projects to help alleviate stress. Some encourage all employees to engage in exercise during their lunch breaks or even on company time. Others provide gymnasiums where employees can easily work out, and many have stress management programs that include in-house counseling. Some places of business even have task forces that evaluate those who are experiencing undue stress. In a few environments, top executives are encouraging their people to minimize the amount of work they take home. Other managers are trying to get their employees to enjoy their work and to experience more job satisfaction.

Many other approaches to stress management are available outside the workplace. Among others, these include diet, exercise, psychotherapy, and various relaxation techniques.

Diet and Exercise Versus Drugs

Pharmaceuticals are commonly used to relieve stress. Modern-day medicine cabinets overflow with countless pills and potions. However, a pill that alleviates one problem may produce another, or it may deplete and contaminate the body, causing health to deteriorate in the long run. Individuals who resort to mind-altering drugs may eventually become dependent upon such external supports to produce an internal state of consciousness.

Instead of drugs, the simplest stress-reducing technique is to maintain good physical conditioning through exercise and diet. Not only can exercise dispel many specific forms of tension; it can also offset the effects of generalized stress. Those in good physical condition also enhance their mental condition and can withstand such stressors as overwork, a quarrel with the boss, or even a virus more easily than someone who is not.

As far as diet is concerned, in one sense, people are indeed what they eat. In this acquisitive and grossly materialistic society, many often feel an emptiness that tempts them to use food as a way to fill the void. Westerners in particular frequently overeat and rely on junk foods. The fast-paced lifestyle in the developed world often leaves neither the time to prepare a balanced meal nor the leisure to sit down and enjoy it in a relaxed manner. The tendency is to resort to fast food, which adds to the general robot-like existence of many who do things in a hurry and seek instant gratification. And the result is predictable: quick, cosmetic, artificial stimulation that later causes complications, for although junk food may be tasty, the effects in the long run can be devastating to the body.

To improve the body's physical condition, therefore, people can take more notice of what they are consuming. For example, cholesterol has been linked to heart disease, and the eating of meat has played a significant role in cholesterol problems. Meat-eating has also intensified humanity's aggressive nature and increased the general level of stress. The body takes on some of the qualities of whatever it ingests, and many animals slain for human consumption are in a state of abject fear at the time of death.

Human beings have the responsibility of rising above animal nature to become more loving, more peaceful, and more godly. Minimizing the intake of meat automatically helps create a more balanced life. The benefits of a vegetarian diet, discussed in more detail later, can play a role in reducing individual as well as collective stress in society at large.

Psychotherapies and Stress

One of the more complicated and expensive ways of dealing with stress in the United States is the billion-dollar-a-year business of psychotherapy. Frequent visits with a psychotherapist may provide the necessary analysis, guidance, and encouragement to free people from the debilitating, even life-threatening effects of stress. However, therapy is often expensive and sometimes makes the person dependent on the therapist.

Self-help groups, which are less complicated and less expensive, have also been effective in relieving stress. These groups usually consist of people with the same type of problem who can share and work out their issues together. Self-help groups have been a great benefit for people addicted to alcohol; together, members can offer strength, guidance and assistance to one another as they cope with the problems of day-to-day life. However, some such groups may be more interested in power and control than in helping the individual. You should pay close attention to the kind of group that you select, or that you encourage others to join.

Biofeedback, Massage, and Hypnosis

Biofeedback is a well-respected technique that has been scientifically investigated and evaluated. It teaches participants to control a specific physiological response by altering the frequency or intensity of a stimulus, such as a sound or a light, connected to a device that monitors bodily processes. Subjects first attain a relaxed state, called alpha–the state immediately below the fully conscious state. This is a light meditative or hypnotic state in which the brain is less agitated. In such a state, individuals can produce such changes as lower blood pressure, more relaxed muscles, a slower heartbeat, or increased blood flow to various parts of the body.[81]

Different types of massage therapies can also relieve stress by stimulating proper energy flow in the body. Massage affects the consciousness as well as the physical organism, allowing clients to release repressed energy blocks and increase their general level of awareness.

Another increasingly popular stress-reduction technique is hypnosis. Hypnosis, which at one time was ridiculed, is now making a comeback, being used widely by therapists and other practitioners to help subjects reach deeper levels of awareness where powerful healing can occur. Further, self-hypnosis is being explored by increasing numbers of people who seek to control their mental faculties or relieve personal suffering through their own power of suggestion.

Meditation and the Relaxation Response

Yet another widely used method to relieve stress is meditation. Many different types of meditation exist, several of which yield spiritual benefits in addition to stress reduction, and a wide variety of individuals and groups teach meditation. In addition, numerous readily available books give instruction on different techniques.

One of the best-known of these is *The Relaxation Response*, by Dr. Herbert Benson.[82] As described in this book, the relaxation response is a stress-reducing meditative practice that produces physiological changes precisely opposite to those brought forth by the fight-or-flight response. During meditation, the overall metabolism of the body slows markedly. For instance, the heart and breathing rates decrease, blood flow to the muscles stabilizes, and blood pressure falls. This relaxation response is achieved by a combination of behavioral techniques, based on Western relaxation methods, Eastern meditative practices, and certain types of prayer.

According to Benson, this technique consists of four basic elements: a quiet environment; a comfortable position; the repetition of a word, phrase, or prayer; and a passive attitude free from thoughts. Besides being a generally useful technique for lowering stress levels, this relaxation response is used therapeutically to treat diseases related to stress and may also be helpful in their prevention.

Several studies have documented the usefulness of the relaxation response. For example, Benson reported that the relaxation response significantly lowered blood pressure in one carefully monitored group of participants suffering from high blood pressure. In another study, subjects accustomed to excessive drug use reported a decrease in their intake of drugs such as marijuana and LSD after practicing the relaxation response.[83]

Take Control: Be Stressed Less

Actually, unhealthy stress is total nonsense! People are responsible for creating their own stress levels, which depend upon the interpretations they give to the situations in their lives.

Because the degree of stress is so dependent upon individual perception and interpretation, specific situations will be naturally more stressful for one person than another. However, this statement is not meant to imply that stress is an illusion–not at all. The actual stress exists. But it does suggest that the meanings people assign to events are at the root of unhealthy stress. This understanding opens a very exciting, empowering door: since everyone has the ability to create stress, everyone also has the capacity to reduce or eliminate it by a simple change of attitude.

Someone who perceives an event as threatening will naturally experience anxiety or want to react with an attack. On the other hand, a person who does not feel threatened and instead responds to the situation constructively, empathically, and competently, will not experience stress. It is only a matter of changing consciousness to a more positive level and recognizing the potential for rising above the difficulty.

In addition to belief systems, habits have a lot to do with minimizing stress. For instance, a regulated daily routine will reduce wear and tear on body and mind. A tendency to do things at a certain time and in a certain way–not out of attachment, but out of a sense of balance–will naturally reduce our unhealthy stress, because even in negative circumstances, we will be preconditioned to carry out the desired activity.

Duality is always present in the material world. In your leadership role, if you become overly attached to either happiness or distress, complications can result. When you are not organized and regulated, your life can become haphazard and subject to fluctuations in your own nature as well as changes in your environment. Further, regulation is necessary in order to develop the higher faculties. As these higher faculties develop, you will naturally become less susceptible to stresses.

Belief, Faith and Detachment

Belief systems are the basis for conscious thought. Therefore, you should be clear about what you create with your beliefs. Examine yourself: Who are you? What is your aim in life? What is important to you? What do you believe in? Reflect upon your goals and evaluate your life based on those reflections. If your accomplishments do not match your goals, reexamine yourself to see if these goals really fit into a harmonious pattern in your life. You can also study your values and constantly use them as a barometer to make your life progress more smoothly.

You can also improve the quality of your faith. A first step is to take inventory to see if you have misplaced faith in things that are superfluous, that impede progress toward your goals, or that do not support your value system. Next, consider your self-image and take note of whether you feel inferior or have a healthy respect for yourself. Obviously, it is important not to overestimate yourself and demonstrate a superiority complex, which would have an adverse effect on your dealings with others. The maturity of your belief system will determine the degree of unhealthy stress that you experience.

One of the most stressful situations for a leader to face is an abrupt change. But with firm goals, a healthy self-concept, strong faith, and a steady aim in life, you can recognize that change is always a part of reality. Seeing yourself not as the proprietor but as the servant of others and of God, try to learn from each change, benefiting from it and seeing it as part of the maturation process. If you view such change as a learning experience, you will reap positive results instead of stress.

To the degree that you still maintain unproductive stress, you need to make adjustments. Look closely to see which situations need attention. If your self-concept is not healthy, you will encounter constant difficulties. In addition, if your beliefs and goals are not strong, constructive and focused, then you are inviting stress into your life.

The Long-Term View

The belief in life after death, and in reincarnation, can help you remain calm in the face of difficulties. You then realize that your problems may be the result of past thoughts and actions, possibly from previous lifetimes. Such a belief helps you realize that you have full control over your life, because your current actions will determine your future. You can deal with problems practically and calmly because your goals, values, and faith allow you to put challenging times in perspective and avoid excessive grief and anxiety. If you accept yourself as a spiritual being, you will not be overly disturbed by any problem because you realize that the true self has not been affected.

Ultimately, most unnecessary stress is the result of an overidentification with the body and the mind. When you become free from this identification, you understand that you are a spirit soul transmigrating into different bodies, putting on new garments and discarding the old ones. As you realize that you are more than just a physical or mental being, you will become less disturbed by your environment and its challenges. At this point you will have developed equipoise, which is real stress management and is also the hallmark of a mature leader.

Highlights

1.   Recent studies demonstrate that stress is a natural part of life. Like seasonings used in cooking, people need to have just the right proportions.

2.   A person's reaction to perceived stress includes specific, measurable physiological reactions such as a faster heart rate, higher blood pressure, hyperventilation, perspiration and a marked increase of blood flow to the muscles. These changes frequently occur in an integrated, coordinated pattern called the "fight-or-flight response," in which the organism prepares to resolve a threatening situation by either fighting or running away.

3.   In present-day society, widespread duplicity and dishonesty contribute to the general level of stress. People say things they do not believe and do things they do not wish to do. Manipulating one another cleverly in a variety of ways, many appear more interested in cosmetic appearances than in the essential aspects of life.

4.   In the modern world, excessive stress is often the product of an environment of rapid technological and economic growth that pushes people to acquire vast amounts of unnecessary commodities. Contemporary society requires its members to work hard, earn sufficient income, and exercise constant vigilance just to maintain the status quo. Such demands, which appear threatening for many, can give rise to fear, insecurity, and loneliness–all contributing factors to unhealthy levels of stress.

5.   Particularly in the West, heart trouble has become one of the greatest killers. Yet in many less "developed" areas of the world, such widespread heart disease does not exist. In these societies, which are more humane and genuinely communal, people see themselves as their brother's keepers and consequently experience less isolation and stress.

6.   As a rule, members of less industrialized societies are more physically active and so more easily convert stress into constructive energy. In contrast, the automated Western way of life actually produces harmful stress because people spend too much time in such sedentary activities as riding in automobiles or watching television, even going so far as to press a button on the remote control to change the channels.

7.   Corporate America has been forced to accept the fact that healthy, stress-free employees are a valuable asset. The cost of stress to companies in health benefits, lost time for sick leave, and inefficiency is staggering. Leaders are beginning to recognize the importance of reducing these losses through programs that reduce stress and increase health.

8.   The simplest stress-reducing technique is to maintain good physical conditioning through exercise and diet. Not only can exercise dispel many specific forms of tension; it can also offset the effects of generalized stress. Those in good physical condition also enhance their mental condition and can withstand such stressors as overwork, a quarrel with the boss, or even a virus more easily than someone who is not.

9.   The relaxation response, besides being a generally useful technique for lowering stress levels, is used therapeutically to treat diseases related to stress and may also be useful in their prevention.

10.   The meanings people assign to events are at the root of unhealthy stress. This understanding opens a very exciting, empowering door: since everyone has the ability to create stress, everyone also has the capacity to reduce or eliminate it by a simple change of attitude.

Mindsets

1.   Refer to the ten essential technologies at the beginning of this book, asking yourself which of them can help you the most to reduce the stress in your life. Select one or two and work with them each day.

2.   As a leader, you run an extremely high risk of encountering stress-related problems. Determine whether or not you have been experiencing some of the psychological and physiological complications of stress mentioned in this chapter. If you have, take steps to remedy the situation.

3.   Be honest and straightforward in your dealings with others. Too much duplicity and dishonesty can cause stress-related problems.

4.   The conveniences of modern life are causing us to amuse, enjoy, and relax ourselves to death. Explore ways in which you can create a more natural lifestyle.

5.   Encourage those you are responsible for to engage in healthy exercise and to eat properly. Do the same yourself.

6.   See that your employees do not have to take work home often. If they usually do, arrange for more vacation time for them.

7.   Engage in regular meditation, especially in chanting or meditating on the holy names of God.

8.   Regulation minimizes stress. Organize and regulate your life, and encourage others to do the same.

9.   Your body and mind have interesting ways of speaking to you. Listen to them. Do not wait until it is too late. Make adjustments

in your consciousness and in your lifestyle as soon as you experience any sign of stress.

10. A weak, conflicted or faulty belief system can cause agonizing stress. If your belief system is value-based, strong, grounded and mature, you will experience few, if any, stress-related problems. However, if you are experiencing constant stress, or if you want to help others who have such problems, then examine the underlying beliefs. Ask some of the following questions: Who am I? What is my aim in life? What is important? What do I believe in?

Part III
Taking Action

Ultimately, as a leader, you can only accomplish the highest material and spiritual goals when you receive full support from those you lead. When you direct your goals and actions to the good of others, and these others know it, the resulting positive energy automatically sets in motion universal forces that can literally move mountains. As a leader, you have an opportunity to tap into this ocean of energy. Indeed, you may be able to singlehandedly change the energy of your family, organization, nation, or even of the entire planet!

10

Providing Protection and Freedom from Fear

Leaders are responsible for the safety of everyone in their charge. Not only do leaders who genuinely love their people implement policies for their benefit; they also make personal sacrifices for them. When people feel valued and cared for in this way, secure in the knowledge that their leaders wish them well, they reciprocate with loyalty and support, readily accepting inconveniences and austerities without complaint.

The Leader Must Set the Stage

Although such attitudes and behaviors may sound idealistic, they are highly possible. Human nature is rather selfish, as demonstrated by the fact that the goal of most behavior is egocentric pleasure and security. When these goals are emphasized, people quite naturally commit themselves to the source of the supply.

One of the greatest human needs is for protection. In ancient times, when the king and his armies provided the only safeguard, the crown received a degree of loyalty unknown in the twentieth century. If practiced today, such mutual love and cooperation between people and their leaders could pull many countries out of their present decline. Leaders who demonstrate their love by offering more protection and a greater sense of security automatically receive more support, cooperation and love in return.

Fearful people manifest specific qualities in their actions and thoughts. They do not trust others; they are slow to reveal their mind; and normally they do not offer love easily or make their best efforts in any endeavor. Sometimes they attack others simply because they anticipate being attacked themselves.

A Catalog of Fears

Fear of the following situations is pervasive in today's societies.

- War: Fear of a third world war; of regional and civil wars; of racial wars; or of religious wars

- Crime: Fear of attack or abuse by criminals, or of exploitation by soldiers or policemen

- Oppression: Fear of denial of civil or human rights

- Inadequate services: Fear of poor medical care or of insufficient educational facilities

- Excessive taxation: Fear of heavy, inequitable taxes

- Destitution: Fear of homelessness; of inability to purchase and maintain a home; or of loss of job, health insurance, or pension

When these fears are eradicated, or at least significantly reduced, people become much more willing to cooperate with their leaders. Given the present economic and political conditions in most countries, many contend that such fears will continue and probably increase. However, this need not be the case. Although some international situations may be difficult to control, the majority of issues can be addressed if leaders employ competent staff and demonstrate by example their personal commitment to help.

The Nuclear Threat

Unfortunately, wars form a constant backdrop for human existence, and fear of war is a global problem. In addition, all of us–especially our children–are aware that most life on the planet can be destroyed by a nuclear war. Indeed, studies report that the majority of adolescents believe that there will be a third world war in their lifetime. Although we have no accurate measure of the psychological effects of such perceived dangers on today's youth, a strong correlation may exist between these fears and the increase in suicides, illicit drug use, and irrational behavior among the young.

Even mature adults are affected psychologically by the fear of nuclear war. The *Bulletin of the Atomic Scientists* has created a "Doomsday Clock" to keep track of humanity's course toward nuclear catastrophe, represented by midnight on the clock's face. The hands, which since January 1988 had stood at six minutes to midnight, were moved back four minutes in 1990 and another seven in 1991 to reflect the end of the Cold War and changes in Eastern Europe.[84] However, since that time, the clock has started ticking again because of the spread of nuclear weapons to other countries of the world, such as North Korea, South Africa and Iraq.

In *The Day After World War III*, author Edward Zuckerman paints a powerful picture of the devastation caused by a nuclear war.[85] He suggests that World War III could kill one billion persons, and that injuries from the blast fires and radiation could kill billions more. Ninety percent of the human population–or up to four billion people–could die from dust and smoke in the atmosphere that would shut out sunlight and produce serious temperature drops. The lack of sunlight and the cold temperature could ultimately cause a drastic decline in agricultural production. This is the phenomenon known as *nuclear winter.*

The entire world could be destroyed by a nuclear winter caused by only one percent of the total nuclear stockpile–an amount found on just one or two modern nuclear submarines. According to the author, nuclear winter produces darkness, freezing cold, toxic gases, radioactivity and, eventually, epidemics. Immediately after a nuclear blast the earth's surface could be plunged into a darkness that might last for months or even longer. Many plants would die from lack of sunlight, resulting in widespread starvation. In addition, because of the temperature drop caused by the lack of sunlight, many animals and humans would freeze to death.

Fires from nuclear blasts could generate huge clouds of toxic fumes that float in the air for long periods of time. The blast would release radioactive particles that cause serious illness and long-term suffering. Once the darkness cleared, the damage to the ozone layer would allow dangerous amounts of ultraviolet radiation to reach the earth, eventually causing cancer and disturbances in the food chain. In other words, a nuclear blast and its aftereffects could devastate the entire planet many times over. And yet, the world's nuclear arsenal in 1986 was sufficient to kill more than 58 billion people–12 times the world's population.

The world's major nuclear powers are the United States, the former Soviet Union, China, France, and the United Kingdom. Although the 1991 collapse of the Soviet Union relieved tensions between the superpowers, many other countries have joined the nuclear club. India, Israel and South Africa have nuclear stockpiles, and other countries–such as Pakistan, Argentina, and Brazil–are gaining in nuclear potential. Still other nations–including Libya, Iran, Egypt, North Korea, South Korea, Taiwan, Japan and Syria–are actively seeking or developing nuclear technology, while Sweden and West Germany have the technology, but are refraining from developing it.[86]

Other Faces of War

Nuclear war is not the only threat. In actual fact, chemical weapons cost less to produce and have been used on battlefields throughout history far more frequently than nuclear or biological weapons. The United States currently has in storage 30,000 metric tons of nerve and blister agents, second only to Russia's stockpile of 40,000 metric tons. Despite public political pledges to destroy chemical arsenals, scientists have charged that new binary chemical agents–substances that would only become toxic when mixed just before deployment–are still being secretly developed.[87] The recent terrorist gas attacks by the Aum Supreme Truth cult in Japan demonstrate the dangers and power of chemical weapons in the hands of terror groups.

Biological weapons, which so far have not come under any form of international control, are perhaps even more threatening. In an article in *The New Republic*, author Robert Wright states unequivocally: "Plain old first-generation biological weapons–the same vintage as the ones Aum Supreme Truth was trying to make–are the great unheralded threat to national security in the 1990s."[88]

Other types of warfare also undermine a nation's well-being. Although nuclear, biological or chemical wars are ultimately far more devastating, local conflagrations can produce a consistent, unnerving, disorienting climate of fear and chaos. Unlike nuclear war, which despite its horrors is still an abstraction for most people, local wars affect the people more directly, tormenting them day and night. These local conflicts are also more likely to recur. While you may not be able to control the international balance of nuclear weapons, you can use your leadership role to help avert regional, civil, tribal, and religious wars closer to home. To do so demands a positive vision of the future and requires you to be strong enough to stand against the tide and take the necessary action.

Skewed Priorities

Depending on the way they are counted, between 150 and 160 wars and civil conflicts have broken out around the globe since the end of World War II, killing roughly 7,200,000 soldiers. Including civilian deaths, the total since World War II is more like 33 to 40 million people, not counting the wounded and other casualties of war. In 1990 alone, the Stockholm International Peace Research Institute counted 31 armed conflicts throughout the world.[89]

The following points appear in *The Strategic Cooperation Initiative or the Star Light Strategy* by retired United States Air Force Major General Jack Kidd:

- According to estimates, the United States and the former Soviet Union account for more than half of the world's military budget and over 80 percent of the world's research budget. These countries have also exported more than 50 percent of the arms sold abroad.
- If the United States military industry were considered to be a national economy, it would rank 13th in the world.
- In the United States, approximately 35,000 businesses have received contracts directly from the Department of Defense, and another 150,000 or so have performed subcontract work.
- The top ten Fortune 500 industrial corporations are all major defense suppliers to the Pentagon.[90]

No wonder there is so much fear. The way societies spend money reveals their priorities and shapes their future. It is imperative that leaders at all levels contribute toward bringing about disarmament and reducing the tremendous threat of war. Leaders cannot receive a high level of cooperation from people who feel unprotected. A fearful family, business or nation is an unproductive one.

Effects of Excessive Military Spending

The expenses of maintaining a large defense establishment are astronomical. Yet, despite the great cost, military spending in the Third World has increased many times over since 1960. If these same financial resources could be channeled into agricultural, medical and educational development, many countries would have a much higher standard of living.

Excessive military spending has also had a negative effect on the technological development of many countries, including America. For instance, U.S. defense spending has greatly stunted the growth of civilian technology in the past 20 years–a period during which America has been losing ground in many technologically oriented industries. On the other hand, China, with one-fifth of the planet's population, is setting an example for the world by mandating a large reduction in military spending to help develop the country in other areas.

If a nation continues to spend only insignificant amounts on health and educational needs, the fears and insecurities of the people will increase. As a leader, you can ensure that everyone receives a basic education and adequate medical care at no charge or at a nominal cost. Excessive concentration on defense, instead of offering more protection and security for a nation or for the world, in fact has the reverse effect. The balance of power becomes a balance of terror, creating greater instability by exposing the world to the dangers of war. Unchecked defense spending also has an adverse effect upon ecological, economic and political stability because it uses up valuable natural resources, contributes to environmental damage, diverts funds from important human needs, and creates discontented, frightened, angry people.

If the present pace continues, in the next few years several additional developing countries will have the technology to produce nuclear weapons. Under such conditions, practically any conflict could produce a serious conflagration endangering the entire planet. No matter what your level of leadership, you can work to avert this possibility.

All-Pervasive Fear of Crime

When criminals have a free hand to terrorize society, all relationships suffer. People who fear attack do not move about freely. Many are afraid to go out at night or to be alone at home or elsewhere. They even hesitate to help someone in distress. Parents worry about the welfare of their children, and this worry produces fear among the children themselves. In many cases people may become aggressive, reacting to perceived threats to their security. General patterns of distrust develop in relationships, because fear cannot easily be compartmentalized. Instead, it becomes a vague undercurrent that affects every perception and interaction.

Criminal activity has become epidemic in many parts of the world. For example, a few years ago two areas of Nigeria–Lagos and Benin–were reportedly under siege by armed robbers. These robbers even attacked police stations and took police weapons to expedite their crimes. Washington, D.C. is said to be infested with drug gangs, which have also taken a heavy toll on other cities such as New York and Los Angeles. In these cities the drug gangs sometimes possess better weapons than the police.

In several Third World countries, criminals have become so powerful that police will avoid them, fearing to arrest them. I personally know of cases in which policemen, witnessing deviant behavior, removed their badges in order not to be recognized by the criminals, who would shoot to kill on sight. In a society so dominated by crime, criminals form powerful alliances with other gangs, or even with existing authorities, to increase their dominion. When this happens, common citizens become afraid to report illegal activity. Even high-ranking government officials, fearing for their lives, will remain silent.

Deterring Crime

Violence, which is both the cause and the effect of crime, has become part of daily life. Every few seconds someone takes the life of another on this planet. The average American child witnesses thousands of murders on television each year.

One theory attributes the increase in violence and criminal activity to a lack of sufficient prison space. However, building more prisons is obviously not the long-term solution. As a matter of fact, prisons are very costly and ultimately counterproductive. Far from being places of rehabilitation, prisons can be cesspools of violence, degradation, and increased racial tensions.

Today, the American incarceration rate is one of the highest in the developed world, with 455 prison inmates per 100,000 population.[91]Among industrialized nations only the former Soviet Union and South Africa have imprisoned as large a segment of their populations. Although these countries have so many prisons, they still have a tremendous and growing amount of criminal activity. For example, between 1973 and 1993, the number of all reported crimes in the United States rose by 42 percent, and of violent offenses, by 82 percent.[92] In addition, the U.S. incarceration rate seems to have a racial component, being disproportionately higher among African Americans. Twenty five percent of all

African American men in their twenties are in jail, on probation or on parole, four times the rate for Caucasian American men.[93]

Undoubtedly, criminal actions call for quick and just penalties that are effective enough to deter crime. Criminals must understand that the law will not tolerate their behavior, and the social environment should label them as deviants rather than accepting, hiding, or even encouraging them. At the same time, it is important to recognize that not all crime is a result of greedy, selfish, or deliberately harmful behavior. Policies to deter crime are more successful when they also include concentrated efforts to remove the causative factors that produce such criminals in the first place. For some, criminal behavior may be the only way to survive. Therefore, one of your responsibilities as a leader is to ensure that the items necessary for basic human survival are available to everyone, reducing the temptation to break the law.

One contributing factor to crime in the United States and certain other parts of the world is the easy availability of guns. No matter what leadership position you occupy, you can develop the courage to support policies that reduce the number of weapons available to the public. The stream of violence in society is exacerbated by the ease with which average citizens, including youth, can arm themselves. In the United States, which has more handguns than any other country in the world, more than one-third of the citizens are armed. The number of crimes and deaths involving firearms is correspondingly high. In the United States, two-thirds of all murders are committed with guns, and 40 percent of all robberies also involve guns.[94]

Use your leadership position to set a positive example. As mentioned in the Bhagavad-gita: "Whatever action a great man performs, common men follow. And whatever standards he sets by exemplary acts, all the world pursues."[95] During the Reagan administration, scores of officials were accused of illegal or unethical activities, and the alleged improprieties uncovered by the Whitewater investigation during the Clinton administration provide another case in point. Such behavior on the part of any leader–even if only suspected–obviously erodes public trust. Citizens who believe that a leader is involved in improprieties or criminal activities will be tempted to seek their own lucrative opportunities for exploitation.

Leaders who want to create thriving countries, organizations or families must set good examples themselves, free from criminal or questionable activity of any kind. In such an environment, people will be afraid to break the law, because of the climate established by the leader's intolerance of crime. A leader who is strict about deviant behavior creates an atmosphere of trust and displays respect for others, who naturally reciprocate in a loving way because they feel protected and valued.

Denial of Basic Human Rights

All over the world, powerful elites deny civil and human rights to the people. For example, in recent years, some of the most popular American news programs, such as *60 Minutes, 20/20,* and *Now It Can Be Told,* have dealt regularly with ways in which the elite cheat and manipulate the average citizen for their own benefit.

Militaristic regimes deny citizens a sense of security and prohibit them from participating in a democratic order–both basic components of a life not dominated by fear. Since the mid-1970s a huge number of countries in Europe and Latin America have moved from dictatorship to elected civillian government. In the 1980s and early 1990s, at least 15 African states departed from dictatorial one-party government and held elections. After 1989, the Soviet bloc followed suit. Despite progressive appearances, though, the military often maintains considerable power. For example, civilian governments have been unable to protect the people from torture and murder in Latin American countries such as Peru, Brazil, Venezuela, Colombia, El Salvador and Guatemala.[96]

The denial of civil and human rights is a worldwide phenomenon, as illustrated by the *Genocide Watch* report, edited by Helen Fein. Over one-third of the countries of the world employ systematic torture. In the early 1990s, atrocities in such nations as Panama, South Africa, Somalia, Ethiopia, Sudan, Liberia, Kuwait, Ireland, and the former Yugoslavia demonstrated the pervasiveness of these abuses.[97]

Throughout world history, holocausts have taken the lives of millions of people. The decimation of Native Americans during the expansion of the United States westward, Jews in Europe during Hitler's regime, and Russian citizens during the Russian revolution are but a few poignant examples. The African slave trade was one of the darkest times in human history, where as many as 100 million Africans lost their lives as they were captured, transported, and sold to the so-called civilized world.

As another example, *The Conquest of America,* by Tzvetan Todorov, contains a powerful description of the effects of the European presence in the New World. The figures speak for themselves and will be devastating to all people of higher consciousness. According to the author, when white European Christians came to America's shores in 1492, there were approximately 80 million people in the Americas. By 1550, in 58 years, only 10 million remained. In Mexico, when Europeans first arrived, there were 25 million Mexicans; by 1600 there were only 1 million. In the West Indies, there was practically total extermination of the aboriginal peoples. In 1492, there were over 1 million inhabitants of Santo Domingo; by 1530, there were only 10,000. In 1492, there were 600,000 Cubans; by 1570, only 290,000 remained.[98]

In addition to physical effects, the denial of human rights can have a profound psychological impact. People who live in constant fear may experience the same deleterious symptoms experienced by prisoners of war. Whether their oppressors torture them one by one or annihilate them en masse is not the point. The very threat of arbitrary imprisonment, torture or execution is a tremendous drain on the psyche.

Ultimately, as a leader, you can only accomplish the highest material and spiritual goals when you receive full support from those you lead. When you direct your goals and actions to the good of others, and these others know it, the resulting positive energy automatically sets in motion universal forces that can literally move mountains. As a leader, you have an opportunity to tap into this ocean of energy. Indeed, you may be able to singlehandedly change the energy of your family, organization, nation, or even of the entire planet!

Inadequate Human Services

In many areas of the world, health care and education cannot compete with military priorities. As *The Gaia Atlas of Green Economics* describes:

> Global military spending, more than $1 billion a minute, amounts to more than the total incomes of the poorest half of humanity. Industrialized countries spend more on the military than on either health or education. And arms imports in many Third World countries have contributed to and exacerbate their already crippling debt burden.[99]

A recent United Nations Development Programme report indicates that just 12 percent of the money spent on weapons could pay for health care, drinking water and sufficient food for the world's starving population.[100] A 1988 article in *The Nation* cites claims by Ruth Leger Sivard, former official of the U.S. Arms Control and Disarmament Agency, that "a single Trident submarine could be traded in for a five-year program of universal child immunization against six deadly diseases, which would prevent 1 million deaths a year."[101]

The global military budget is vastly larger than the total amount of humanitarian aid provided by the world's nations. If countries spent less on defense, more money would be available to improve medical and educational services. Of course, a functional defense system is necessary, but it should not take away from other significant priorities such as education. After all, children are this planet's greatest natural resource and the future depends upon how they are cared for now.

Fear of Heavy Taxation

Many people are expert at finding ways to avoid paying taxes, or to pay as little as possible. Of course, taxes are a necessary, logical, and healthy government policy that allows those who benefit from services to help offset their cost. However, the problem in most countries is that citizens view the government as alien, different from themselves and determined to exploit them. But, once again, when leaders are seen as well-wishers, protectors, and genuine servants, then citizens will understand more clearly that their tax dollars are being spent to help them. In such a situation, governments can even impose heavy taxes without causing resentment.

Given the selfishness of human nature, however, people generally want to know what they will gain personally from their tax contributions. If leaders can make tax benefits tangible to their people, allowing them to realize how they are helping themselves, they will offer less resistance. People will be more willing to pay taxes to improve the quality of their lives instead of lining the pockets of the elite or increasing a nation's ability to kill others.

The important goal is to create an atmosphere of trust that allows people to take pride in paying taxes to support government programs. Given proper security, affection, and love, people naturally want to be generous rather than selfish, because giving brings joy, especially when the gift produces positive results in their lives. With a proper level of love, giving in the form of taxation will not be viewed as an imposition.

The Ravages of Homelessness

Homelessness has always been a problem in Third World countries and in war-torn nations, where large portions of the population are forced to flee for their lives. But homelessness has now also become a major problem in countries like the United States, where leaders have allowed the well-being of the people to become a low-level priority. The undisputed fact is that the number of people without shelter is increasing daily throughout the world.

Across cultures, people share a common dream of having safe, comfortable homes for their families. However, millions of people on this planet are homeless. The number of people living in slums and squatter settlements is increasing faster than the rate of growth for the overall world population. Globally, housing conditions have worsened since 1976, especially in most Third World countries.[102] Even in economically successful Western countries like the United States and Japan, people are living in crowded conditions because they cannot afford their own homes, or because suitable housing is not available. Husbands and wives must both work even to acquire a much smaller house than that of their parents.

In Japan, as well as in many other countries, even members of the middle class must wait a long time for an available apartment or house. And, in the United States, many of those who do manage to buy a house find it difficult to make their mortgage payments, so that the banks foreclose. Others are evicted, finding all of their clothes, furniture, and other personal possessions literally cast out on the streets.

Worse yet are the refugees, who have had to flee their homes, and often their countries as well. In 1992, over 16 million refugees fled to foreign countries.[103] Almost nothing is more devastating to people than to fear their own country so much that they risk their lives to leave it.

The flight of citizens to another country is a sign of a major failure in leadership. What could be more terrible than to have no control over the feeding, sheltering and protecting of loved ones? Parents who flee with their families suffer daily watching their relatives, and many others, helplessly die. This is surely a nightmare of the worst order. International indifference to people living in refugee camps or roaming as involuntary nomads often condemns them to a slow death or, at best, to a highly uncertain future.

Even if many people disagree with your policies, your responsibility as a leader is always to act in their best interest. This is true at any level of leadership. Once again, when leaders protect those in their charge–even in the face of mistakes and confusions–people will stay where they are because they know the leader is working on their behalf. On the other hand, when their fears are aroused, people will retaliate or flee–both dangerous situations for a leader. When too many people rebel against government or organizational policies, the government or organization becomes unstable. Further, people who flee upset those who remain behind and may bring in reinforced opposition from the outside. In addition, refugees can cause conflict with citizens of other countries and bad relationships between neighboring governments.

Consider those whom you lead to be your family. Although a family always has problems, disputes, and confusions, like a caring parent you can consistently create order out of chaos, being determined but loving and providing adequate security and protection. If you are compassionate in your leadership, you will not cause anyone to suffer helplessly or run away. When you make every possible effort to provide proper protection for others, you are deeply loved and protected in return, and will surely be praised even after you leave this world. Such leaders have a profound impact on others, and make their mark in history.

Highlights

1.   Not only do leaders who genuinely love their people implement policies for their benefit; they also make personal sacrifices for them. When people feel valued and cared for in this way, secure in the knowledge that their leaders wish them well, they reciprocate with loyalty and support, readily accepting inconveniences and austerities without complaint.

2.   Fear of the following situations is pervasive in today's societies.
    • *War:* Fear of a third world war; of regional and civil wars; of racial wars; or of religious wars
    • *Crime:* Fear of attack or abuse by criminals, or of exploitation by soldiers or policemen
    • *Oppression:* Fear of denial of civil or human rights
    • Inadequate services: Fear of poor medical care or of insufficient educational facilities
    • *Excessive taxation:* Fear of heavy, inequitable taxes
    • *Destitution:* Fear of homelessness; of inability to purchase and maintain a home; or of loss of job, health insurance, or pension

3.   No wonder there is so much fear. The way societies spend money on armaments reveals their priorities and shapes their future. As a leader at any level, you can do everything within your power to bring about disarmament and reduce the tremendous threat of nuclear war.

4.   When criminals have a free hand to terrorize society, all relationships suffer. People who fear attack do not move about freely. Many are afraid to go out at night or to be alone at home or elsewhere. They even hesitate to help someone in distress. Parents worry about the welfare of their children, and this worry produces

fear among the children themselves. In many cases people may become aggressive, reacting to perceived threats to their security.

5. Sanctions obviously need to be effective enough to deter crime. Criminals must know that the law will not tolerate them, and that their actions will bring severe, immediate penalties. In addition, such a strict approach is most productive when it is complemented by genuine efforts to remove the causative factors that produce such criminals in the first place.

6. In addition to physical effects, the denial of human rights can have a profound psychological impact. People who live in constant fear may experience the same deleterious symptoms experienced by prisoners of war.

7. If a nation continues to spend only insignificant amounts on health and educational needs, the fears and insecurities of the people will increase. As a leader, you can ensure that everyone receives a basic education and adequate medical care at no charge or at a nominal cost. Excessive concentration on defense, instead of offering more protection and security for a nation or for the world, in fact has the reverse effect.

8. If leaders can make tax benefits tangible to their people, allowing them to realize how they are helping themselves, they will offer less resistance. People will be more willing to pay taxes to improve the quality of their lives instead of lining the pockets of the elite or increasing a nation's ability to kill others.

9. The flight of citizens to another country is a sign of a major failure in leadership. What could be more terrible than to have no control over the feeding, sheltering and protecting of loved ones? Parents who flee with their families suffer daily watching their relatives, and many others, helplessly die. This is surely a nightmare of the

worst order. International indifference to people living in refugee camps or roaming as involuntary nomads often condemns them to a slow death or, at best, to a highly uncertain future.

10.   Consider those whom you lead to be your family. Although a family always has problems, disputes, and confusions, like a loving parent you can consistently create order out of chaos, being determined but loving and providing adequate security and protection.

Mindsets

1. Review the ten essential technologies at the beginning of this book, especially numbers 3 and 7. Make efforts to understand the feelings and perceptions of those you lead, and behave as if God were watching your every action.

2. Remind yourself and those who work for you that the more others feel protected and secure, the more they will automatically offer support, cooperation and love.

3. In order to minimize fear and uncertainty among those whom you lead, make sure that your policies are clearly explained and communicated.

4. As much as possible, tend to the basic needs of those for whom you are responsible, providing adequate income, shelter, education, food, and medical care. If you cannot provide these, you are forcing them to seek relief elsewhere.

5. Now that the world has become one global village, remember that tribal, civil, or religious wars anywhere affect everyone and can even be the catalyst for a world war. Be aware that when you resolve local conflicts, you are helping create world peace, and that if you allow these conflicts to continue, you are endangering the planet.

6. Because criminals can undermine the authority of any government or organization, creating a climate of fear and anxiety, you must deal with them efficiently and effectively. If people know that their leader is honest and genuine, they will be less likely to engage in crimes themselves. Everyone is affected by the tone set by the chief, and will follow a leader's example. Therefore, be sure to provide a positive role model.

7.   Publicly reward those who display altruistic concern, whether these be other leaders, officials, employees, family members or unknown individuals. In addition, encourage other departments or organizations to do this regularly, in order to support such behavior as the norm. To create greater awareness of altruism, invite as many people as possible to participate in selecting the award-winners. Place pictures of the winners in prominent places, and do whatever else is needed to make these awards a very popular yet serious process.

8.   As funds become available that were formerly spent on defense, you will have more opportunities to invest in health and educational programs. Be careful to balance these areas effectively so that one does not suffer because of the other.

9.   Show by clear example that you will neither take advantage of others nor tolerate any exploitation of the people by your representatives. If someone does exploit others, deal with that person quickly and firmly.

10.   Make it a matter of pride to be fair and respectful in all your dealings with others, and encourage others to follow your example.

11

The Dangers of Overconsumption and Misdirected Development

*O*ne of the most important activities of a compassionate leader is to help ensure a viable future for everyone by protecting the environment, which contains the earth's life-support systems. To this end, leaders at any level can design programs and implement policies that do not waste valuable resources and that maintain the delicate balance of planetary ecosystems. In line with this approach, the most constructive form of economic growth and development is people-oriented, based on appropriate technology–technology that is on a human scale–and does not consider economic profit as its sole measure of value.

Overconsumption: A Contagious Disease

The United States, with its entrenched patterns of excessive consumption, has unfortunately become the role model for most developing nations. Although America is home to only about six percent of the world's population, it consumes disproportionately large percentages of the world's advertising, energy, and resources. In societies such as the United States, where success is measured by economic growth and consumption, advertising has become a major industry, encouraging people to buy what they often do not even need.

The average American supermarket has thousands of items on display, and Europe now has mega-markets that stock even more products. The United States currently uses hundreds of times more energy than such countries as Nepal or Burkina Faso. In addition, the industrialized world's rapid consumption of resources destroys countless acres of land each day, and this excessive use of resources is also accelerating the extinction of plant and animal species.

Each year, the United States produces 5 billion tons of solid waste from manufacturing, mining and farming–twice the amount created by any other country in the world. At home and in the workplace, Americans generate another 230 million tons of trash annually. Every year, the United States throws away 16 billion disposable diapers, 1.6 billion ball-point pens, 2 billion disposable razor blades, and 216 million pounds of plastic soda bottles and milk containers.[104] Such prodigious overconsumption and waste of resources indicate tremendous insensitivity to the global situation.

Americans are the most entertained people in the world, depending extensively on movies, videos, television, and spectator sports. Ninety-eight percent of all homes have at least one television set and over one-third have two or more, so that the average American spends almost 17 hours each week watching television.[105]

Although Americans are reputed to have the best diet in the world, they still have many health problems. One reason is that a high percentage of the food purchased in supermarkets is bought in response to misleading advertisements and does not provide optimum nourishment. Each year, the average American digests several pounds of food additives, which can cause cancer and other diseases. Americans also overeat, and the United States population is the world's fattest. Millions of Americans use drugs and low-calorie food to lose weight, despite the fact that most of them ultimately gain back the weight they have lost.

Misdirected Development

In most cases, the contemporary ideal of success–whether for a country or for a human being–is inappropriate and unnatural. Unfortunately, modern societies seem to admire individuals and nations for acquiring and using as many commodities as possible. The more assets they amass, the greater their apparent success. For a nation, and for human civilization in general, such a focus on rapid growth and massive consumption is suicidal. Humanity can no longer afford such excesses and cannot continue to ignore the consequences of its activities. One of the responsibilities of a leader is to offer a stable and secure future to everyone by being more conscientious about the effects of each decision upon the world's environment and resource base.

Industrialized countries, which contain only about one-quarter of the world's population, control most of the world's goods and are responsible for the bulk of its production. Such disproportionate resource use is causing the entire global community to suffer. The sad irony is that these excesses are not only harmful to the immediate consumer, but to future generations as well.

The industrialized nations, with their emphasis on overconsumption and industrialization at any cost, are effectively bequeathing an environmentally imperiled planet to the children of the entire world. Leaders of developing nations who mistakenly emulate Western standards of consumption are dooming their constituents to a lifestyle that may superficially appear luxurious and desirable, but is, in fact, ultimately destructive.

Staggering Toll on Humans and Society

The emphasis on self-gratification in Western societies has important sociological ramifications as well. For example, the steady deterioration of moral and ethical standards is one by-product of an overly self-indulgent society. Moral and ethical degradation leads not only to increased promiscuity, crime and exploitation, but also to a heightened sense of hopelessness and despair. The suicide rate among the young is rising. Between 1970 and 1986, the rate among children ages 10 to 14 increased two and one-half times, while for teenagers between the ages of 15 and 19, it almost doubled. In general, the suicide rate for young people in the 15 to 24 age range has risen steeply since the 1950s.[106] Where the immediate concerns of parents 25 or 30 years ago centered around economic growth and consumerism, today parents face a veritable cornucopia of problems resulting from the moral decline in society.

Rampant sexual promiscuity has contributed to an increase in AIDS and other sexually transmitted diseases, abortions, single parenting, children having children, incest and child abuse. Americans spend billions each year on pornography. In 1992, 45,472 new cases of AIDS were reported in the United States–jumping to 103,500 in 1993 because of new reporting methods–in addition to over 600,000 cases of other sexually transmitted diseases.[107] A 1980 Cosmopolitan magazine survey indicated that 21 percent of respondents–American women–had engaged in intercourse by the age of 15, and another 69 percent had experienced sexual relations by the age of 20. Fifty-four percent of the married women in the survey had been unfaithful to their husbands, 11 percent reported being victims of incest, and 26 percent had experienced rape or sexual molestation at some point in their lives.[108]

America's preoccupation with self-gratification at all costs has profoundly affected U.S. industries. In order to finance a lifestyle replete with an ever-increasing supply of material possessions, both parents must now work, leaving the children of the nuclear family to be raised by day-care centers and babysitters. The competitive workplace environment creates stress which impairs the quality of work and contributes to workplace illness and absenteeism. For instance, in 1988, the U.S. National

Institute for Occupational Safety and Health (NIOSH) identified psychological disorders as one of the ten leading work-related diseases in the United States. In addition, a 1991 survey conducted by Northwestern National Life Insurance Company found that 72 percent of the workers surveyed experienced stress-related conditions that could raise health-care costs.[109]

Present patterns of industrial growth and scientific advancement in the United States may eventually reduce the number of jobs on the assembly line by half. An inexpensive robot can work two shifts a day for years at a low hourly cost, in contrast to a worker who might receive $15 or more per hour plus many expensive benefits for the same job. Viewed solely from the perspective of immediate economic growth, the use of machines to replace people may seem beneficial. After all, a machine works much faster, is more reliable, and does not require overtime pay. But in the long run, the costs to human beings will far outweigh the benefits. As economist Richard Douthwate observes, "New technologies almost always destroy more jobs than they create."[110]

Costs of Western-Style Development

Therefore, although industrial growth and material development have produced undeniable advantages, in recent times the associated costs have become increasingly apparent. Suppose that Americans were asked to vote on whether to accept or reject a new technology with the following price tag: tens of thousands of fatalities each year; millions of people disabled; billions of dollars in property damage; urban sprawl and inner-city decay; sexual promiscuity and weaker parental control; increased air pollution and accompanying health problems; dependence of the United States on Middle Eastern countries; disappearance of thousands of acres of farm land under asphalt; ugly billboards; large personal debts; and a landscape dotted with automobile junkyards.

Would such costs be acceptable to the public? Neither the American people nor their representatives in Congress ever voted to develop the automobile, for which everyone now pays such a terrible price. All things considered, the deleterious effects may well outweigh the gains. It is incumbent on the leaders of society to carefully weigh the prospective benefits and detrimental effects of a technology upon the people before any implementation begins.

Willis Harman, former president of the Institute for Noetic Sciences, has extensively studied the costs and benefits of modern industrial civilization, identifying several "problems of success" that accompany the undeniable advantages. For example, the sophistication of science and technology that has made life easier also has made mass destruction possible via nuclear, chemical and biological weapons. The ability to prolong human life has been counterbalanced by the growing problems of the aged. Widespread automation has produced unemployment and dehumanization of the workplace. The general affluence of Western societies has polluted the earth and depleted its resources, and also caused a widening gap between the rich and poor nations of the world.[111]

Similarly, Herman Kahn and Barry Bruce-Briggs, in *Things To Come*, have identified "mixed blessings of progress," including loss of privacy, increased institutional power over individuals, dehumanization, a loss of human scale, increasing vulnerability of centralized administrative and technological systems, a rapid pace of change that makes successful adjustments difficult, and increasing complexity and uncertainty of choices without the proper knowledge to choose wisely.[112]

Leaders of developing nations, as well as other leaders at all levels around the world, would be wise to support development programs that direct people toward a healthy, simpler lifestyle—one focused on compassionate relationships with all life instead of the Western world's example of abuse, misuse, and exploitation of nature and people. The long-term global consequences of any leadership decision can be examined with these goals in mind.

Using Local and Natural Resources

Historically, because of a culturally inherent respect for nature, leaders in some developing nations have protected their environment more than their counterparts in the West. It is imperative that they continue to work hard to revitalize and maintain such values for the sake of the children, the nation and the planet. All leaders can learn from the mistakes of the industrialized world, developing the resolve to save their people from the heavy toll exacted by the "disease" of overconsumption. In order to more fully develop the capacity for caring and sharing, two mottoes must echo around the world: "Simple living with high thinking" and "Small is beautiful."

Leaders can best actualize healthy growth through appropriate technology, which means technology on a human scale, suitable to local needs, capabilities and conditions. The use of appropriate technology can become a top priority for all developing countries, many of which still tend to emulate Western patterns of large-scale development. Instead of following the Western model, leaders must consider the specific needs of each nation and its people, including physiology, psychology, environment, weather conditions, available resources and the existing talent pool of human skills.

All too often countries have measured their achievements by a Western barometer without first determining the success of a project in human terms and evaluating its suitability for their own unique environment or stage of development. Developing nations have wasted billions of dollars on equipment and projects that either have no use, are harmful, or cannot work in the developing world.

Particularly disastrous for developing countries are projects that depend on raw materials from other nations. Such an approach creates a dependency that can exhaust assets through foreign exchange purchases. Volumes could be written about such cases, which are numerous and often ridiculous. All leaders of developing countries should make it a top priority to avoid this plight. This can be done by planning developmental goals and projects that the people are willing to accept and able to implement, and by determining the capacity of the country's resources and existing infrastructures to support them.

A nation can continue to produce locally manufactured products, even if these are not polished or sophisticated, using locally available manpower and resources to improve quality, rather than buying these resources and skills outside of the country. Foreign expertise can instead be used to help develop locally available assets so that the nation can avoid increasing dependence on imports, which can create serious trade imbalances.

Avoiding Past Mistakes

Leaders of Third World countries are in an excellent position to escape many of the problems that the developed world can now only alter with serious difficulty. By approaching the issue of development with prudence and circumspection, it is possible to avoid embarking on the self-destructive journey of misdirected development and mad consumption so avidly pursued by the Western world.

As a leader at any level in any part of the world, you can evaluate all your decisions in light of their effect upon others and upon the planet. You can implement policies that use a minimal amount of resources, and you can recycle those materials that have already been used. In addition, anyone who is seeking to sell unnecessary or harmful equipment, commodities, and projects to Third World nations would be wise to remember that the world is now one global village. What happens to your neighbors inevitably affects you, and everyone else as well.

In the long run, everyone will benefit from leaders who constantly examine the potential impact of their projects and proposals. There are valuable source books available concerning the importance of limited growth, the pitfalls of development, and realistic planning methods for success. Leaders can study them with care. In addition, organizations exist that emphasize the role of appropriate technology in Third World development and provide invaluable assistance. One such organization is England's Intermediate Technology Society, which publishes a journal about appropriate technology and advises interested groups and individuals pursuing projects in the Third World.

Those who ignore the lessons of history are doomed to repeat them. Although it would be wise to act immediately to avoid the pitfalls inherent in Western technology, the glitter of an apparently comfortable, opulent lifestyle shines so brightly that it often blinds both leaders and the led, who believe that they can have the pleasure and circumvent the pain.

Take care not to be deceived. You can fulfill your responsibilities by planning development to fit your own culture and natural environment. Then people will embrace your policies, and the nation will move toward harmony and self-sufficiency. Even if you are not a political leader, but the leader of a family, business or organization, you can take steps to implement a simpler, more self-sufficient and less wasteful lifestyle. The world is depending on you.

Highlights

1. Leaders at any level can design programs and implement policies that do not waste valuable resources and that maintain the delicate balance of planetary ecosystems. In line with this approach, the most constructive form of economic growth and development is people-oriented, based on appropriate technology–technology that is on a human scale–and does not consider economic profit as its sole measure of value.

2. In most cases, the contemporary ideal of success–whether for a nation or for a human being–is inappropriate and unnatural. Unfortunately, modern societies seem to admire individuals and nations that acquire and use as many commodities as possible. The more assets they amass, the greater their apparent success. For a nation, and for human civilization in general, such a focus on rapid growth and massive consumption is suicidal.

3. Despite the fact that the world's resources are limited, most countries still try to follow the example of America and other Western nations, whose excesses are causing the entire global community to suffer. The sad irony is that these excesses are not only harmful to the immediate consumer, but to future generations as well.

4. The emphasis on self-gratification in Western societies has important sociological ramifications. For example, the steady deterioration of intrinsic moral and ethical standards is one by-product of an overly self-indulgent society. Moral and ethical degradation leads not only to increased promiscuity, crime and exploitation, but also to a heightened sense of hopelessness and despair.

5. Neither the American people nor their representatives in Congress ever voted to develop the automobile, for which everyone now pays such a terrible price. All things considered, the deleterious effects may well outweigh the gains. It is incumbent on the leaders of

society to carefully weigh the prospective benefits and detrimental effects of a technology upon the people before any implementation begins.

6.   Historically, because of a culturally inherent respect for nature, leaders in some developing nations have protected their environment more than their counterparts in the West. It is imperative that they continue to work hard to revitalize and maintain such values for the sake of the children, the nation and the planet.

7.   All leaders can learn from the mistakes of the industrialized world, developing the resolve to save their people from the heavy toll exacted by the "disease" of overconsumption. In order to more fully develop the capacity for caring and sharing, two mottoes must echo around the world: "Simple living with high thinking" and "Small is beautiful."

8.   Leaders of developing nations, as well as other leaders at all levels around the world, can support development programs that direct people towards a healthy, simpler life—one focused on compassionate relationships with all life instead of the Western world's example of abuse, misuse, and exploitation of nature and people.

9.   Those who ignore the lessons of history are doomed to repeat them. Although it might be wise to take immediate steps to avoid the pitfalls inherent in Western technology, the glitter of an apparently comfortable, opulent lifestyle shines so brightly that it often blinds both leaders and the led, who believe that they can have the pleasure and circumvent the pain. Take care not to be deceived.

10.   Even as the leader of a family, business or organization anywhere in the world, you can take steps to implement a simpler, more self-sufficient and less wasteful lifestyle. The world is depending on you.

Mindsets

1.   Reread the ten technologies at the beginning of this book. Consider how each of them can assist you in caring for this earth and making wise environmental decisions. Select one or two to keep in mind as you make decisions that affect the well-being of this planet's resources and ecosystems.

2.   Look closely at your own lifestyle and notice areas where you are excessive or overindulgent. Make a list of these areas and what you plan to do about each. As you make an actual change, cross out that category until you have eliminated all areas.

3.   When is the last time you took a simple camping trip, spent some time in a village or in the country, or just went for a walk in a forest or park? Try to make this a weekly or at least a monthly affair. Admiring nature and simple villages, or communing with the elements, can raise your consciousness tremendously. Such rejuvenating activities are essential for your well-being.

4.   Note your own leadership style. Where are you emphasizing monetary concerns and minimizing quality of life? See how many improvements you can make before the year is over. Arrange your future planning to consider the effects of your policies.

5.   Educate those you lead. Use the motto "simple living with high thinking" in your conversations and speeches. Avoid over-corrupted, complicated living and whimsical, selfish, exploitative thinking.

6.   Do not hesitate to study all of your major projects to see if the plans meet the practical needs of your people. Leaders in the developing world should use local and national resources and appropriate technology as much as possible, even to the point of occasionally sacrificing quality. Self-sufficiency can go hand-in-hand with material and spiritual development.

7. Become familiar with limited growth and "small is beautiful" approaches to development. Study recent literature or contact such groups as the Intermediate Technology Society of England and others. Use the material and expertise available to you to plan healthy, effective development.

8. Observe the birds, squirrels, insects, fish and other forms of life. Notice how simply they live and how God provides for them so nicely. These reflections will help you release many fears and attachments.

9. Be aware of the impact of all decisions you make as a leader. Think carefully about their short-term and long-term effects on your family, your immediate community, your nation and your world, and about their influence on future generations. If you discover potentially harmful consequences, reconsider your decisions and make new, more constructive, choices. Encourage others to do the same.

10. Read some of the newest information about recycling and about conserving energy. See how your organization, community, or country can be more efficient and less wasteful.

12

Agricultural Development and Basic Nutrition

Two of humanity's most fundamental needs are food and water. Any species of life unable to acquire them in sufficient quantity cannot survive. For these reasons, leaders at all levels should consider carefully the issues of agricultural development and diet in order to ensure a sustainable future for everyone.

Lack of Food and Water

A family, a community, or a society that cannot feed itself or protect itself from disease is in a very precarious situation. Unfortunately, many people in the world find themselves in just such circumstances. For instance, much of the world's population has no access to safe water. Because so many people have no clean water source, vast numbers die each year from diseases—such as guinea worm infestation or cholera—contracted from contaminated water.

In Third World nations, many children die in their first year, and a large percentage of the survivors will contract serious diseases, all because of unclean water. It is a depressing sight to tour many Third World villages, witnessing the effects of water-related illnesses on person after person, knowing full well that the water supply that helps the inhabitants maintain their livelihood is itself responsible for many sicknesses and even deaths.

In addition to serious water problems, lifelong hunger and malnutrition affect countless people on this planet. About one-quarter of the population in Africa is chronically hungry. The United Nations Food and Agricultural Organization (FAO) estimated in 1992 that about one-fifth of the Third World population, or about 800 million people, suffered from serious malnutrition. Around the world, the numbers of undernourished children are increasing.[113]

Obviously, current agricultural planning and programs are inadequate. For example, per capita cereal grain production around the world has declined. This trend started in the 1970s in Africa, Eastern Europe and the Soviet Union; it has continued during the 1980s in Latin America and North America; and it is beginning to appear in Western Europe and West Asia.[114] Despite the fact that cropland on the African continent has increased, food production per person has declined by 20 percent since 1970. One cause of this decline is the high percentage of degraded farmland that has developed under the pressures of rapid population growth, harmful environmental policies, and competing demands for fuelwood and pasture land. Africa has become a food importer since the 1970s and many African countries are now dependent on food aid to survive.[115] As Anthony McMichael, author of *Planetary Overload*, concludes, "Millions now face serious malnutrition in the immediate sub-Saharan countries....Clearly, the challenge of attaining food security in Africa is huge, and strict political and economic programmes that are attuned to ecological sustainability will be needed."[116]

Contributing Factors to World Hunger

There are numerous causes for the inability of much of the world to feed itself. One major stumbling block is the failure to recognize the role of women in agricultural production. For instance, although women grow most of the food in Africa, the majority of the training, technology, and investments are currently channeled to men.[117] The significance of women in agricultural development needs to be acknowledged, so that the proper resources and equipment can be placed in the hands of those who actually produce.

Another important factor contributing to the world's food shortage is a distorted sense of priorities. In pounds per person, more explosives exist in the world than food. In the 1980s, African governments, similarly to many Third World nations, allocated less than 10 percent of their budgets to agriculture, with a far greater proportion dedicated to police and the military.[118] The world's governments spend almost $1 trillion annually in military investments, many overspending to such an extent that they place themselves in extreme financial difficulty. If this capital were rechanneled into the agricultural sector, everyone could have a better chance for survival in a healthy environment.

Another absurdity is the fact that nations can store millions of tons of surplus grains a year, while spending billions per year on food subsidies. This is a tragic paradox: while famine ravages so many areas of the world, the developed countries pay farmers millions of dollars not to farm, or to abandon or destroy their produce, in order to balance the economy. For example, in 1989, corn in the United States was selling for $2.26 per bushel on the open market, but because the government had promised the growers $2.84 per bushel, American taxpayers footed a bill of $3.5 billion for this subsidy. In addition, the government required farmers who participated in this subsidy program to take 10.8 million acres of cornfields out of production.[119]

Around the world, financial and economic issues increasingly receive greater priority than human welfare. Unfortunately, not all economically feasible decisions are humanly sound and many of them can contribute to global instability. For instance, some prosperous African countries, instead of investing in the agricultural sector, emphasize hotels, high-rise buildings, and other facilities that do not address the central needs of the people. As another example, between 1960 and 1980, the Nigerian government earned billions from crude oil exports, much of which could have been, but was not, effectively invested in the agricultural sector.

Yet another problem in many Third World countries is the storage of agricultural produce. A large proportion of grains, fruits and vegetables produced in these regions go to waste because of improper storage facilities. Obviously, in addition to improved farming methods, the development of adequate storage is a critical factor in the elimination of food shortages.

Even those developing countries that recognize the importance of the agricultural sector often do so more in theory than in practice. To remedy this situation you can take initiatives to ensure that farming is a respected occupation and to provide positive incentives to those in agricultural work. Not only can you speak often about the importance of farming, but you can also demonstrate your interest by visiting agricultural projects and encouraging successful farmers to serve as role models for others.

Ultimately, the global food crisis can be attributed to humanity's ineffective use of the 20 percent of the earth's land surface available for agriculture. Alarming, too, is the fact that much of the world's arable land is threatened by desertification. Clearly, the world must change its approach to food production. However, in order to develop a comprehensive solution, it is important also to examine the other side of the equation: worldwide patterns of food consumption.

Vegetarianism: A Solution on Many Levels

As a leader, naturally you want to keep your mind and body fit for service to others. Because food has a profound effect on human well-being, one major way to develop a more sound mind and body is through diet. Indeed, diet affects not only your personal health, but the health of the entire planet and all its inhabitants. For these reasons, a vegetarian diet becomes the most compassionate and agriculturally sound approach to a more positive future in which humanity can feed itself and world ecosystems can maintain their balance.

A significant shift toward vegetarianism, especially in the developed world, could help to eradicate a major portion of the world's hunger. Currently, grain crops that could be channeled to impoverished people around the world are being used to feed animals for slaughter. Most of the grains produced in America feed animals that are, in most cases, placed on someone's dinner table. This means that in order for the rich to satisfy their palates with flesh, the poor are deprived of grains to meet their most basic survival needs.

In a 1974 report for the World Food Conference in Rome, René Dumont, an agricultural economist at France's National Agricultural Institute, made this blunt statement: "The overconsumption of meat by the rich means hunger for the poor."[120] A similar idea appears in _Proteins, Their Chemistry and Politics_, by Dr. Aaron Altschul. He notes that a diet of grains, vegetables, and beans uses 20 times less land than a diet of meat.[121] Also in 1974, the CIA warned that global food shortages might occur in the near future "unless the affluent nations make a quick and drastic cut in their consumption of grain-fed animals."[122]

If the earth's available land were used primarily for the production of vegetarian food, the planet could easily support a much larger population. As stated in _The Higher Taste_, an excellent exposition of the advantages of vegetarianism, facts such as these show that much of the global hunger problem is illusory, created by deliberate human choices. Even now, the earth is producing enough food for everyone. Unfortunately, however, it is being allocated inefficiently.[123]

Even as far back as ancient Greece, Socrates claimed in Plato's writings that a vegetarian diet could allow a country to use its agricultural land more effectively. He warned of a crisis if people continued eating animals, because this practice would create a constant need for more grazing land.[124] Therefore, as you plan your allocation of resources, keep in mind that the amount of grazing land needed to produce 1 ton of meat can yield 10 to 20 tons of grain. Or, to look at it another way, to produce 1 pound of meat, an animal must be fed 16 pounds of soy and grain.[125]

This means that by eating flesh people sacrifice the earth's land 10 to 20 times, and its grains about 16 times, more than necessary. On the other hand, just by minimizing the intake of flesh, human beings can increase the available land and grains by the same proportions. Such statistics can motivate you as a leader–whether of a family, organization, business or nation–to try a vegetarian diet and to encourage others to do so as well.

Meat-Eating and the Human Body

Physiologically speaking, meat-eating is an unnatural imposition on the human biological system. The human body is naturally designed for eating vegetables and fruits. As *The Higher Taste* explains, a comparison of carnivorous and herbivorous animals reveals some interesting facts:

- Species that have a body designed for eating meat have claws. Humans have no claws.

- Meat-eating animals perspire through the tongue. Human beings perspire through the pores of the skin.

- Those species with a natural ability for eating meat have sharp, long front canine teeth for tearing at flesh; they rarely have flat teeth for grinding. Humans do not have such prominent canine teeth, but instead have flat rear molar teeth for grinding plants, nuts, and seeds.

- The length of the intestinal tract in meat-eaters is different from that of plant-eaters. Carnivores possess a tract three times their body length, so that the rapidly decaying meat can be expelled quickly. The human intestinal tract is twelve times its body length, and is therefore not structured for the rapid expulsion of decaying meat.

- Those species with a body built for eating meat have very strong hydrochloric acid in the stomach. Human stomach acid is approximately 20 times weaker than the stomach acid of carnivorous animals. Natural meat-eaters eat flesh raw and hunt their own prey. *Homo sapiens* are the only meat-eating species that has to cook meat to help break it down, because meat is not its natural diet.[126]

By eating meat, people turn their bodies into graveyards, ingesting a corpse without even knowing what caused the animal's death. In addition, the additives in animal flesh can be carcinogenic. Although

Americans supposedly have the best diet in the world, they rank twenty-third in longevity. This may partly be because of so many additives in meat that, despite appearances, can cause tremendous harm.

Health Effects of Meat-Eating

In their book, *Poisons in Your Body*, Gary and Steven Null describe the procedures used in large-scale animal farms owned by big corporations. Their findings indicate that numerous potentially hazardous chemicals, of which consumers are generally unaware, are present in meat and meat products. The animals are fed a constant diet of tranquilizers, hormones, antibiotics and 2,700 other drugs. Although these drugs remain in the meat when it is sold, the law does not require producers to inform the consumer of that fact.[127]

As far back as 1961, the *Journal of the American Medical Association* noted that a vegetarian diet could prevent almost all heart disease, the cause of over 50 percent of American deaths.[128] As research continues, evidence linking meat-eating to other forms of cancer is building at an alarming rate. As the National Academy of Sciences reported in 1983: "People may be able to prevent many common cancers by eating less fatty meats and more vegetables and grains."[129]

In his Notes on the *Causation of Cancer*, Rollo Russell writes: "I have found of 25 nations eating flesh largely, nineteen had a high cancer rate and only one had a low rate, and that of thirty-five nations eating little or no flesh, none had a high rate."[130]

As *The Higher Taste explains:*

> In addition to dangerous chemicals, meat often carries diseases from the animals themselves. Crammed together in unclean conditions, force-fed, and inhumanely treated, animals destined for slaughter contract many more diseases than they ordinarily would. Meat inspectors attempt to filter out unacceptable meats, but because of pressures from the industry and a lack of sufficient time

for examination, much of what passes is far less whole-
some than the meat purchaser realizes.[131]

In America, the U.S. Department of Agriculture has frequently been negligent in enforcing its own low standards. For example, a 1972 U.S. government report listing carcasses that passed inspection after diseased parts were removed gave these figures: nearly 100,000 cows with eye cancer and 3,596,302 cows with abscessed livers passed inspection. The U.S. government also once permitted the sale of chickens with a pneumonia-like disease that causes pus-laden mucous to collect in human lungs.[132]

Research has furnished proof that a balanced vegetarian diet can be more nutritional than meat. As described in *The Higher Taste*, Dr. Irving Fisher of Yale University conducted comparative endurance tests demonstrating that vegetarians could last twice as long as meat-eaters. In fact, by reducing the non-vegetarians' protein consumption by 20 percent, Dr. Fisher found that their efficiency increased by 33 percent. Furthermore, another study at the University of Brussels showed that vegetarians could endure physically strenuous tests two to three times longer than meat-eaters. In addition, vegetarians were able to recover fully from fatigue in a fraction of the time needed by meat-eaters.[133] Those who believe they need to eat meat for physical strength should remember that some of the strongest animals–such as the horse, the elephant, and the ox–are themselves vegetarians.

Religious Traditions and Meat-Eating

Many references in the Bible support vegetarianism. In Genesis 1:29, God proclaims, "Behold, I have given you every herb-bearing seed, which is upon the face of all the earth, and every tree, in which is the fruit of a tree-yielding seed; to you it shall be for meat." Genesis 9:4-5 directly forbids meat eating: "But flesh with the life thereof, which is the blood thereof, shall ye not eat. And surely your blood of your lives will I require; at the hand of every beast will I require it." In later books of the Bible, major prophets also condemn meat-eating.

Many people, noting specific references in the Bible, believe that Jesus himself ate meat. However, as *The Higher Taste* explains, many Christian scholars take issue with such interpretations, because the vast majority of the words translated as "meat" in the Bible come from the Greek *trophe* or *brome*, which mean "food" or "eating" in the broader sense. This means that the original words did not refer to meat, but rather to food and the taking of nourishment. When, in Luke 8:55, Jesus raises a woman from the dead and commands that she be given "meat," the original Greek word in this case is *phago*, which means "to eat." Therefore, Christ actually ordered that she simply be given something to eat.[134]

Jesus was quite possibly affiliated with the Essenes, a religious sect known for austere vegetarianism. Isaiah 7:14, predicting Jesus' appearance, says: "Behold, a virgin shall conceive, and bear a son, and shall call his name Immanuel. Butter and honey shall he eat, that he may know to refuse the evil, and choose the good." Also, although many early Christians were vegetarians, they were so persecuted that they had to practice both their Christianity and their vegetarianism underground. St. John Chrysostom, one of the early church fathers, did not approve of meat-eating. St. Benedict, who founded the Benedictine order in A.D. 529, established a diet based on vegetables for his monks. Even today, many Trappist monks are vegetarians.[135]

The practice of vegetarianism also exists in many non-Catholic religious traditions–Christian and non-Christian. The Seventh Day Adventists strongly recommend vegetarianism for their members. Buddhism, Jainism, and Hinduism all emphasize vegetarianism, and the Sufi mystic priests of Islam are usually vegetarians. The Koran contains many stipulations concerning meat-eating. For example, verse 22:38 states: "Their flesh reaches not Allah nor does their blood, but it is your righteousness that reaches Him." According to the Koran, one should not eat pork or an animal that has been strangled, has fallen off a cliff or has been beaten to death. If eating meat is such a problem, might it not be better to avoid it altogether?

Some may argue that all edibles are a form of life, so that people are also killing when they eat plants. In some cases, this is true. However, when one eats vegetarian foods such as fruits, nuts, milk, and grains, a plant's life is not taken. Even in those situations in which killing occurs, the plant's pain and trauma are very likely much less than those of an animal, because the plant's nervous system is not as developed. As *The Higher Taste* says: "Clearly, there is a vast difference between pulling a carrot out of the ground and killing a lamb."[136]

Meat-Eaters, Violence, and Karma

Leading thinkers from the East and West have made observations about meat-eating. Gandhi said, "I do feel that spiritual progress does demand at some stage that we should cease to kill our fellow creatures for the satisfaction of our bodily wants." Thoreau had a similar view, stating, "I have no doubt that it is a part of the destiny of the human race, in its gradual improvement, to leave off eating animals."[137] Tolstoy himself wrote: "By killing, man suppresses in himself unnecessarily the highest spiritual capacity–that of sympathy and pity toward living creatures like himself–and by violating his own feelings becomes cruel."[138] He considered flesh-eating immoral, because it is based upon the act of killing, which is contrary to the nature of the spirit soul. French philosopher Jean-Jacques Rousseau also espoused vegetarianism. He commented that meat-eaters are generally more violent than vegetarians, and concluded that a vegetarian diet could make a person more compassionate. In addition, he advocated that butchers be banned from testifying in court or sitting on juries.[139]

In America today, no other industry, including coal mining or construction, has a higher injury or illness rate than the slaughterhouse business. Each year, nearly one-third of American meat-packing employees suffer job-related injuries that require medical attention.[140] Further, the annual employee turnover rate for slaughterhouse workers in the United States is higher than for any other occupation. As one example, in 1980 a slaughterhouse run by the Excel Corporation in Dodge City, Kansas had a turnover rate of 43 percent per month.[141] These statistics shed a very gloomy light on the practice of slaughtering animals for the satisfaction of human palates.

Not only is violence employed to produce meat for human consumption, but the ingestion of meat itself may make human beings more violent. Despite impressive progress in science and technology, the world faces an unrelenting crisis of aggression in the form of war, murder, terrorism, vandalism, abortion, and child abuse. With political and social solutions to these problems conspicuously failing, perhaps it is time to analyze these issues from a different perspective: that of the law of karma.

Undoubtedly, the callous and brutal slaughter of countless, helpless animals is a powerful contributing factor to this wave of uncheckable violence. The law of karma requires that those who unreservedly kill so many animals be slaughtered like animals themselves. Is it any coincidence that in the West, where slaughterhouses are maintained without restrictions, a major war breaks out every five or ten years in which endless numbers of people are butchered even more cruelly than the animals? In addition, soldiers sometimes torture and kill their enemies in very cruel ways. Many spiritual teachings recognize these situations as karmic reactions brought about by unrestricted animal killing.

The Energy Levels Surrounding Food

On a more personal level, eating habits can have a profound effect on individual well-being. For example, be mindful of the atmosphere in which you take your food and be careful when someone is watching you eat. If you eat while another person, perhaps a beggar, is lusting over the food, or while an extremely hungry person is present, psychically that person will transmit lust, greed, or envy into the food. In such circumstances, the negative energy can affect you and even make you sick.

You may also want to be selective about who cooks your food. The mentality, or energy, of the cook inevitably enters into the meal that is being prepared. That is why many leaders either prepare their own food or consistently keep the same cook. In addition, believe it or not, people sometimes put substances into food in an attempt to influence a leader's mind. This practice is better known in the developing world than in the West, with the result that people in the developing world are more cautious about the preparation of food. Westerners need to become more aware of the energy transfer that occurs during food preparation, giving more attention to consuming "live" vegetarian food prepared by loving hands.

Not only is it wise to minimize the intake of meat, eliminating it from the diet if possible, but it is also important to reduce or stop the intake of stimulants such as caffeine. Caffeine has harmful effects upon the body and can become habit-forming, resulting in nervous complications and digestive problems.

Food and the Modes of Nature

Foodstuffs are not all the same. They generate energy at different levels because, like everything else in nature, they are governed by different principles. As discussed earlier, these principles are referred to in the *Bhagavad-gita* as the different modes of nature–specifically, the modes of goodness, passion, and ignorance. Each has a different effect on our consciousness. The *Bhagavad-gita* states:

> Foods that are dear to those in the mode of goodness increase the duration of one's life. They purify one's existence. They give strength, happiness, health and satisfaction, and such foods are wholesome and pleasing to the heart. Foods that are too bitter, too salty, too sour, too pungent, and dry are dear to those in the mode of passion. Such foods cause distress, misery and various kinds of diseases. Foods prepared more than three hours before being eaten, food that is tasteless, decomposed, putrid, consisting of remnants and untouchable things are dear to those in the mode of darkness.[142]

Foods in the mode of goodness, such as fresh vegetables and fruits, help to increase intelligence and clarify perception. Foods in the mode of passion cause agitation, tension, and uneasiness. Foods in the mode of ignorance, or darkness, make people sluggish, morbid, depressed, and aggressive.

Consider the Future

Proper water and food are two of the most essential factors for the growth of any person, community, or society. A hungry person, or an unhealthy one, will not be able to render the most effective service to society, and the leader who keeps people in such states of deprivation is in a very precarious situation.

As the popular saying goes: "You are what you eat." Therefore, for the sake of the world food problem and for the future of this planet, you should endeavor to minimize your intake of meat and encourage others to do the same. If for no other reason than the simple desire to live longer–sociological studies show that non meat-eaters have greater longevity than meat-eaters–vegetarianism is a wise choice for everyone. As a leader, you are a primary example-setter, and therefore you can alert people to the dangers of meat-eating and its physical and spiritual effects, as well as its deleterious impact on the planet.

A drastic shift in diet to one that excludes meat obviously represents a major step for many, especially since great numbers of people were brought up to be meat-eaters. However, vegetarianism has such important global, national, and personal benefits that all those who care about this planet's future should consider seriously changing their eating habits in this radical way. Actually, influenced by factors varying from health and economics to ethics and religion, many people around the world are already turning toward a vegetarian diet. In particular, leaders who want to guide humanity into the twenty-first century can make the deliberate choice to take such a revolutionary step themselves, making personal sacrifices for the benefit of the whole.

Vegetarianism can contribute to harmonious coexistence, which is a desirable condition on many levels ranging from the family to the global community. In these times when humanity faces the possibility of massive worldwide destruction, a nonviolent approach to nutrition and food production can contribute to world peace and produce beneficial karmic circumstances for everyone.

Highlights

1. A family, a community, or a society that cannot feed itself is in a very precarious situation. Unfortunately, many people in the world find themselves in just such circumstances. For instance, much of the world's population has no access to safe water.

2. In addition to serious water problems, lifelong hunger and malnutrition affect countless people on this planet.

3. There are numerous causes for the inability of much of the world to feed itself. One major stumbling block is the failure to recognize the role of women in agricultural production. Another important factor is a distorted sense of priorities. In pounds per person, more explosives exist in the world than food.

4. A significant shift toward vegetarianism, especially in the developed world, could help to eradicate a major portion of the world's hunger. Currently, grain crops that could be channeled to impoverished people around the world are being used to feed animals for slaughter.

5. By eating flesh, people sacrifice the earth's land 10 to 20 times, and its grains about 16 times, more than necessary. On the other hand, just by minimizing the intake of flesh, human beings can increase the available land and grains by the same proportions.

6. Physiologically speaking, meat-eating is an unnatural imposition on the human biological system. The human body is naturally designed for eating vegetables and fruits.

7. As far back as 1961, the *Journal of the American Medical Association* noted that a vegetarian diet could prevent almost all heart disease, the cause of over 50 percent of American deaths. As research continues, evidence linking meat-eating to other forms of

cancer is building at an alarming rate. As the National Academy of Sciences reported in 1983: "People may be able to prevent many common cancers by eating less fatty meats and more vegetables and grains."

8. Leading thinkers from the East and West have criticized meat-eating. Gandhi said, "I do feel that spiritual progress does demand at some stage that we should cease to kill our fellow creatures for the satisfaction of our bodily wants." Thoreau had a similar view, stating, "I have no doubt that it is a part of the destiny of the human race, in its gradual improvement, to leave off eating animals."

9. In America today, no other industry, including coal mining or construction, has a higher injury or illness rate than the slaughterhouse business. Each year, nearly one-third of American meat-packing employees suffer job-related injuries that require medical attention. Further, the annual employee turnover rate for slaughterhouse workers in the United States is higher than for any other occupation.

10. The law of karma requires that those who unreservedly kill so many animals be slaughtered like animals themselves. Is it any coincidence that in the West, where slaughterhouses are maintained without restrictions, a major war breaks out every five or ten years in which countless people are butchered even more cruelly than the animals?

Mindsets

1.   Reread the ten essential technologies at the beginning of this book, concentrating on numbers 3, 4 and 8. Imagine that an animal awaiting slaughter could speak to you; what might it say? Remember that animals, too, are energies of God. Keeping in mind that your role as a leader is to be an example of love in action, reconsider your attitude about killing animals for food.

2.   If you eat meat, reflect on the direct role your meat-eating plays in maintaining world hunger. Because of meat-eating, the world has 10 to 20 times less land for agricultural development and 6 to 7 times less grain available for human consumption. If you have not already done so, make the sacrifice to become a vegetarian for the benefit of humanity and for your own health and consciousness.

3.   Realize that by being a vegetarian you are inspiring others to follow your example. Take specific steps to encourage vegetarianism among those you lead. Aside from its other benefits, vegetarianism will help reduce heart disease and cancer, two of the most devastating diseases on the planet.

4.   The next time you are tempted to partake of meat, imagine the inhumane environment in which many animals are raised and slaughtered. Do you want to support such practices? Do you want the energy of suffering, terrorized animals as part of your diet?

5.   Visualize the last time you encountered the body of a dead animal on the street–how it had already started to rot and had such an intense odor. Remember that such decay happens to the human body as well. Consider whether you actually want decomposing flesh inside your stomach.

6.   If you need additional encouragement to become vegetarian, here are some graphic reflections for you. Every time you eat flesh, you are making your body a graveyard, because you are taking a

corpse into your system. Realize as you eat the animal's heart, breast, neck, back, legs and even feet–along with its blood–that some might perceive your behavior as cannibalistic.

7. As a powerful reconditioning practice, spend a few moments observing some pigs. Notice how they eat anything: rats, worms, even stool. Then, if you eat pork, consider that you are also indirectly partaking of the same abominable diet. Also, if you like the idea of tapeworms eating your insides, then continue with your meat diet. Tapeworms thrive on dead flesh.

8. Visit a slaughterhouse or an area where animals are lined up, awaiting slaughter. You may be surprised to notice how desperately they cry out; indeed, some cry out all day long and sound like small children.

9. As you know, according to karmic law, violence breeds violence, and the slaughter of animals can increase hostility among human beings even to the point of war. Be happy to see yourself contributing to world peace as you abstain from eating meat. Whenever you are tempted to eat flesh, affirm to yourself that you are an agent of world peace and not of destruction.

10. Be mindful to eat foods in the mode of goodness; pay attention to who prepares your food; and be careful when eating in public.

13
_____

Harnessing Sexual Energy
for World Peace

In these perilous times, the issue of human survival on this planet has come into serious question, and the attainment of world peace has become a number one priority. In view of this situation, the global community has come to understand that a sustainable peaceful world order depends upon improvements in international, political, economical, and social relationships.

However, these global improvements cannot occur without better interpersonal relationships within families and between individuals. As a matter of fact, individuals need to find peace within themselves first, which primarily comes from properly controlling and regulating the sexual energies. If human sexual energies remain unharnessed, unintegrated, and unappreciated, personal or planetary peace and stability will continue to elude everyone's grasp.

Effects of Misdirected Sexual Energy

The family unit is a microcosm of the family of nations. When people create harmonious relationships within their families, they automatically improve community, national and international cooperation. Global peace is in its current precarious state because of a lack of harmony within the family, which can be largely attributed to the pursuit of lust and self-satisfaction instead of authentic love.

Sexual energy is an extremely powerful force. Properly channeled, it is an expression of love. Misdirected, it becomes a vicious agent of destruction that manifests in negative, abusive ways. Poorly harnessed sexual energy can literally enslave an individual, a family, and even a nation, stimulating people to act irresponsibly and violently, ultimately endangering the planet. On the other hand, properly regulated sexual energies can become part of the universal love force that fosters selflessness and compassion. Truly, everyone needs to learn to make genuine love and not war.

History provides numerous examples of promiscuous world leaders who ultimately were completely devastated by their uncontrolled sex lives. Many wars have, in the final analysis, been fought over sexual desires–motivated by anger over a frustrated sex life or a desire to conquer the opposite sex. The biographies of Cleopatra, Napoleon, and Adolf Hitler are replete with stories of personal and sexual problems that helped engender wars.

Best friends have become sworn enemies because of poor control of the sex drive. In religious as well as secular environments, leaders have fallen prey to uncontrolled carnal desires and thereby lost the respect of their followers. During the Renaissance, several popes led lives of debauchery and had many illegitimate children. In more recent times, revelations of sexual abuses within the Catholic church have caused great disturbance, as have the downfall of Christian evangelists such as Jim Bakker and Jimmy Swaggart. These latter two cases became international news because of the dramatic way in which these men of the cloth, who preached against illicit sexual behavior, ultimately fell victim to it themselves. Also, in the political arena, the public witnessed the downfall of a U.S. presidential candidate, Gary Hart, who had to abandon the race because of an illicit affair.

Sexual Energy and Effective Leadership

Some people contend that behavior in private life has nothing to do with a leader's effectiveness in public. However, this is a farce, because how a leader thinks and lives inevitably affects the quality of service offered to others. How can a leader give everything to the service of the people if mind and body are dedicated to the pursuit of lustful experiences? A self-centered person who desires to exploit the opposite sex will surely manifest these traits in dealings far beyond the personal sphere.

Therefore, a serious leader understands that strict control of the senses is necessary in order to be a servant of the people. Leaders who do not possess enough strength to regulate their own senses naturally cannot presume to regulate those of tens, hundreds, thousands or millions of people.

Among other problems, leaders who cannot control their sexual desires pose a great threat to the security of the governments or organizations they lead. They are vulnerable to espionage, which has employed the opposite sex to solicit confidential information since time immemorial. In the future, espionage will be an even greater problem because the gathering of secrets and the spreading of lies is one of the world's biggest growth industries. For example, the U.S. Central Intelligence Agency employs thousands and works with many individuals throughout the world who assist in the analysis of information and engage in deceptive practices. Illicit sexual affairs almost guarantee that a leader will become vulnerable to attack from these sources, or even toppled from power.

Sexuality therefore poses many problems for leaders, not only personally but also in the course of fulfilling more public responsibilities. As a leader, you may be forced to confront several difficult issues–such as sexually transmitted diseases, abortion, or sexual abuse–deriving from misdirected sexual energy. How you address these may well define your success or failure in leading others.

Sexually Transmitted Diseases

Among the many threats to human survival on this planet, sexually transmitted diseases deserve special attention. In 1990, the World Health Organization estimated that 3.5 million new cases of syphilis and more than 25 million new cases of gonorrhea occur in the world each year.[143] In 1992, about 450,000 cases of full-blown AIDS were reported around the globe. During this same year, there were an estimated 2 million unreported cases and 10 million HIV-positive individuals.[144] By mid-1994, the World Health Organization estimated that over 16 million adults and over one million children had been infected by the AIDS virus.[145]

Speculation and statistics concerning AIDS can be heard in every corner of the globe. Some experts predict that, unchecked, the AIDS epidemic could make 40 million people HIV-positive by the year 2000, most of them in the developing world. One in 250 adults is now HIV-positive, and 5000 people are newly infected each day.[146] The World Health Organization predicts that "the deaths of as many as one-fifth of young and middle-aged adults over a short period of time will lead to social turmoil, economic disruption and even political destabilization in many countries."[147] This is reminiscent of the bubonic plague in the 14th century, which killed about 30 million people out of a total world population of 75 million!

Whether one accepts a conservative or more liberal prognosis, AIDS is proving to be a great threat to humankind. To minimize the danger, people have come to recognize the importance of avoiding promiscuity and of exercising greater control over their sexual practices and sexual energy in general. Not only does this improve moral character; it has become a matter of human survival.

Abortion

Although abortion is a controversial topic, anyone who claims the responsibility of leadership may need to address it at some point. Clearly, if people had better control of their sex lives, fewer abortions would occur, and these would only be for extreme situations such as rape, incest, or the risk of death to the mother. As always, the most secure contraceptive method still is abstinence, and couples should learn to value sex so high-ly that they reserve it primarily for procreation.

But in actual practice, abortion has become a contraceptive device used to counteract lack of responsibility for sexual behavior. Today mil-lions of people in the world are killing their own seed through abortions. A 1990 abortion report estimates that 40 to 60 million abortions are perfomed each year around the world, with China and the former Soviet Union alone accounting for 25 million of these.[148] Official reports for many years generally stated that abortions in the Soviet Union averaged one or two per live birth. However, informal estimates have placed the abortion rate in the former Soviet Union at a much higher level: two abortions for every three pregnancies–or even four for every five–so that the average Soviet woman may have up to nine abortions during her lifetime.[149]

In 1991, the abortion rate among American women was 339 per 1000 live births, for a total of 1,388,937 abortions.[150] Abortions are more fre-quent among African Americans than among white Americans. In 1986, African American women had 634 abortions for every 1000 live births, almost double the national average.[151]

Abortion is intimately associated with atheism. The U.S.S.R., among the first countries to legalize abortion, did so in 1920, followed by Japan in 1949, England in 1967, and other parts of Europe and the United States over the next 20 years.[152] The practice of abortion in many coun-tries derives in no small part from the belief that no God, or soul, exists, and that the fetus is not yet a human being.

However, science demonstrates that a fetus is a living entity. It can be transferred from one womb to another and still remain alive. In just three weeks, the heartbeat of a fetus becomes audible. In seven weeks, the unborn child has developed its own brain tissue, a sign of the presence of life in humans already born. Nonetheless, despite these facts, the tech-niques and terminology of abortion encourage potential parents to believe that they are just eliminating some superfluous tissue.

Although abortion will continue to be highly controversial, collectively people must become more conscious of how they handle the future of the unborn, and individually each person should make decisions that result in tranquility within.

Sexual Misuse, Abuse, and Exploitation

Marital relationships are suffering severely. In the United States, 66 percent of marriage partners have been unfaithful at some point in their lives.[153] It may come as no surprise that about half the marriages in the United States do not last.[154] In Sweden, almost all couples live together before marriage, and 25 percent of these never marry at all. Forty-six percent of Swedish babies are born out of wedlock, compared to a rate in the United States of 21 percent.[155]

Only 16 percent of American girls and 12 percent of American boys have not had sexual relations by the age of 20, and only 55 percent of sexually active teenagers use birth control. The United States has the highest rate of teenage pregnancy of any developed country; more than one-third of all children in the United States born out of wedlock are born to teenagers.[156] In addition, each year about 800,000 Americans seek treatment for venereal diseases.[157]

In 1991, the FBI's Uniform Crime Report data, which counts reported and substantiated rapes only, indicated that 106,593 rapes had occurred in the United States, which means that 292 rapes took place every day, or 12 rapes every hour. To make matters worse, a 1992 study discovered that only one rape in six is ever reported to the police. At that rate, the actual number of rapes in the United States is estimated to exceed 600,000 annually, making the total number of rapes committed during the 20-year period from 1972 to 1991 more than 12 million.[158]

Sexual abuse of children is also rampant. Studies indicate that in the United States, between 25 and 35 percent of women and 10 to 20 percent of men–at least one in six Americans–have been sexually abused as children. And the incidence is increasing, so that up to one in three girls and one in five boys face sexual abuse by the age of 18. In 1990 alone, about 376,000 American children were reported to be victims of sexual abuse.[159] Such rape and abuse statistics are horrifying. They suggest that the women and children of America are under virtual attack from the (mostly) male population.

During the 1970s, many women looked to feminist groups for support against the constant abuse and harassment by men, no longer willing to accept sexual exploitation in order to keep their jobs or get promotions. In addition, the 1990s have revealed an increasing number of cases in which even psychotherapists have sexually abused their clients. The problem is so severe that some states are making special laws to stop–or at least curtail–such offenders. It is a sad commentary on the state of the world that certain individuals entrusted to help free their clients from distress, anxiety, and misplaced sexual energy have now become offenders and abusers themselves.

It is not difficult to understand why sexual promiscuity and deviancy are on the increase. In America, at every turn, programs and advertisements in the media provide relentless sexual stimulation. Advertisements for numerous products on the market contain sexual overtones. Indeed, much subliminal advertising is designed so that consumers will associate sexual feelings with a particular product. No wonder people try to achieve sexual gratification by whatever means necessary.

Inasmuch as this is a time when there are practically no bars to sexual activity, it may come as no surprise to hear accounts of extreme behavior. Humankind is becoming more and more animalistic, acting instinctively according to whatever feels good, regardless of the consequences. As a leader, you must be aware of the devastating effects of such uncontrolled sexual behavior and seek to educate others about its inherent dangers. Silence and inaction represent a shared complicity. The victims of these abuses have a right to expect protection from their leaders.

Controlling and Channeling Sexual Energy

Uncontrolled sexual energy manifests itself in subtle, as well as obvious, ways. For example, strong desires to receive distinction, adoration, or profit are generally signs of an uncontrolled sex drive, although the connection with sexuality may not be immediately apparent. Such aspirations usually indicate an extremely active false ego that can lead, in its quest for self-gratification, to more apparent sexual disturbances if not channeled or properly checked.

Sexual energy can either rise to a higher level where it supports creative endeavors, or fall to a low, degrading level of destructive behavior. If the energy is used for lower purposes, overtly sexual anxieties and frustrations occur. Channeled into higher pursuits, such energy produces great achievements, realizations, understandings, and discoveries, and also helps increase physical perseverance and stamina.

Many years ago, world heavyweight champion Muhammad Ali would introduce me as "my friend the Swami who is a celibate monk." During his reign as world champion, Ali mentioned to me that for many months before a given fight his trainers would instruct him to abstain from sex, which could detract from his ability to fight as effectively as possible. After a release of seminal fluid, the body requires several weeks to build itself up again, because a man must drink and eat a great deal to produce just a few drops of semen.

Actually, a few drops of semen are equal to many pints of blood. In ancient times, yogis knew that controlling and channeling their sexual energy would enhance their ability to attain self-realization. Indeed, celibate students were able to remember colossal amounts of information. In contrast, today many people have to write almost everything down, still often forgetting where they have left their notes. This forgetfulness, at least in men, is associated with the constant release of vital fluids.

The more that people engage in sex, the more habituated they usually become, seeking a greater number and variety of experiences. However, a man or woman need not be a slave to the senses, because enslavement to anything jeopardizes opportunities to achieve the higher goals of life. There is nothing wrong with a religiously oriented sex life. The important point is to remember the need for self-regulation and control. Ultimately, no genuine higher, God-conscious realization is possible without mastery of the senses.

Others Speak about Sexual Energy

Leading authorities throughout the ages have recognized the importance of regulating sexual energy. For example, Mahatma Gandhi revealed that his capacity for significant achievement in the world was based on control of his sexual passion. By rechanneling sexual energy to a higher purpose, he became more clear and focused, as well as more compassionate and loving–a powerful combination. Here are some other comments from well-known sources about sexual matters:

- In the degree in which a man's mind is nearer to freedom from all passion, in that degree it is also nearer to strength. –*Marcus Aurelius*
- To control the sexual impulse efficiently has always been and ever will be regarded as the highest test of human wisdom. –*Auguste Comte*
- Sex is a thing of bodies, not of souls. –*Hermes Trismegistus*
- Sexual activity weakens man in his most essential aspect, spiritual expression. –*Leo Tolstoy*
- No obtainable object of desire can give lasting satisfaction. It can produce merely a fleeting gratification. Desires last long, the demands are infinite, the satisfaction is short. The satisfied passions lead more often to unhappiness than to happiness. As long as we are given up to the throne of desires, we can never have lasting happiness or peace. –*Arthur Schopenhauer*
- While contemplating the objects of the senses a person develops attachment for them; from such attachment lust develops; and from lust anger arises. From anger, delusion arises, and from delusion bewilderment of memory. When memory is bewildered, intelligence is lost, and when intelligence is lost, one falls down again into the material pool. –*Bhagavad-gita*
- Sexual relations unfavorable to the rearing of offspring must tend toward degradation. –*Herbert Spencer*
- Sexual desire has been given to man not for gratification of pleasure, but for the continuance of the human race. When you have escaped the violence of this secret destruction implanted in your very vitals, every other desire will pass you by unharmed. Carnal pleasure is a low act, brought about by the agency of our inferior and base members. There is nothing grand about it, nothing worthy of man's nature. –*Seneca*

Rebalancing Male-Female Interactions

In almost every way, women are much more sexually powerful than men–although men do not normally admit it. Therefore, women have an important role to play in regulating the sexual passions of humanity to create proper balance and control.

For example, in contrast to modern clothing styles that expose a woman's figure, women can dress in a less revealing way that does not tempt men to become preoccupied with their female form. If nothing else, women who are mothers can at least think in terms of the well-being of their own sons and dress accordingly. A woman's voice has a powerful subtle effect on men without their conscious awareness. In addition, a woman's gestures, mannerisms, and body language send signals to men that can make them agitated, consciously or subconsciously. A woman's eyes can also exert great power.

Therefore, in society, women can make efforts to avoid agitating men unnecessarily. Otherwise, men tend to use this agitation as an excuse for exploitation and abuse. For their part, men can begin to think of all women as "mothers," appreciating them as the basic carriers of the culture. A man who views all women as mothers will have respect, love, and affection for them instead of seeing them as sexual objects for his egocentric sense enjoyment. Nor will he tolerate others who abuse women. He will see all members of the opposite sex as people of value to be cherished because they carry the life force. Societies become time bombs ready to explode when women are abused, misused, exploited, unappreciated, or denied their right to protection. The stability of a civilization depends upon how the genders treat one another.

Today, radical feminism has become an important social movement, creating even more fragmentation. However, men are largely accountable for this situation, because it is their improper activities that have produced such a reaction. Men in society–via the police, the court system, and even the lawmakers–have failed to address the escalating abuse of women. Therefore, many women believe that they are on their own and can find their only protection by banding together. Both genders can solve this problem cooperatively and stimulate a healing process that will result in more harmony, equanimity, and equality.

How People Love

In today's society, the importance of the sacred institution of marriage is declining. Many men continue to withdraw from responsibility, abandoning their families and creating a new group of poor and homeless. Increasing numbers of women, perceiving the institution of marriage as a poor return on their investment, either choose to remain single or to leave their husbands in numbers unprecedented in human history.

Marriage needs to be revitalized in such a way that people have a greater appreciation for each other. Ideally, married life is an institution of mutual sharing in which both partners can develop higher consciousness. Spiritually speaking, married life is also an excellent opportunity to bring children who are highly evolved souls into this world, where they can make major contributions to humanity.

Advanced spiritual teachings such as the Vedic scriptures explain certain interesting points about procreation. For example, they teach that the consciousness of the man and woman at the time of conception helps determine the kind of child that is attracted to the womb. A soul waiting to take birth will be drawn to a couple based on the consciousness and quality of love between the man and woman.

Spiritualizing Sexual Activity

Sexual activity is meant to take place under circumstances diametrically opposed to those that are commonplace in today's society. People often want to be in dark places, intoxicated, and as animalistic and self-centered as possible. However, a spiritually focused couple understands that the man and woman can prepare themselves mentally and spiritually for the sexual exchange so that the encounter will become a divine experience in which the parties are sharing energies of a higher nature.

Before engaging in sexual activity, if a couple meditates, chants, and prays so that the consciousness becomes surcharged, the exchange becomes a divine encounter and a service. On the other hand, sex life occurring in a state of lower consciousness, when the partners are intoxicated or do not desire children, lacks this sacred quality.

There are no accidents concerning the circumstances under which a particular soul enters into this world and the conditions that it will experience in its coming life. These factors are evaluated before the soul takes birth in a particular family, and many nonphysical beings assist in arranging the circumstances of that soul's next existence. Also, many higher authorities help guide the soul as it enters its chosen body and undergoes a period of adjustment. The more people know about the science of birth and death–the science of the transmigration of the soul–the more they will understand the importance of everything they say, think and do concerning sexual activity.

By understanding and appreciating the law of karma, which states that for every action there is a corresponding reaction, individuals will become much more giving, caring, and humane in all of their activities, including sexual exchanges. They will be less involved in pursuing self-centered pleasures based on the physical stimulation and gratification of bodies and become more interested in attaining higher levels of happiness and ecstasy through activities that uplift consciousness.

To seek God-consciousness does not mean to lead a life of deprivation weighed down by rules and regulations or restrictions. Instead, it means to experience the higher pleasures of the senses by regulating and controlling the lower ones in order to become free from the stimuli of the immediate environment. In addition, when people seek higher levels of awareness, they are not functioning in a mere three-dimensional way, but instead are able to penetrate the more subtle levels of existence and move closer to true ecstasy.

How People Eat

As discussed in the previous chapter, diet affects human beings in many ways. Those who are serious about the impact of sexual self-control on world peace will choose to avoid eating meat, poultry, fish, or eggs in any form, because these are "passionate" foods that have generally become available through violence. Those who wish to subdue the flesh would be wise not to eat the flesh of others. A spiritually minded person is naturally compassionate to all living entities, always trying to remember God and declining to take the lives of others just to satisfy the senses.

In addition, a balanced diet is essential. Those who do not eat sufficiently can grow weak and become unable to maintain proper sense control. On the other hand, those who eat too much can fall prey to sexual agitation, obesity, and lethargy.

Controlling the Senses

Leaders who are genuinely interested in world peace should seek inner peace first by controlling the senses, regulating the sexual energy, and refusing to perceive others as mere sex objects. To be a leader means not being a slave to passions or senses. You will not be in harmony with your soul if you do not master the temptations of the material world, because the soul, being of a higher, subtle, divine quality, cannot express itself unless your mind and body are aligned with your true nature.

As leader and caretaker, it is your duty to live as you would like others to. What better way than to be genuinely loving and compassionate, unafraid of the AIDS epidemic, immune to sexual temptations, and unwilling to view others as objects of sexual gratification?

If you as a leader are not controlled in your personal life, how can you expect others to cooperate with you to create a better family, organization, nation, or world? If you are preoccupied with immediate gratifications and pleasures, where will you find the intelligence and insight for mature, long-term planning and development?

Everything starts at home, and your most immediate home can be considered to be this particular body with its senses. Effective leadership starts by setting a good example, which means that you have conquered the senses rather than being manipulated or destroyed by them. You can then channel your life force–your sexual energy–in such a manner as to achieve higher insights. The accompanying power will give you the opportunity to serve humanity compassionately, constructively and wisely.

Highlights

1.   Global peace cannot occur without better interpersonal relationships within families and between individuals. As a matter of fact, individuals need to find peace within themselves first, which primarily comes from properly controlling and regulating the sexual energies. If human sexual energies remain unharnessed, unintegrated, and unappreciated, personal or planetary peace and stability will continue to elude everyone's grasp.

2.   Sexual energy is an extremely powerful force. Properly channeled, it is an expression of love. Misdirected, it becomes a vicious agent of destruction that manifests in negative, abusive ways. Poorly harnessed sexual energy can literally enslave an individual, a family, and even a nation.

3.   Some people contend that behavior in private life has nothing to do with a leader's effectiveness in public. However, this is a farce, because how a leader thinks and lives inevitably affects the quality of service offered to others. How can a leader give everything to the service of the people if mind and body are dedicated to the pursuit of lustful experiences?

4.   A serious leader understands that strict control of the senses is necessary in order to be a servant of the people. If leaders do not possess enough strength to regulate their own senses, then naturally they cannot presume to regulate those of tens, hundreds, thousands or millions of people.

5.   AIDS is proving to be a great threat to humankind. To minimize the danger, people have come to recognize the importance of avoiding promiscuity and of exercising greater control over their sexual practices and sexual energy in general. Not only does this improve moral character; it has become a matter of human survival.

6. It is not difficult to understand why sexual promiscuity and deviancy are on the increase. In America, at every turn, programs and advertisements in the media provide relentless sexual stimulation. Promotions for numerous products on the market contain sexual overtones. Indeed, much subliminal advertising is designed so that consumers will associate sexual feelings with a particular product. No wonder people try to achieve sexual gratification by whatever means necessary.

7. Uncontrolled sexual energy manifests itself in subtle, as well as obvious, ways. For example, strong desires to receive distinction, adoration, or profit are generally signs of an uncontrolled sex drive, although the connection with sexuality may not be immediately apparent. Such aspirations usually indicate an extremely active false ego that can lead, in its quest for self-gratification, to more apparent sexual disturbances if not channeled or properly checked.

8. Sexual energy can either rise to a higher level where it supports creative endeavors, or fall to a low, degrading level of destructive behavior. If the energy is used for lower purposes, overtly sexual anxieties and frustrations occur. Channeled into higher pursuits, such energy produces great achievements, realizations, understandings, and discoveries, and also helps increase physical perseverance and stamina.

9. Today, radical feminism has become an important social movement, creating even more fragmentation. However, men are largely accountable for this situation, because it is their improper activities that have produced such a reaction. Men in society–via the police, the court system, and even the lawmakers–have failed to address the escalating abuse of women. Therefore, many women believe that they are on their own and can find their only protection by banding together. Both genders can solve this problem cooperatively and stimulate a healing process that will result in more harmony, equanimity, and equality.

10.   Sexual activity is meant to take place under circumstances dia-
         metrically opposed to those that are commonplace in today's
         society. People often want to be in dark places, intoxicated, and as
         animalistic and self-centered as possible. However, a spiritually
         focused couple understands that the man and woman can pre-
         pare themselves mentally and spiritually for the sexual exchange
         so that the encounter will become a divine experience in which
         the parties are sharing energies of a higher nature.

Mindsets

1.   Refer to the ten essential technologies at the beginning of this book, paying special attention to numbers 6 and 8. Assess your sexual behavior and attitudes in terms of accountability and love. Do you act in ways for which you are willing to be accountable to God? Do you express love in action?

2.   Be aware of the climate you establish in your family, organization or nation. Create an environment of respect and love that does not condone promiscuity or sexual exploitation of others.

3.   Remember that your personal life has an impact upon your effectiveness as a leader. Evaluate your sexual habits to discover any inconsistencies between what you say publicly and what you do privately. If you find discrepancies, take steps to align your private behavior with your desire to lead and serve others.

4.   Examine your ability and willingness to regulate all of your senses in order to bring your life more into harmony with divine will. To the extent that you serve your senses, you are unavailable to serve others or God.

5.   Develop and implement policies to minimize the spread of sexually transmitted diseases. Remember that an important preventive measure is a climate that does not condone sexual excesses.

6.   Rather than avoiding the issue, take some time to consider deeply your attitudes and feelings about abortion. Remember that every living being is an energy of God and that the Supreme is monitoring all your actions. Do these considerations have an impact upon your point of view?

7.   Monitor attitudes toward sexual abuse and sexual harassment within yourself and among those you lead. Create an environment that does not tolerate abuse and harassment in any form.

8.   Cultivate the higher pleasures of the senses by developing your awareness of the more subtle levels of existence and opening yourself to the possibility of spiritual ecstasy. Encourage others to do the same.

9.   Ensure that women are taken seriously and treated with respect, and be vigilant for subtle forms of sexual exploitation or condescension. Bring these into the open and make it clear that they are not acceptable.

10.   Be aware of the types of sexual stimulation to which those you lead are exposed. Help reduce the amount of sexual overtones in the media, and encourage those who produce movies, television programs and advertisements to consider the impact of what they present to the public. Develop incentives for more constructive programming.

14

Mind Control and Manipulation: Keys to Progress or Destruction?

The vast potential of the mind allows human beings to perform amazing feats. However, the mind's power also has a dark side that permits deliberate exploitation of others. Consequently, mind manipulation and mind control have become ominous threats to the future of humanity. Leaders have a responsibility to understand such phenomena in order to be effective against these onslaughts on the human psyche.

The Science of the Mind

The *Bhagavad-gita* contains a fascinating discussion about the nature of the mind. According to this sacred scripture, the mind at times can be an individual's greatest friend, because no one else is as close and has such an influence on day-to-day activities. A mind that is enthusiastic, enlightened, and at peace is a great comforter and ally. However, at other times the same mind, because it is such an intimate companion and knows all one's secrets, can be tremendously destructive if it is uncontrolled or lacks direction.

Therefore, although the mind is powerful and can perform a vast number of amazing feats, this very power can be used in harmful ways. When people are not attentive, their minds can become subject to deliberate exploitation by others. Mind manipulation and mind control are great dangers to society when its members are unaware of the threat and fail to exercise careful vigilance.

Mind Control: A Growing Industry

Mind control promises to be one of the most critical issues of the twenty-first century. Even now, it is a major problem, because the manipulation of the mind has a devastating effect upon human development. Mind control constantly violates free will, sometimes through the agency of other individuals, but most often in modern societies through the influence of the media. It is frightening to consider that much of the present world-view in industrialized nations is shaped by advertisers and public relations executives paid by corporate and political clients to manipulate the public. People are constantly told what to think, how to perceive the world, and what ultimately to consider as reality.

In the eighteenth century, Voltaire skillfully described the docility of the masses. The situation is not much different today, when the majority of people are influenced by prevailing norms—whatever these happen to be—and automatically accept them as necessary, righteous, and beneficial. However, as a leader, you cannot afford to be swept up by trends, fads, or superficial distractions. You can instead remain somewhat detached from normally accepted societal patterns, so that you are able to be more circumspect in decision-making and therefore more effective in your leadership.

Advertisements in the media have devastating effects on each individual's consciousness, especially in America, where the average consumer is exposed to considerably more advertising per year than in Canada,

England or France. Americans tend to be influenced by advertising techniques that constantly create new needs or desires.

One of the most effective mind control agents is television. Americans watch hours of television every day–much of it full of violence, sex, and cruelty. People are constantly subjected to psychologically unhealthy images, which can cause mental disturbance unless each person deliberately screens out these negative thought patterns and pictures. One obvious way for people to protect themselves is to remain outsiders, being more contemplative, relishing the silence, being in this world but not of it, cherishing the aloneness as they go deeper, and communicating with their inner essence rather than with the superficiality of external material things.

An article in the January 1987 issue of *Time* magazine mentions another aspect of mind control: gathering secrets and spreading lies. The article claims that this surreptitious activity is one of the world's biggest growth industries, wherein the United States and the former Soviet Union each spend billions of dollars on intelligence and espionage activities.[160] The net result of these activities is confusion in the public about the difference between truth and propaganda. Exorbitant amounts of propaganda circulate throughout the world, causing chaos and uncertainty in the minds of people. As a leader concerned about the welfare of the people, it befalls you to relinquish propaganda and speak the truth in order to assist others along a more certain and auspicious path.

Subliminal Suggestion

Most people have heard of subliminal suggestion–the attempt to influence the subconscious mind in order to stimulate action on the conscious level. Subliminal suggestion is used particularly in advertising and brainwashing, where sophisticated psychologists create hidden images that register within the subconscious mind. Many hidden and persuasive techniques have been employed in daily life to encourage people to behave in certain specific ways.[161]

For example, at the movies, subtle images can be spliced between film frames. These images implant impressions in such a way that the normal eye does not "see" them, yet they affect the subconscious mind.

Supermarkets have sometimes implanted audible suggestions behind the music that plays over the sound system, and many stores have found that reminders encouraging people not to shoplift make a significant difference.

Individuals who are public speakers can use subliminal suggestion to manipulate or control others without their knowledge, sometimes even against their will. In addition, certain kinds of music have the ability to put consciousness into an alpha state, which makes the mind far more receptive to suggestion. Marching to music also creates a form of self-hypnosis, and different forms of chanting and meditation produce altered states of consciousness, allowing various influences to affect the mind more easily. Therefore, some people who speak in public may even pipe in music or sound vibrations covertly behind the hum of the air conditioning system in order to have an effect on the audience.

Another example of subconscious manipulation is called ELF, or extremely low frequency waves. In the mid-1970s, Soviet researchers reported that sailors who worked in close proximity to ELF generators showed an abnormal number of psychiatric problems, central nervous system disorders and stress related symptoms. Dr. Elizabeth Rauscher, head of the Technic Research Lab in San Leandro, California has tested ELF frequencies on human volunteers. Among others, she has discovered a frequency that induces nausea, and another that provokes laughter. She states: "Give me the money and three months, and I'll be able to affect the behavior of 80 percent of the people in this town without their knowing it. Make them happy–or at least they'll think they're happy. Or aggressive."[162]

Mind Conversion: A Powerful Tool

There is an agency in Los Angeles that caters specifically to evangelist ministers, guaranteeing to increase the fund-raising ability of their church through mind conversion and subliminal suggestion techniques. The agency emphasizes the speaker's body language, and lighting and sound effects in the room, that can make church members more amenable to manipulation. Powerful events can occur when a charismatic speaker addresses an audience. Mind conversion takes place–whether those listening are conscious of this fact or not.

Mind conversion techniques are used instinctively by many people unaware of what they are doing. Of course, experts also exist who are highly skilled at using such techniques deliberately. For example, a religious speaker could employ mind conversion methods to create tension and fear within participants who have a desire to repent and "wipe their slates clean." Wiping the slate clean allows room for new input in any form that the speaker wishes to implant. Sometimes a speaker will give commands in a monotone, intimidating people or causing them to become so confused that they lose the ability to be rational.

Preachers, politicians, advertisers, lawyers, and certain human potential groups use mind conversion techniques daily. Some organizations–such as the military–can use these methods to "break" a man, deliberately undermining his self-confidence in order to mold him into what they want. A person who is "broken" loses many psychological props that once provided security, and will vigorously, sometimes desperately, try to find new ones. In addition, sometimes mind conversion practitioners will purposely distract the left brain in order to activate the right brain, making the subject more "open" and receptive to whatever stimuli are available.

Because the brain is an electrical receiver as well as a transmitter, it can accept mental transmissions from the minds of others via electrical waves similar to those that transmit radio signals. This is how a person's mental space can be deliberately invaded by others. For example, sometimes individuals may find that their moods change abruptly as a result of thoughts that are not their own–although they are not often aware that they are receiving mental projections from others. In humanity's present state of evolution, such manipulations are unfortunately quite common.

Perhaps the worst kind of mental disturbance is possession, when another being–embodied or disembodied–literally forces itself into someone's mental domain, taking control of that person's thoughts and influencing subsequent actions. This is probably one of the most invasive mind control and manipulation techniques, because it is not just a temporary attack upon an individual's mental space, but an ongoing intrusion that interferes with the ability to exercise free will.

Russian Superiority in Psychic Research

Some people contend that at one time other continents existed on earth that either sank into the ocean or were otherwise destroyed. According to these sources, thousands of years ago the continents of Mu and Atlantis contained highly evolved civilizations possessing a tremendous amount of technological and psychic knowledge, far beyond anything understood today. These civilizations were allegedly annihilated because of their abuse of this knowledge.

There are those who believe that the same scenario is about to repeat itself today due to our misuse of science and technology. Some predict that unless there is a significant change in world priorities, our technological achievements, instead of enhancing the quality of life, may destroy human civilization as we know it today.

One example of the misuse of science and technology is the surreptitious use of extrasensory perception (ESP) behind the former Iron Curtain, in the United States, and perhaps in other countries, for espionage and military activities. Russia and her former satellites are said to be far ahead of the West in analyzing and using psychic phenomena for such clandestine purposes. The world today is dominated by a weapons culture, a culture that is extremely bellicose, and some of its greatest minds are unfortunately using parapsychology to enhance the abilities of the military complex to annihilate human life.

Consider how dangerous such techniques could be in the hands of those who seek to dominate others. For example, remote viewing (the ability to witness activities far away from the immediate environment), the ability to read minds, or the capacity to invade the mental space of others could be used to confuse diplomats and world leaders. Envision the consequences of being able to see sensitive military targets or of using massive psychic energy to manipulate the minds of millions.

Russian and American Psychic Research

Psychic Discoveries Behind the Iron Curtain, written in 1970 by Sheila Ostrander and Lynn Schroeder, examines the study of parapsychology in the formerly communist countries and gives an interesting evaluation of the differences between America and these nations in their respective appreciation of psychic phenomena. Several major points from their book warrant attention:

- The former Soviet government supported parapsychological research to the tune of 12 to 20 million rubles a year. In the United States, the government's contribution to such research is apparently very little. Also, in America, ESP research is generally centered around establishing statistical proof of its existence, whereas in Russia and other communist countries, the research is geared toward the use of psychic phenomena in various techno-logical applications.

- In the United States, few universities recognize ESP research, whereas in Russia, many highly esteemed scientists and even members of the Soviet Academy of Sciences view parapsychologi-cal research favorably. Psychic research in Russia is regarded as a new field in the natural sciences, called bio-information, biocy-bernetics, or biotelecommunication. In other words, parapsychological research in the formerly communist countries is conducted by mainstream scientists.

- In the West, where there is a lot of competition, psychic researchers tend to work unilaterally or with just a few others in the same field. In Russia scientists work as a cooperative team.

- Although most Westerners know very little about their psychic research, the Russians are very cognizant of all aspects of Western parapsychological research.

- Basic Russian psychic research is mostly physiological, whereas Western research is generally psychological and philosophical.

- Several popular journals and periodicals in the former communist countries include articles about parapsychological phenomena, whereas in America, parapsychological research is rarely welcomed by regular scientific journals or popular magazines. Instead, it is confined to specialty publications read by a limited audience.[163]

These are only a few of the major differences specifically outlined by Ostrander and Schroeder, who have studied psychic phenomena in both countries. These differences make it easy to appreciate the progress of the former Soviet Union and its former satellite countries in being able to understand and manipulate psychic phenomena.

Applications of Psychic Research

Even more significant than Russia's research into psychic phenomena are its plans for the application of such knowledge. In Israel and other countries, emigres from Russia who were involved in psychic research, or who were psychics themselves, have expressed great concern that psychic research might be used against the Western world.

Josef Stalin himself was extremely interested in a mystic known as Wolf Messing, who was no ordinary mentalist. Messing was a celebrated psychic tested by such persons as Freud, Einstein, and even Gandhi. In their book, Ostrander and Schroeder recount one of Stalin's well-documented tests of the psychic's abilities:

> Stalin knew of Messing's alleged ability to telepathically project his thought into another person's mind, to control or cloud their mind....Stalin ordered a straightforward, horrendous trial of Messing's talent. He was to pull off a psychic bank robbery and get 100,000 rubles from the Moscow Gosbank where he was unknown. "I walked up to the cashier and handed him a blank piece of paper torn from a school notebook," says Messing. He opened an attaché case and put it on the counter. Then he mentally willed the cashier to hand over the enormous sum of money. The elderly cashier looked at the paper. He opened the safe and took out 100,000 rubles. Messing stuffed the banknotes into

the case and left. He joined Stalin's two official witnesses in charge of the experiment. After they had attested that the experiment had been satisfactorily performed, Messing returned to the cashier.[164]

Psychics can put persons to sleep by telepathy, a phenomenon known as "telepathic knockout." Dr. K. I. Platonov, a Russian psychologist, performed an interesting experiment on one young girl in front of a congress of psychoneurologists. Out of the range of her sight and hearing, he mentally repeated the words "sleep, sleep" over and over, vividly imagining the girl's face. According to Platonov, the most important element of telepathic control is wishing. He wished the girl asleep until he felt a "sort of ecstasy of triumph" that indicated to him that she had indeed fallen asleep, which in fact she had.[165]

Dr. Stefan Manczarski, head of Poland's team for international geophysics in 1957, considers telepathy an unusual and effective way of spreading propaganda. His experiments have led him to believe that telepathy, which consists of electrically charged thought forms, could utilize the air waves and then be amplified like radio waves or any other electrically based waves in everyday use, such as TV, shortwave radios, or radar. He predicts that, once telepathy is technologically enhanced and amplified like a telephone, architects may find themselves with a new problem: how to screen apartments from unwanted telepathy. In general, he believes that telepathy could become a subtle new medium for the influencers of the world.[166]

Czech biochemist Dr. Milan Ryzl states the following in his book, *Psychic*: "The bulk of recent telepathy research in the U.S.S.R. is concerned with the transmission of behavior impulses–or research to subliminally control an individual's conduct."[167] While visiting Russian psychic laboratories in 1967, Dr. Ryzl reports being told:

> When suitable means of propaganda are cleverly used, it is possible to mold any man's conscience so that in the end he may misuse his abilities while remaining convinced that he is serving an honest purpose. The U.S.S.R. has the means to

keep the results of such research secret from the rest of the world and, as practical applications of these results become possible, there is no doubt that the Soviet Union will do so.[168]

Psychotronic Generators as Weapons?

Considering the phenomenal capabilities of the human mind, there is nothing more frightening than the possible abuse of psychic phenomena. Most disturbing is the existence of machines called psychotronic generators, produced in Czechoslovakia, that can harness energy from humans, store it, and use it to affect people mentally and physiologically. Employing the same procedures that psychics would use, the generators are much more powerful than any one individual.

In their research on psychic phenomena behind the Iron Curtain, Ostrander and Schroeder report seeing psychotronic generators demonstrated in a film shown by Czechoslovakian scientists at an International Parapsychological Conference in Moscow. They also explain how these generators draw bioenergy from individuals, and describe different types of machines to accomplish specific goals. The following passage from *Psychic Discoveries Behind the Iron Curtain* gives insight into the possible applications of these devices:

> Generators turn wheels, step up plant growth, purify polluted water, perhaps changing its molecular structure....Some, we believe, could speed healing of wounds and recovery from various illnesses. Others have a harmful effect....At a distance of several yards, we beamed this energy from a generator toward [a young woman's] head. The EEG showed it caused a change in her brainwaves. [She] became dizzy–her spatial orientation was affected, and she began to swirl around.[169]

Given that the world today is weapons-oriented, locked in a struggle for domination and power, and that many of the greatest minds in the world are being used for research related to mind control, espionage, and defense, is it difficult to conceive that these psychotronic generators might be used on people around the world? Actually, some believe that such psychic manipulation is already widely employed. In 1976, a new radio signal was discovered around the world, emitted by a huge transmitter in the Ukraine. A year or two later, people in the northwestern United States and Canada–especially in Eugene, Oregon–complained of mysterious symptoms such as ringing in the ears, head pressure and pain, numbness, fatigue, anxiety, insomnia and lack of coordination. These symptoms indicated radio or microwave irradiation that engineers concluded most likely originated in the Soviet Union.[170] While Russia is much more advanced in its psychic research than America, America is dabbling in these areas for military purposes as well.[171]

The Need for Vigilance

Many cities and nations around the world are besieged by crime. In the near future, will countries and continents also be under siege from mind control technologies? Closer investigation produces a frightening discovery: people are already subject to extensive mind control and mind conversion as part of their day-to-day experience.

Whether the issue is general mind conversion techniques employed in advertising and politics, more harmful subliminal techniques, or influences from psychic generators, all such manipulative practices are highly disturbing. Could this perhaps be one of the reasons that Russia is more eager to eliminate nuclear arsenals than the West? Perhaps they have a much more sophisticated arsenal–the weaponry of psychotronics.

Unfortunately, most mind conversion and mind control techniques, as well as many psychic intrusions, go unnoticed. It is rare for a brainwashed person to be aware of the process or its ultimate effect. Cases have been recorded in Stockholm of brainwashed prisoners who were not only unaware of the brainwashing, but began to admire those who were abusing them–even to the point of becoming attracted to them. If a situation arose where thousands, or even millions, of people fell under such subjugation, a civilization could be reduced to a robotic level. Human and spiritual factors would mean less and less, and societies would be subjected to the control and manipulation of power elites in the most overwhelming and frightening ways.

The knowledge of mind control and manipulation is accessible to any-one who wishes to use it. In today's world, everyone is more or less affected by it, so that the issue is not whether an individual is under the influence of mind control, but to what degree. Therefore, to protect them-selves and others, leaders can learn how to recognize such influences, how to minimize them, and how to avoid being devastated by them. Indeed, unethical parapsychological intrusions may occur even more intensely in the future. It is imperative that leaders appreciate the gravity of the situation and choose not to use such knowledge in harmful ways.

Because you are in a leadership position, you should learn how to pro-tect yourself psychically since, more than most, you are likely to be under psychic attack from many different sources. However, it is not the inten-tion here to present a detailed discussion about psychic self-defense. Such information is better provided in more personal exchanges, because defense techniques need to be prescribed according to the nature of the psychic attack and the particular constitution of the individual. Instead, the following sections will emphasize more general approaches.

The Power of Love

Because the manipulative negative influences of mind control affect everyone's equilibrium, you should learn to create strong mental barriers against them. The most powerful way to do so is to maintain a kind and loving attitude, feeling a strong "heart love" for every person in your envi-ronment, whether you know the individual or not. This creates such a powerful radiation that any negative influences directed toward you will simply be absorbed into your loving energy field.

When you are involved in obviously negative situations, try to raise the level of consciousness of those around you by thinking loving, positive thoughts about them. Actually envision a ray of love streaming from your heart to theirs. Negative energies are attracted to discordant situations, where they can find similar vibrations, and are correspondingly repelled in the presence of positive, loving energy. If you are careful to monitor your emotional and psychological states, such energies will not easily dis-turb you.

Control the Mind

Another important step in psychic self-defense is understanding and taking control of the mind. Those who recognize the mind's strengths and weaknesses are able to protect their minds more effectively. This requires people to see the mind as different from themselves, remembering that a human being is more than the mind. Each individual has intelligence, senses, a physical body, and a subtle body–in addition to the soul. At any given time all of these aspects are operating in different ways.

Individuals who separate themselves from their minds realize that the mind is a tool under their control. They are then less likely to respond automatically to some of its desires and fixations. Indeed, the mind can behave as an enemy, as it does when it accepts without question the normal dictates of day-to-day interactions. If people do not protect themselves from the mind-disturbing phenomena that are a part of this daily environment, they can become susceptible to influence or attack.

The mind is similar to a clown who accompanies someone throughout the day. This clown constantly acts as a jokester trying to throw the person off balance or to provide ingenious distractions. Those who recognize the mind's ability to harass and agitate them will be less inclined to follow its unfocused erratic whims.

A metaphor may clarify the situation. The physical body can be compared to a chariot with the soul as the driver holding the reins. The reins are the mind, which controls the five horses that represent the five senses of touch, sight, hearing, taste, and smell. A person can maintain control of the senses by disciplining the mind, rather than allowing the senses to be in control. Someone who views the mind and the senses in this way will not be caught off guard even in disturbing situations. If the mind–one's sensation-driven, practical aspect–is guided by the intelligence–the aspect controlled by the soul–and if the intelligence stays attuned to a spiritual and transcendental platform, then even though the mind has the potential to be undisciplined, it will be less likely to cause chaos.

Monitoring the Energy Around You

You can further protect yourself by creating a powerful atmosphere around you. One way to accomplish this is to associate with "high-energy" people–"high" in terms of the quality, not the speed, of the energy. The nature of the people you associate with will dictate the kind of energy absorbed. Correspondingly, the energy you take in influences the kind of energy that you radiate and determines the quality of your protective shield. Everyone has experienced the drain that comes from associating with people of low, poor-quality energy.

You should also be very careful in selecting your associates. Association is one of the most important influences in the formation of character and in the fulfillment of individual aspirations. Sometimes, however, you cannot avoid associating with "low-energy" people. Therefore, you will need some techniques to revitalize yourself so that you do not become a candidate for psychic manipulation.

For example, around people of negative energy, you can concentrate on sharing your own energy rather than absorbing theirs, creating a protective barrier around yourself while maintaining a kind and friendly attitude. The primary objective in such a situation is to give them more of your energy, your understanding, and your essence rather accepting theirs. In such a situation, you can even imagine light emanating from within you and encompassing them, clearing and cleansing all undesirable energy from the environment.

Some self-defense techniques involve using the third eye, the psychic center in the forehead that has an amazing ability to channel psychic energy. One such technique involves refusing to accept the intruding influence and literally projecting counterbalancing energy outward from the third eye as a direct confrontation.

Regulating the Sounds that Affect You

Sound encompasses a variety of energy vibrations, including the harmonious tones of a voice, a symphony orchestra, or a rushing stream, and the disharmonious and disorienting vibrations generated by rock music, urban traffic, or psychic generators. You should remain aware of this all-encompassing, never-ending world of sound and the way it affects you and others.

Sound vibration has a powerful effect on both matter and consciousness. You should be very attentive to the kind of sound vibrations that you utter and that you internalize. The quality of the words that you speak and the sounds that you hear will either increase your physical, psychic, and spiritual strength, or tear them down.

Defense techniques employing sound include uttering uplifting words, avoiding speech that unnecessarily offends, and engaging in mantra chanting. Mantra chanting is the repetition of sacred words and sounds, particularly the various names of God. Chanting will help build spiritual strength, which in turn can minimize the ability of low vibrations and psychic attacks to penetrate your consciousness.

A mantra can be obtained from several sources: traditional literature, a spiritual leader, or even yourself. Some examples from traditional literature are the following:

Christianity:
Lord Jesus Christ Have Mercy on Me

Hinduism:
Hare Krishna, Hare Krishna, Krishna Krishna, Hare Hare,
Hare Rama, Hare Rama, Rama Rama, Hare Hare

Judaism:
Barukh Attah Adonai

Islam:
Allahu Akbar

Buddhism:
Kwanzeon Bosatsu

These techniques are for prevention as well as for defense against psychic attack. The repetition of the various names of God can act like a sword–a laser beam of light–that severs the "tentacles" of the negative mental projections directed at you. The energy activated by calling on a name of God literally sets higher forces in motion that can support, sustain, and defend you. Indeed, a person engaged in regular deep meditation and mantra chanting will have a subtle body that is much more fortified against psychic attack than a person who is just pursuing sense gratification or superficial religiosity.

One of the most pervasive vehicles in Western culture for depleting human consciousness is rock music, particularly hard rock. Not only are the words of many hard rock songs devastating, sinister, and downright offensive, but the music itself has an intense effect on the lower chakras–those associated with sexual, material desires. Chakras are energy centers in the body, located between the base of the spine and the crown of the head, that contain a storehouse of psychic energy that can be harnessed for a person's benefit or harm.

During experiments in which hard rock music was played to plants, the plants died very quickly. In contrast, beautiful music of a completely different nature–less aggressive and less lustful–has the ability to speed up the growth of plants. Most people have experienced the way in which rock music attacks the senses by putting the consciousness and the body in a frenzy. Such music can produce a state of agitation or disorientation and drive someone to seek immediate sense gratification. These effects are negative, because they can cause a person to lose full control and deny responsibility for reckless behavior.

Refusing to Feed the Lower Nature

In addition to encouraging the spread of rock music, many of the forces of oppression are expertly bombarding the world with drugs as a way of making people more susceptible to control. Drug addiction offers a very powerful way to enslave people to passions and to their lower natures. One defense strategy is to avoid the use of drugs steadfastly and to refuse to associate with those who are addicted to them.

Drugs are a drain not only on the physical body, but also–and primarily–on the subtle body, which becomes vulnerable to all kinds of attack. Alcohol produces the same effect. Everyone has heard how alcoholics or drug addicts sometimes see monsters and other lowly evolved creatures that frighten them in different ways. This is not imaginary. A person whose vibrations become lower is more attuned to negative energies.

Diet can also be a defense strategy. The body literally houses the spirit of God and, when it is respected and treated as the sacred temple that it is, it affords protection. What a person puts into the body is naturally going to influence the organism's effectiveness and its ability to protect itself. Flesh–meat, poultry, fish, and eggs–lowers one's vibratory energy and makes a person more likely to be a captive of the senses and to attract various negative influences. Bad dietary habits block out much of the divine protection available to a person, because divine energy will not be attracted to an unclean temple whose caretaker is driven by self-indulgence and negativity.

Gambling is also a widespread activity that feeds the lower nature. Everyone knows of people who are addicted to trying to make a fortune in an instant. However, habitual gamblers, and even those who merely gamble "a lot," invariably lose more money than they make. Worse still, gambling enslaves the mind and promotes irrational behavior. It also causes a person to lose control of the normal faculties of discernment. Anything that makes people prisoners of the lower nature is obviously not spiritually progressive, and anyone who becomes intoxicated by gambling has a weakened mentality that invites psychic attack and mind control.

As discussed earlier, sexual energy is a powerful force that can cause many problems if it is misdirected or abused. The consciousness of a person controlled by sexual desire is vulnerable to negativity, because psychic attack and mind conversion techniques depend upon lust. The confusion of lust with love can be very dangerous. Sexual promiscuity has become so accepted that in many parts of the world a person who does not engage in free sex is considered to be repressed. Of course, the spread of sexually transmitted diseases is beginning to change this perception. However, the problem is being addressed superficially as long as the focus remains on medical and physical solutions. At a deeper level, human enslavement to sexual gratification intensifies the desire for egocentric, self-centered pleasure and therefore increases susceptibility to psychic attack and mind control.

When people lack control of their sexual energy, what would normally develop into love remains as lust. In other words, what could have evolved into a higher-self expression remains a manifestation of the lower self. One of the consequences of undisciplined or illicit sex is that people dishonor the womb rather than glorify it. Such disrespect ultimately leads to dehumanization, with the result that human beings naturally become more like robots subject to the manipulation of sinister forces.

Ultimately, however, love is still the most significant factor in conquering these negative attacks. Available in unlimited quantities, it is the only power capable of defeating all negative forces. Leaders can make the deliberate choice to express it freely. It would be a tragedy to have the power to win the war and simply fail to use it.

Using Your Power

As a leader, you must learn to control fear. Fear is poisonous energy that throws you off balance and draws your attention to the mundane rather than the transcendental. Everyone's mental space is bombarded every day by various intruding factors. However, even when you know that you are under direct attack in this way, it is not wise to become angry. Instead, remember to use the power of love and light to upgrade the attacker. Upgrading the attacker gives you the ability to neutralize the attack and, hopefully, to make the attacker your friend and supporter. As explained earlier, by uplifting the energy of other people, you can neutralize their negativity. In addition, your refusal to lower your energy to the level of those who try to abuse you can provide a great service. Your immunity to their maneuvers and your ability to prosper despite them may inspire them to rethink the whole scheme of their existence.

If you have affected someone in a positive way, that person will affect another. Many people can ultimately benefit from your willingness to use your energy constructively. Eventually, even more positive energy will return to you because, as the saying goes, "what goes around comes around." These are the beneficial results you stand to gain from exercising wise, compassionate leadership.

Highlights

1. The mind at times can be an individual's greatest friend, because no one else is as close and has such an influence on day-to-day activities. A mind that is enthusiastic, enlightened, and at peace is a great comforter and ally. However, at other times the same mind, because it is such an intimate companion and knows all one's secrets, can be tremendously destructive if it is uncontrolled or lacks direction.

2. Mind control constantly violates free will, sometimes through the direct agency of other individuals, but most often in modern societies through the influence of the media. It is frightening to consider that much of the present world-view in industrialized nations is shaped by advertisers and public relations executives paid by corporate and political clients to manipulate the public.

3. As a leader, you cannot afford to be swept up by trends, fads, or superficial distractions. Instead, remain somewhat detached from normally accepted societal patterns, so that you are able to be more circumspect in decision-making and therefore more effective in your leadership.

4. Exorbitant amounts of propaganda circulate throughout the world, causing chaos and uncertainty in the minds of people. As a leader concerned about the welfare of the people, it befalls you to relinquish propaganda and speak the truth in order to assist others along a more certain and auspicious path.

5. Unfortunately, most mind conversion and mind control techniques, as well as many psychic intrusions, go unnoticed. It is rare for a brainwashed person to be aware of the process or its ultimate effect.

6.   Most people have heard of subliminal suggestion–the attempt to influence the subconscious mind in order to stimulate action on the conscious level. Subliminal suggestion is used particularly in advertising and brainwashing, where sophisticated psychologists create hidden images that register within the subconscious mind.

7.   One example of the misuse of science and technology is the surreptitious use of extrasensory perception (ESP) behind the former Iron Curtain, in the United States, and perhaps in other countries, for espionage and military activities. Russia and her former satellites are said to be far ahead of the West in analyzing and using psychic phenomena for such clandestine purposes.

8.   Because the manipulative negative influences of mind control affect everyone's equilibrium, you should learn to create strong mental barriers against them. The most powerful way to do so is to maintain a kind and loving attitude, feeling a strong "heart love" for every person in your environment, whether you know the individual or not. This creates such a powerful radiation that any negative influences directed toward you will simply be absorbed into your loving energy field.

9.   Sound vibration has a powerful effect on both matter and consciousness. You should be very attentive to the kind of sound vibrations that you utter and that you internalize. The quality of the words that you speak and the sounds that you hear will either increase your physical, psychic, and spiritual strength, or tear them down.

10.   Control the mind; monitor the energy around you; regulate the sounds that affect you; avoid feeding the lower nature; and remember the power of love.

Mindsets

1. Revisit the ten essential technologies at the beginning of this book, considering how each of them in turn can help your mind avoid manipulation and control by others. Select one or two of the most powerful ones for you, and work with them whenever you feel the need for protection.

2. Envision the mind as a clown constantly trying to harass you, and visualize yourself as unaffected by its attempts.

3. Be mindful of your associations. Seek out people of higher energy levels and avoid those who drain you. If you find yourself in the presence of someone emitting negative energy, remember to use the energy of love to upgrade that person's state and protect yourself.

4. Be careful about the sounds you hear as well as those you emit. Sound has a powerful influence upon the mind. Play different types of music and notice how you are stimulated differently by each style.

5. Keep in mind the importance of mantras and affirmations that call on the name of God. Whenever you feel vulnerable, remember that these are a powerful defense. Use them.

6. Avoid alcohol and drugs, because they can make you more susceptible to lower vibrations, psychic attacks and intrusions.

7. As discussed earlier, change to a vegetarian diet if you have not already done so. You are harming yourself by eating meat, which after all is part of a dead body.

8.   Do not enslave your mind by gambling. It makes you susceptible to control by negative influences.

9.   Avoid illicit sex. Pursue true love, not lust. Negativity, psychic attack, and mind control feed on lust.

10.   Assess your mind's strengths and weaknesses, and make a list of your vulnerabilities. Then write down steps you can take to improve. Take those steps, knowing that every improvement is an additional protection against mind control and manipulation by others.

15

Encouraging Religious Tolerance

In these days of multiple religious conflicts, when millions of people in the Middle East, Europe, Asia, and Africa are killed because of religious fanaticism, leaders may find it a dangerous business to encourage any form of religious practice. Some of the greatest threats to world stability, even in those countries that have recently gained their independence, can be traced to religious differences. Nigeria, for instance, has had hundreds of religious riots since gaining independence. In addition, countries that have been autonomous for centuries are facing similar conflicts.

Religious Belief: A Powerful Force

Today, people widely accept that religion should be kept separate from politics and that governments should remain secular, devoid of religious affiliations. Indeed, a government that attempts to establish a single "national" religion may succumb to the dangerous temptation of suppressing other bona fide religious institutions. Such suppression creates a constrictive environment that destroys the ultimate meaning of religion. The variety of world religions originally evolved from one common essence into different forms to suit time, place and circumstance. When respected, such variety can be healthy, but when condemned, the same variety may create conflicts and lead to the denial of religious freedom.

Billions of people throughout the world readily identify with one particular religious orientation. The World Christian Encyclopedia estimates that 1.5 billion people, almost one-third of the world's population, consider themselves Catholics; 750 million call themselves Muslims; 600 million view themselves as Hindus; and 300 million say they are Buddhists.[172] Besides these major world religions, many other religions are practiced by smaller numbers of people. There are thousands of African religions alone, and even within America, numerous religious sects are now active.

Religious feelings represent some of the most passionate emotions known to humankind. Millions of people are willing to die for their religious beliefs, and some do just that. Of course, others are eager to kill in the name of religion, ready to accept any degree of punishment in the belief that their destructive actions are justified on religious grounds. Some people bequeath entire fortunes to religious communities and others make large contributions during their lifetimes to their religious institutions. Still others remain in debt for the rest of their lives because they have made tremendous sacrifices to complete sacred pilgrimages.

Such focused determination demonstrates that dedication, strength and commitment can be extremely dynamic forces when they are directed toward endeavors that directly help to elevate the human condition. This power is so strong that it cannot be denied, but must be properly channeled so that it may become a valuable resource to be used in constructive ways.

Service, Not Sectarian Religion

Human beings in their essence are spiritual beings. When spirituality is denied, psychological disturbances occur and horrendous atrocities can take place. A society deteriorates and becomes hedonistic when it operates on the assumptions that its members are merely material creatures without souls and that God does not exist at all. As such a society minimizes the truths of life, it becomes capable of producing a high degree of immoral, self-centered activity.

Religion, because it provides the foundation for morals, ethics, and standards of socialization, can play a productive role in society. However, religion must be distinguished from pseudo-religiosity or sectarianism. In the present era, many people practice religion in a sectarian way, as if God belonged only to their own group. Even in heaven these individuals might be capable of asking, "Where is the area for the Catholics? for Presbyterians? for Sufis? for Suni Muslims?" Obviously, this is absurd. Anyone who practices in such a superficial way is spiritually immature and not seriously God-oriented. Just as God recognizes no distinctions among human beings, God expects human beings not to use sectarianism as a divisive element. The distorted perceptions of pseudo-religiosity and sectarianism are detrimental to human development and spiritual evolution, whether these appear in the form of nationalism, racism, tribalism, chauvinism or religious intolerance.

Ultimately there is only one God and one religion. That one religion is love–and it is about service to God. Therefore the outer form of religion itself is not the issue. One can be born a Christian and later become a Muslim, a Buddhist, or a Taoist. One can be born in a Buddhist community and accept its teachings, but later become a Christian. The particular religion and its structure are not ultimately significant. Rather, the important aspects are the tenets and conditions one has agreed to accept in order to render service to God and other human beings.

God relates to human beings according to their degree of sincerity and their willingness to love and serve–certainly not according to their religious affiliation. In the ancient *Bhagavad-gita* is a quotation that substantiates this point:

> As all surrender unto Me, I reward them accordingly.
> Everyone follows My path in all respects, O son of Prtha.[173]

In this passage, God is saying that He rewards people according to their degree of surrender. No one can cheat God, nor can He be bribed. He is not lazy, and He does not take any vacations or breaks. Instead, He is constantly monitoring each person's level of devotion and reciprocating in kind. He is not interested in the particular denomination with which persons align themselves, but is taking notice of their actual genuine devotion. Does anyone really want to serve a God who allows the majority of His children to be damned and only favors one particular group?

"Love thy neighbor as thyself" is a precept that applies to humanity anywhere in the world. God has given each person the capacity to love literally every single being in existence, and one can always strive to achieve this ideal in practice. Such an understanding of spiritual life can bring solace, because people know that their relationship with God is completely up to them, and that His greater plan encompasses everyone, regardless of sectarian associations.

Exoteric and Esoteric Approaches

The practice of religion is based upon two distinct systems: the exoteric and the esoteric. Most people approach their religion exoterically, fully absorbed in the rituals, institutions, and mindsets that have come to be a part of that system. It is these exoteric practitioners who often fight among themselves, creating riots, conflicts and ongoing tensions that threaten humanity's present survival. Their own insecurity causes them to attack other groups in an attempt to eliminate, deny or suppress those who do not share the same religious views. They try to push others down as a way of pulling themselves up. Obviously this behavior is not an expression of brotherly or sisterly love. Those who really love their neighbor will raise others up, realizing that these people are but extensions of themselves.

Esoteric practitioners are those who seek self-realization by trying to penetrate beyond form and rituals. More simply, they are interested in discovering the essence of their spirituality and in attaining communion with God. Although some people may consider it impossible to have contact with God, indeed such a connection is possible. For example, the

Bible says, "Blessed are the pure in heart; for they shall see God."[174] The El Hadith, a complement to the Koran, says, "The highest experience in paradise is to behold the vision of Allah."[175] All the scriptures allude to the fact that one can have various experiences with the Lord.

Because so few people, even among those on a spiritual path, have reached this level of communion, sectarianism is widespread. However, those who penetrate deeply beyond superficial, exoteric forms discover a great comradeship with all true religious seekers and uncover a common thread connecting all religions. Such esoteric practitioners, eager to see the immature levels of God-consciousness evolve, are pleased whenever they find true God-consciousness. They understand that religion, pursued according to the bona fide scriptures and prophets, is simply a matter of service to God. This concept of service applies not only to religion, but to all relationships. Whether you are in a superior, inferior, or equal position, you are always serving or being served.

The Message is Consistently the Same

The writings of those who have experienced deep God-consciousness teach people not to be overly concerned about the externals of religious practice. The critical task is to use the external practices to go deeper within to seek the essence, which is pure love and service to God. Ultimately there is only one God who sends various bona fide prophets to enlighten people according to a particular time, place, and circumstance.

A close examination of the messages of these prophets reveals universal teachings that keep reappearing through the ages: love God with all your heart and soul; love your neighbor as yourself; do not consider this world to be your real home; and engage in self-purification in order to enter into the kingdom of God. Although the details may vary, these differences are minute compared to the similarities.

Actually, any religious leader who preaches that God has only one prophet is insulting God. How can anyone think that God, who is the greatest, most merciful, most magnanimous divine Parent, would instruct humanity in only one particular approach by one particular messenger? How presumptuous! Even ordinary human beings can bring more than one child into this world. To think that the Mother-Father God, the greatest of progenitors, can produce only one teacher is to attempt to place a limit on God's great power and compassion. Out of love and concern, God repeats the same teachings in different forms, via as many messengers as necessary, until the instruction is complete. Human beings are the ones who have created so much religious confusion.

The compilation of spiritual teachings collectively known as the Vedas is older than most. A close look at these scriptures demonstrates the profound unity among the teachings of the representatives of God. For example, the Vedic scriptures predicted Buddha's coming to the world thousands of years ahead of time. Also, the *Bhavisya Purana* anticipated the appearance of Jesus, and other Vedic scriptures mentioned Ramanujacarya and Madhavacarya, two great realized souls, many years before they were born. True followers of the Vedic wisdom have little difficulty appreciating other religions that remain faithful to their prophets' teachings of love and unity.

Although the prophets' teachings are very similar to each other, their messages have been constantly distorted, changed and misused. Many of their teachings were recorded after the prophets' disappearances by individuals who lacked a full understanding of the message or who had their own agendas.

Even during their lifetimes, these great spiritual leaders were not appreciated, and suffered trying to give their wisdom to the world. For instance, Zoroaster, a Persian mystic of the sixth century B.C. who founded Zoroastrianism, was stabbed to death. The Greek philosopher Socrates (470-399 B.C.) was charged with corrupting the minds of the young and condemned to die by poison. Gautama Buddha (563-483 B.C.) was stoned by orthodox Hindus. Jesus was crucified, when the people chose to spare Barabbas, a common murderer. Mohammed (570-632 A.D.) was poisoned in an assassination attempt, and although he survived, he suffered pain constantly for the last seven years of his life.[176]

If people attacked these prophets and their messages so intensely when they were on the planet, how could there fail to be confusion, abuse, and distortion in their teachings after their departure?

Distortions of the Message

Christianity offers a prime example of how the messages of a great spiritual teacher can become distorted. Since the disappearance of Jesus, many changes have taken place within Christianity itself, several of them the result of decisions made by ecumenical councils that have met periodically over the centuries. Leading religious "authorities" have decided what should be kept, eliminated, or altered in the Bible.

Today, Christian bookstores offer dozens of different versions of the Bible: the Good News version, the King James version, the Roman Catholic version, the Greek Orthodox version, or the Revised Standard version, to list just a few. The translations vary widely, and some Bibles contain more, or different, books than others. Since the discovery of the Dead Sea Scrolls a few decades ago, these variations have become even more pronounced. In the Dead Sea Scrolls, researchers have discovered several striking facts that contradict traditional biblical tenets. As a result, many of the newer translations have made serious changes in their interpretations.

Christians of a particular denomination may consider their version of the Bible to be the complete and absolute word of God. However, a study of history explains how each version evolved and reveals that, because of human fallibility, distortions have occurred. Despite this fact, the essence remains intact and can be discovered at a deeper level.

Translations into many languages have increased the distortion of the Bible's message. The fact that the Bible was originally written in Hebrew, Aramaic, and Greek, has made accurate, consistent, word-for-word translations difficult. Even among many Christian scholars there is confusion about how to interpret certain passages.

The *American Encyclopedia* mentions that there are over 30,000 errors in the Bible.[177] Many sections of the Bible are apparently copied from others, with resultant inconsistencies. For example, in II Chronicles 9:25, Solomon had 4,000 stalls for horses and chariots, but possessed 40,000 in I Kings 4:26. David slew 700 men in II Samuel 10:18, but killed 7,000 in I Chronicles 19:18. Matthew and Luke seem to have taken major portions of their work from Mark. Some other biblical passages are copied quite accurately, as for example the 38 verses of II Kings 19 that also appear in Isaiah 37, or the verses from Psalm 18 that also are included in II Samuel 22.

New Discoveries

The Dead Sea Scrolls reveal that certain words attributed to Jesus were not originally his. For example, the Sermon on the Mount, which many have considered unique and original, is found in an earlier Essene text and therefore was not originated by Jesus himself.[178] This revelation is all the more believable, given that Jesus may have actually belonged to the Essenes.

Jesus' teachings to his disciples may in part have been a result of his Essene orientation. In the process of seeking self-realization, the Essenes often manifested mystical powers and were therefore able to perform the "miracles" demonstrated by Jesus. Clairvoyant and telepathic, they believed in reincarnation and could exercise control over the material world, healing the sick or the infirm and–as Jesus demonstrated–raising the dead.

The discoveries from the Dead Sea Scrolls have produced various changes in the more recent Bibles, the most noticeable being a shift away from considering the attainment of Jesus as unique. The past emphasis on the exclusivity of the spiritual mastership of Jesus led Christians to believe–contrary to Jesus' own message–that only Jesus could attain such a high level of God-consciousness. However, Jesus himself said: "He that believeth in me, the works that I do shall he do also."[179] The misinterpretation of Jesus' teachings has allowed Christians to believe that they cannot achieve his state. It also enhances Christian sectarianism by considering Jesus to be the world's only divine personality and representative of God. The perpetuation of such religious sectarianism is dangerous in any religion.

All great teachers would be disturbed to be evaluated in such a way. Actually, the cosmic Christ is present in every tradition, in contrast to the historical figure of Jesus, who is not represented in most other religions. The cosmic Christ is God's all-pervading universal love, the "offspring" of the Mother-Father God. In the Bible we find the statement, "God is love;

and he that dwelleth in love dwelleth in God, and God in him."[180] This is why people who practice esoteric Christianity are not disturbed by different religious dogma. They realize that the same loving Lord, along with His representatives, permeates all religious systems despite differences in dogma and ritual.

The point of this discussion is to demonstrate that the external forms of scripture and ritual that exoteric religionists rely on are confusing and contradictory at best. In contrast, the esoteric practitioner fully realizes that scripture, although significant, is only one part of the total picture. In esoteric spiritual life, the study of scripture is accompanied by teachings from authorized practitioners who exemplify the revealed writings and give insight into how they acquired perfection. Unlike exoteric approaches, esoteric spirituality seeks direct contact with the spiritual world and helps bring practitioners closer to a state of self-realization. Reliance on scripture alone produces narrow minds and an increase in sectarianism and confusion.

Allow Diversity; Encourage Tolerance

People feel strongly about their religious beliefs, which often comfort and sustain them. As a leader, you can encourage religious tolerance and diversity rather than obliterating or discouraging distinctions. You can be happy to see people feeling sufficient conviction and dedication to say, "My religion is the best," so long as they do not force their beliefs on others or cause nonbelievers to suffer. At the same time, if a religious system is not working, you can encourage people to explore other approaches. Help them realize that any true spiritual path, if one goes deeply enough into it, will give great realization, power, strength, and love as it helps them harmonize their relationships with God and their fellow human beings.

Trying to deny variegation is quite unnatural and unhealthy. A beautiful symphony requires a variety of instruments and different levels of expertise. No one would want to hear only one instrument played by musicians all having the same caliber of accomplishment. It is the uniqueness of each instrument and musician that produces a harmony of great distinction.

Similarly, different races, tribes, nations and religions can complement each other, helping to reinforce each person's ability to enjoy life on a higher level. A leader should be an expert in bringing this understanding to the forefront, emphasizing universal truths and the inner essence of each situation while helping to minimize the importance of external practices and superficialities. Spirituality, which is the natural state of human beings, is an intimate part of life. A government or organization that tries to suppress it may experience unfortunate consequences. In my extensive travels throughout the world, I have noticed, even in the former communist countries where religion was once heavily suppressed, a strong, natural proclivity toward spiritual life.

Many people even risk their lives to get their hands on a holy book such as the Bible, Koran, or Torah. Something innate drives humanity in the direction of ever-greater philosophical, psychic, and spiritual development. Leaders can take a significant step toward uniting a country, organization or family by helping people appreciate that everyone has the same God. Those leaders who promote religious tolerance are making an important contribution to world stability and peace.

Calling on the Names of God

Leaders sincerely interested in encouraging religious tolerance, and thereby reducing conflict, can encourage the collective practice of calling on the names of God, emphasizing that these many names all refer to the same God. Remind those in your charge that all great scriptures emphatically declare that peace and well-being are the result of humanity's recognition of God's supremacy. Calling upon the names of God is a most effective process for creating peace.

The following scriptural passages emphasize this point:

- Everyone who calls upon the name of the Lord shall be saved. –*Romans 10:13*
- From the rising of the sun to its setting, the name of the Lord is to be praised. –*Psalms 113:3*
- Call upon Allah, or call upon Rahman: By whatever name ye call upon Him (it is well): For to Him belong the most beautiful names. –*Koran 17.110*

- The most beautiful names belong to Allah; so call on Him by them. *–Koran 7.180*
- The greatest name carries the highest vibration. The vibration produces a special result. *–Abdu'l-Baha*
- Call upon His Holy Name, cry unto Him for mercy, cry unto Him in your homes morning, midday, and evening. *–Book of Mormon, p. 282, verse 17*
- By chanting any of the Names of God one can purify the mind and become undisturbed by the material world. *–Your Right to Know, p. 102, from Eckankar*
- Of sacrifices, I am the chanting of the Holy Names. *– Bhagavad-gita 10.16*

These quotations demonstrate that many great scriptures of the world emphasize the importance of calling upon the names of God to acquire more unity, peace and divine blessings. When crises, emergencies and natural calamities occur, as part of the recovery process leaders can request that religious groups or individuals call upon the holy names according to their particular tradition.

Not only can these groups call on the names of God in silent prayer, but they may also want to chant the names aloud. Sound vibration has a powerful impact on the physical world, influences the atmosphere, and affects the collective consciousness of those in the environment. Because calling on the names of God can be so valuable, as a leader you can help everyone around you reap the benefits of this practice.

Whether you are a world leader or a leader in another capacity, you can recognize the importance of spirituality, honoring its power to create unity within diversity as it allows people to go more deeply within themselves and understand more of their spiritual essence, which can then become a significant common ground to share with others. You can remind everyone that they are all of the same family, ultimately having the same God.

You can also promote harmony by visiting the major religious festivals of each tradition, associating with people from all spiritual paths, and emphasizing the need for unity. The spiritual dimension of your leadership can create a higher level of consciousness among nations, organizations and families, and such an approach can give you access to a very sacred aspect of the lives of those you lead, who will consider you as supportive of their individual and collective aspirations.

Highlights

1. Today, people widely accept that religion should be kept separate from politics and that governments should remain secular, devoid of religious affiliations. Indeed, a government that attempts to establish a single "national" religion may succumb to the danger-ous temptation of suppressing other bona fide religious institutions. Such suppression creates a constrictive environment that destroys the ultimate meaning of religion.

2. Human beings in their essence are spiritual beings. When spiritu-ality is denied, psychological disturbances occur and horrendous atrocities can take place. A society deteriorates and becomes hedonistic when it operates on the assumptions that its members are merely material creatures without souls and that God does not exist at all.

3. Just as God recognizes no distinctions among human beings, God expects human beings not to use sectarianism as a divisive ele-ment. The distorted perceptions of pseudo-religiosity and sectarianism are detrimental to human development and spiritual evolution, whether these appear in the form of nationalism, racism, tribalism, chauvinism or religious intolerance.

4. Ultimately there is only one God and one religion. That one reli-gion is love–and it is about service to God. God relates to human beings according to their degree of sincerity and their willingness to love and serve–certainly not according to their religious affilia-tion.

5. "Love thy neighbor as thyself" is a precept that applies to human-ity anywhere in the world. God has given each person the capacity to love literally every single being in existence, and one can always strive to achieve this ideal in practice. Such an understanding of

spiritual life can bring solace, because people know that their relationship with God is completely up to them, and that His greater plan encompasses everyone, regardless of sectarian associations.

6.   Actually, any religious leader who preaches that God has only one prophet is insulting God. How can anyone think that God, who is the greatest, most merciful, most magnanimous divine Parent, would instruct humanity in only one particular approach by one particular messenger? How presumptuous!

7.   The practice of religion is based upon two distinct systems: the exoteric and the esoteric. Most people approach their religion exoterically, fully absorbed in the rituals, institutions, and mindsets that have come to be a part of that system. It is these exoteric practitioners who often fight among themselves, creating riots, conflicts and ongoing tensions that threaten humanity's present survival.

8.   In esoteric spiritual life, the study of scripture is accompanied by teachings from authorized practitioners who exemplify the revealed writings and give insight into how they acquired perfection. Unlike exoteric approaches, esoteric spirituality seeks direct contact with the spiritual world and helps bring practitioners closer to a state of self-realization. Reliance on scripture alone produces narrow minds and an increase in sectarianism and confusion.

9.   People feel strongly about their religious beliefs, which often comfort and sustain them. As a leader, you can encourage religious tolerance and diversity rather than obliterating or discouraging distinctions. You can be happy to see people feeling sufficient conviction and dedication to say, "My religion is the best," so long as they do not force their beliefs on others or cause nonbelievers to suffer. At the same time, if a religious system is not working, you can encourage people to explore other approaches.

10.   Different races, tribes, nations and religions can complement each other, helping to reinforce each person's ability to enjoy life on a higher level. A leader must be an expert in bringing this understanding to the forefront, emphasizing universal truths and the inner essence of each situation while helping to minimize the importance of external practices and superficialities. Spirituality, which is the natural state of human beings, is an intimate part of life. A government or organization that tries to suppress it may experience unfortunate consequences.

Mindsets

1.   Reread the ten essential technologies at the beginning of this book, with a view to understanding how many different religions address each of these concerns. Make an effort to grasp the universality of these themes across all forms of religious practice.

2.   Meditate on different examples of the way in which all activities are a form of service, involving one person serving another. Consider how the essence of religion is service and love of God.

3.   If other religions make you insecure or if you find them intolerable, then it is time to examine your own religious system much more deeply. If you are unable to do so, at least consider a change in attitude. Sectarianism on your part means you have chosen to limit your reality, and therefore you can only be a leader of a narrow sect rather than of all people. A good leader seeks to achieve unity in diversity, and any serious endeavors toward local and world peace must be based upon this approach.

4.   Remember the three universal truths given by many prophets:

    •Love God with all your heart and soul and put nothing before God.
    •Love your neighbor as yourself.
    •Seek the kingdom of God because this world is not your home.

Let these common threads help you see the universality of all bona fide prophets and religious traditions.

5.   Use the following three-way check system to validate the genuineness of religious systems. A healthy religion is supported by:

    • bona fide scriptures
    • bona fide present-day saints

- bona fide self-realized individuals of the past and present who have transcendental contact, such as sons of God, ascended masters, saints or gurus

When a religion meets all of these criteria, you can feel secure about its validity. In addition, each of the three criteria themselves should be validated by the other two.

6. Make it a practice to remind those you lead that although God has many names, there is only one Supreme Being, the Mother-Father of us all. Remind yourself that you, as the leader, play the role of an earthly parent. Check to see that you treat your people with a parental loving spirit.

7. A dynamic leader enjoys working with powerful individuals, and people who have made religious commitments can manifest tremendous strength. Do not try to deny or suppress such strength, but instead guide it properly for the unity of your nation, organization or family, and for the higher good of humankind.

8. In order to create more unity among those in your charge, and to counteract negative influences, encourage them collectively to call on the sacred names of God according to their own traditions. For instance, during celebrations or calamities, or at regular weekly or monthly gatherings, invite people to chant and meditate profoundly on the Lord's holy names.

9. Help create more unity by periodically visiting the major religious festivals of each tradition, or by finding some other way to honor the religious traditions of those you lead. Constantly remind people about the need for unity and religious tolerance, and encourage everyone to make their religious commitments manifest through service, helping to improve the quality of life in all areas for all people.

10.   Take a moment to study your own religious feelings and commit-
        ments. Do your beliefs tolerate the faith of others? How long has it
        been since you had an interfaith dialogue?

Epilogue

As a leader in today's world, you face a daunting task. Not only must you remain centered amidst great uncertainty and confusion, but you also have the job of guiding others to integrate ancient spiritual wisdom and modern material knowledge in ways that allow them to fulfill the purpose of human life. Your inner connection with the divine and your willingness to be of service can sustain you in this process, helping you balance a broad vision with practical, skilled, creative action.

As you fulfill your daily responsibilities, keep in mind that your success as a leader depends upon your willingness to express love and to follow its counsel. When others perceive your love as genuine, they will reciprocate it, creating an atmosphere of trust that allows you to implement even the most painful policies, should the need ever arise. An important goal of your leadership, in all situations, should be to increase the amount of love experienced by those you lead.

Truly effective leadership is based upon a spiritual awareness of what a human being is and upon a proper understanding of the material world. Ultimately, whether you lead a family, an organization or a nation, your most essential function is to create an environment in which people can eventually find their way back home to God. When you are aware of the true purpose of human life, you gain the ability to base your decisions, programs and policies upon a solid spiritual foundation, one that will hold steady in the face of self-serving criticisms and attacks from others. You will not be swayed by desires for personal gratification nor will you be deluded by the idea that material wealth, comforts and pleasures constitute the primary goals of life.

Also keep in mind that you are responsible for the energy that you generate, recognizing that whatever atmosphere you create will permeate your family, organization or nation. Constant self-examination is an essential ingredient of leadership for those who wish to develop the self-knowledge to serve without seeking gratification of the ego or the senses. The energy emanating from leaders reflects their intentions, which to be constructive must be devoid of lust, greed, manipulation or any wish for self-aggrandizement. In addition, to be effective, leadership requires an equilibrium between masculine and feminine energies, reflecting the inherent androgyny of human beings and, particularly at this time in history, the earth's need for balance.

Leaders in today's world must understand and harness the vast potential of the human mind. Not only can the mind affect the health of the body, produce incredible paranormal phenomena, or perform amazing feats of superlearning; it can also be manipulated in ways that are disruptive to human autonomy and well-being. As a leader, you should be careful about the ways in which–consciously and unconsciously–you use your own mind and how you affect the minds of others. Your leadership can only benefit from your unwillingness to manipulate others and your refusal to abuse power. In addition, the mind can be of great help as you use the resources of your own unconscious to assist you in your role. Let your dreams serve as a reservoir of guidance and inspiration.

As a leader, you are first and foremost a servant–a servant of the people and of God. Understanding the value of empathy and compassion, recognize that your power to lead is strengthened by your deep awareness of the needs of others. Remind yourself that God is ultimately in control of every situation, and so develop tolerance and patience, which are essential components of wise decision-making.

In order to make effective decisions, learn to look beneath the surface of events to discern their deeper meaning. Suppressing a symptom is only a short-term fix, postponing the eventual need to discover the true cause of a situation that ultimately must be addressed. In addition, many conflicts in the world are the result of failing to look beyond superficial differences to discover the universal spiritual principles that unite all human beings. When apparently opposing factions are able to discover their common bonds, struggles abate and disputes can be more easily settled to the mutual benefit of everyone.

Improper time management and inability to address conflict are contributing factors to high levels of stress. For this reason, leadership skills include the ability to manage time, resolve conflicts and minimize stress. Remember that all time belongs to God, and that you are accountable for how you spend it in your leadership role, as well as in your personal life. As for stress, each individual is ultimately responsible for creating it, because a person's level of stress is based upon interpretations of experience rather than the experiences themselves. Take the initiative to change your perspective of the situations that are causing you stress, and encourage others to do the same.

The contemporary world situation presents numerous stressful challenges. Your role is to set a positive tone, at the same time being aware of the difficulties and taking specific, practical actions to remedy them. Millions of people around the world who live in the grip of fear–as a result of war, crime, injustice, inadequate education, poor medical care, poverty or homelessness–need strong, compassionate, capable leaders to protect them and offer assistance. Widespread industrialization has created much suffering around the globe, and responsible leaders will seek ways to encourage more humanly oriented forms of development, promoting simple lifestyles that safeguard precious resources and provide more opportunities for fulfilling lives.

As a conscious leader, you must be aware of the wasteful agricultural practices ingrained in the world's economic system. In whatever environment you find yourself, take steps to eat more simply, consuming foods lower down on the food chain–becoming vegetarian, if possible, and encouraging others to do the same. On another front, the harmful results of misused human sexuality are everywhere apparent–in sexually transmitted diseases, abuse, infidelity, divorce, abortion and promiscuity. Let these circumstances help you remember the importance of regulating your own sexual behavior, so that you may serve as an example to others and create a climate in which sexuality can serve its sacred function.

In this age of sophisticated technology and increasing understanding of the human brain, mind control is a constant and growing threat. You should be vigilant about how others may be using such techniques against you and those you lead. Always remember that the greatest protection against harmful influences is the power of love. This is why it is so important for a leader to develop the capacity to love and to express this love freely. Such behavior encourages others to follow your example, if you make it safe for them to do so.

Throughout the world, many wars between nations and conflicts among groups originate from religious fanaticism and intolerance. These disputes arise because of an attachment to outer, exoteric religious forms that ignore the fundamental unity beyond all differences. Ensure that all your actions as a leader demonstrate your understanding that there is one God, and that sectarianism has no place in your family, organization or nation. This means establishing a climate that accepts and is enriched by religious diversity, and encouraging those you lead to call upon the names of God in their own unique ways.

❖❖❖❖❖❖❖❖❖

In these turbulent times, never has the world been more in need of centered, spiritually aware, compassionate, firm leadership–leadership that is practical yet visionary. Too much is at stake for you as a leader to limit your view to the horizons of your personal, organizational or national agendas, however worthy these may be. The increasing interdependence of all forms of life on this planet requires a broader perspective that looks outward to embrace the entire globe, forward in time to care for future generations, and inward to honor the Lord in your heart.

This means that your role as a leader is far more than bowing to the least common denominator or seeking to enjoy the so-called prerogatives of power at the expense of others. Rather, your function is to remind yourself and others that no one is the proprietor of anything on this earth. Instead, human beings are stewards who care for whatever comes into their temporary possession. Stewardship is based upon an appreciation of the sacred nature of what is being cared for, and requires a relationship of love, appreciation and tender attention that respects the value of each part in the whole. Ownership, on the other hand, relies upon the assumption that the material world exists mainly for human sense gratification, and encourages a grasping and clinging to pieces that are often ripped out of the web of life with greed and aggression.

Self-serving behavior, whether in leaders or others, eventually brings harm to those touched by it and turns back to hurt the instigators themselves. In today's world, which suffers from the effects of intensified exploitation and competitive self-gratification, everyone is affected by such actions. The planet can ill afford leaders who continue in the same vein. Far from being impractical, when you act with clarity from a spiritual platform, you are offering what the earth and its inhabitants most need in these times: a vision based on love, a sense of higher purpose and a commitment to manifest compassion, integrity and wisdom in all transactions.

When you lead in this way, you are fulfilling your role as an intermediary between heaven and earth, turning inward and upward for divine guidance and inspiration and translating your revelations into concrete, productive expression in the physical world. You are in the world but not of it, respecting material existence as an arena that makes the return back home possible, and yet not becoming trapped in the belief that the material world is all there is. At all levels, your leadership can then demonstrate courage, insight and strong resolve to guide, inspire and encourage those in your charge to fulfill their responsibilities and to express their love to one another, to all living beings, to the earth and to God.

And so, dear leader, this book concludes where it began: with an acknowledgment of the significance and power of love. Within the pages of this book, you have been instructed by a loving unseen coalition. We care for you, and we have grown to love you even more from this association. We have offered you simple yet profound advice for your own survival, well-being, and success.

The greatest problem facing the world is a crisis in leadership. Proper thoughtful, loving leadership from a metaphysical perspective can inaugurate a new era for humankind–truly an age of higher consciousness.

Beloved, will you help provide leadership for an age of higher consciousness?

Notes

1. This is a theme from *A Course in Miracles* (Tiburon, CA: Foundation for Inner Peace, 1976).
2. See Diane Collinson and Robert Wilkinson, *Thirty-five Oriental Philosophers*, (New York: Routledge,1994).
3. See Kirtanananda Swami Bhaktipada, *Rama. The Supreme Personality of Godhead.* (New Vrindaban, WV: Palace Publishing, 1989).
4. For tested and successful techniques to combat misery, atheism, materialism, impersonalism, and voidism see A.C. Bhaktivedanta Swami Prabhupada, *The Path of Perfection: Yoga for the Modern Age* (Los Angeles: The Bhaktivedanta Book Trust, 1979) and Jerry Savells, "The Amish Life-Style in an Era of Rapid Social Change," in *Social Psychiatry Across Cultures: Studies from North America, Asia, Europe, and Africa,* Rumi Kato Price. Brent Mack Shea. and Harsha N. Mookherjee, eds. (New York: Plenum Press, 1995).
5. 1 John 2:15-17.
6. 1 Cor. 15:40-50.
7. 2 Cor. 5:6.
8. 2 Cor. 4:18.
9. Diane Collinson and Robert Wilkinson, *Thirty-five Oriental Philosophers* (New York: Routledge, 1994).
10. Satsvarupa dasa Gosvami, *Elements of Vedic Thought and Culture* (Bombay, India: Bhaktivedanta Book Trust, 1977), 28-29.
11. The changes in the body result from the six laws of material nature: birth, growth, maintenance, transformation, deterioration, and finally death. See A.C. Bhaktivedanta Swami Prabhupada, *Sri*

Isopanisad: Discovering the Original Person, [5th ed.] (Los Angeles: The Bhaktivedanta Book Trust, 1974), 79-84.

12. A.C. Bhaktivedanta Swami Prabhupada, *Bhagavad Gita As It Is* (Los Angeles: Bhaktivedanta Book Trust, 1986) 2.13.

13. Matt. 7:1-2.

14. Manley P. Hall, *An Encyclopedic Outline of Masonic, Hermetic, Qabbalistic and Rosicrucian Symbolical Philosophy: Being an Interpretation of the Secret Teachings Concealed within the Rituals, Allegories and Mysteries of All Ages*. Full-Page Illustrations by J. Augustus Knapp,Golden Anniversary Edition, Reduced Facsimile, (Los Angeles: The Philosophical Research Society, 1977), XLV-XLVII.

15. A.C. Bhaktivedanta Swami Prabhupada, *The Laws of Nature: An Infallible Justice*, (Los Angeles: Bhaktivedanta Book Trust, 1991), 1-3.

16. A.C. Bhaktivedanta Swami Prabhupada, *Teachings of Lord Kapila The Son of Devahuti* (New York: Bhaktivedanta Book Trust, 1977), 16-18.

17. Jon F. Dechow, "Origen and Early Christian Pluralism: The Context of His Eschatology," in *Origen of Alexandria: His World and His Legacy* ,eds. Charles Kannengiesser and William L. Petersen, (Notre Dame, Indiana: University of Notre Dame Press, 1988). See also "Transmigration of the Soul" in *Encyclopedia of Religion and Ethics*, vol.8, ed.,James Hastings,(New York: Charles Scribner's Sons, 1915), 601.

18. Henri Crouzel, *Origen*, trans. A.S. Worrall (San Francisco: Harper & Row, 1989). See the following books for history and discussion on Origen and Origenism: Jean Danielou, *Origen*, trans. Walter Mitchell (New York: Sheed and Ward, 1955) and Charles Bigg, *The Christian Platonists of Alexandria* (Amsterdam, 1968).

19. For the sixth century church and the Fifth Ecumenical Council of Nicaea, see Judith Herrin, *The Formation of Christendom* (Oxford: Basil Backwell, 1987), 119; Emperor Justinian, see J.B. Bury, *A History of the Later Roman Empire from Arcadius to Irene (395 A.D. to 800 A.D.)*, vol. 2 (Amsterdam: Adolf M. Hakkert, 1966), 1-5. For the reaction against Origenism, see William Fairweather, *Origen*

and Greek Patristic Theology (Edinburgh: T. & T. Clark, 1901), 248-251.

20. Matt. 14:1-2.
21. Rom. 9:13-15.
22. Luke 9:18-19.
23. In 1993, based on a single national survey in England, 26 percent of the population polled believed in reincarnation. See Elizabeth Hann Hastings and Philip K. Hastings, eds., *Index to International Public Opinion, 1992-1993* (Westport, CT: Greenwood Press, 1994), 438. Emerging trends in American opinion on reincarnation have been compiled from several Gallup Organization surveys. See Opinion Research Service, *American Public Opinion Index*, 1993, vol. 2, I-Z (Bethesda, MD: ORS Publishing), 559.
24. A.C. Bhaktivedanta Swami Prabhupada, *A Second Chance* (Los Angeles: Bhaktivedanta Book Trust, 1991).
25. Matt: 8:8.
26. A.C. Bhaktivedanta Swami Prabhupada, *Srimad Bhagavatam* (Manila, Philippines: Bhaktivedanta Book Trust. 1972), 4.8.80-82.
27. James Allen, *As a Man Thinketh* (Marina del Rey: DeVorss & Company), 11.
28. Job 3:25.
29. Matt. 5:44.
30. Three Initiates, *The Kybalion: A Study of the Hermetic Philosophy of Ancient Egypt and Greece* (Chicago: Yogic Publication Society, 1912),39.
31. Ibid., 113.
32. Steven J. Rosen, *Sri Panca Tattva. The Five Features of God* (New York: Brhat Mrdanga Press, 1994), 7-8.
33. Merlin Stone, *When God Was a Woman*, (San Diego: Harvest/HBJ, c1976),32-48.
34. Matt. 5:44.
35. The Institute of Noetic Sciences, *The Heart of Healing* (Atlanta: Turner Publishing, Inc., 1993), 14-16. Other examples are discussed elsewhere in the book and in *Spontaneous Remission–An Annotated Bibliography* published by the Institute of Noetic

Sciences.

36. Sheila Ostrander and Lynn Schroeder, *Psychic Discoveries Behlnd the Iron Curtain* (Englewood Cliffs, NJ: Prentice-Hall, 1970), 291.

37. Ibid.

38. Norman Kiell, *Freud Without Hindsight: Reuiews of His Work (1893-1939)*, with translation from the German by Vladimir Rus and the French by Denise Boneau (Madison, CT: International Universities Press, 1988) 200.

39. See Gerhard Wehr, *Jung: A Biography*, translated from the German by David M. Weeks (Boston: Shambhala Publications, 1987), 9-21.

40. Ibid., 68-75.

41. Ostrander and Schroeder, *Psychic Discoveries*, 77, 197, 210-211.

42. Ibid., 196-197.

43. Ibid., 198-209.

44. Carl Jung, *Memories, Dreams, Reflections*, (New York: Vintage Books,c1963),305.

45. Swami Prabhupada, *The Laws of Nature*. 28.

46. Swami Prabhupada, *Bhagavad-gita*, 15.15.

47. Childress, David H., *Vimana Aircraft of Ancient India and Atlantis*, (Stelle, IL: Adventures Unlimited Press, cl991).

48. George Gallup, Jr., *Adventures in Immortality*, (New York: McGraw-Hill Book Company, 1982), 135-139.

49. Richard L. Thompson, *Alien Identities: Ancient Insights into Modern UFO Phenomena* (San Diego: Govardhan Hill Publishing, 1993), 110.

50. Ibid, 38.

51. See *Alien Identities* above and Thomas C. Claire, *Occult/Paranormal Bibliography: An Annotated List of Books Published in English, 1976 through 1981* (Metuchen, NJ: Scarecrow Press, 1984).

52. Swami Prabhupada, *Srimad Bhagavatam*, 3.27.28-29 and 3.6.2.

53. For discussions on expansion of awareness via dreams, phenomenology of dreams and recent advances in psychophysiological theories of dreaming, see Ernest Lawrence Rossi, *Dreams and the Growth of Personality* (New York: Brunner/Mazel, 1985). For a ready reference for current developments and history as well as a

mechanistic approach to the dream state, see Fred Alan Wolf, *The Dreaming Universe: A Mind-Expanding Journey Into the Realm Where Psyche and Physics Meet* (New York: Simon & Schuster, 1994). For discussions on the history and significance of dreams and dream interpretation in religion or dream interpretation in anthropology, surrealism, neuroscience, analytical psychology, cognitive psychology, etc., see Kelly Bulkeley, *The Wilderness of Dreams: Exploring the Religious Meanings of Dreams in Modern Western Culture* (Albany: State University of New York Press, 1994). For sources specifically discussing the religious significance of dreams and dream interpretation, see Morton T. Kelsey, *God, Dreams, and Revelation: A Christian Interpretation of Dreams* (Minneapolis: Augsburg, 1991) and Monford Harris, *Studies in Jewish Dream Interpretation* (Northvale, NJ: Jason Aronson, 1994).

54. For an example of a spiritual dream from the Vedic tradition, see A.C. Bhaktivedanta Swami, "The Meeting of Usa and Aniruddha", in *Krsna, The Supreme Personality of Godhead*, vol. 2 (New York: Bhaktivedanta Book Trust, 1970).

55. Mark 11:23.

56. See Swami Prabhupada, *Srimad Bhagavatam*, 7.1.13-20 and 7.2.1-61.

57. See Michael Wessells, *Computer, Self, and Society* (Englewood Cliffs, NJ: Prentice Hall, 1990) and Marike Finlay, *Powermatics: A Discursive Critique of New Communications Technology* (New York: Routledge & Kegan Paul, 1987). For effect of automation on society, see Raymond Barglow, *The Crisis of the Self in the Age of Information: Computers, Dolphins, and Dreams* (New York: Routledge, 1994). For psychological effects of automation, see the view of cognitive scientists in Eric Dietrich, ed., *Thinking Computers and Virtual Persons: Essays on the Intentionality of Machines* (New York: Academic Press, 1994). See Steven R. Holtzman, *Digital Mantras* (Cambridge: MIT Press, 1994) for use of the computer in language, music, art, and virtual reality.

58. 1 John 2.15-17.

59. Milton C. Hallberg, Robert G.G. Spitze, and Daryll E. Ray, eds.,

Food, Agriculture, and Rural Policy Into the Twenty-First Century: Issues and Trade-Offs (San Francisco: Westview Press, 1994), 153.

60. See M.F.C. Bourdillion, *"Street Children in Harare"*, Africa 64, no. 4 (1994),516-532.

61. For a detailed discussion, see A.C. Bhaktivedanta Swami Prabhupada, *The Hare Krsna Challenge: Exposing a Misdirected Civilization* (Bombay: Bhaktivedanta Book Trust, 1990).

62. Young Back Choi, *Paradigms and Conventions: Uncertainty, Decision Making and Entrepreneurship* (Ann Arbor: The University of Michigan Press, 1993).

63. See A.C. Bhaktivedanta Swami Prabhupada, *The Science of Self Realization,* (Los Angeles: Bhaktivedanta Book Trust, 1980).

64. See Hedrick Smith, ed., *The Media and the Gulf War* (Washington, DC: Seven Locks Press, 1992) and Hamid Mowlana, George Gerbner & Herbert I. Schiller, eds., *Triumph of the Image: The Media's War in the Persian Gulf–A Global Perspective* (Boulder: Westview Press, 1992), 35.

65. Jim Oliver, *The Randy Weaver Case* (American Rifleman: Vol. 141 No.11),40-43.

66. Sigmund Freud, *Sexuality and the Psychology of Love* (New York: Macmillan Publishing Company, 1993).

67. Richard Dimbleby and Graeme Burton, *More than Words: An Introduction to Communication* (New York: Methuen, 1995), 91-201 and Marike Finlaay, *Powermatics,* 126.

68. Holly Idelson, *Plans to Expand Police Powers Following in Bombing's Wake* (Washington, DC: Congressional Quarterly April 29, 1995), 1177- 1180 and Jack Dawson, *We Will Never Forget: A Tribute to the Federal Employees of Oklahoma City* (Washington, DC: Federal Bar Association Vol. 42 No. 5, 1995), 26-31.

69. Swami Prabhupada, *Srimad Bhagavatam,* 3.26.15.

70. Swami Prabhupada, *Bhagavad Gita,* 12.13-14.

71. Alan Lakein, *How to Get Control of Your Time and Your Life,* (New York: Penguin Books, 1973), 158-160.

72. "If all items are arranged in order of value, 80 percent of the value would come from only 20 percent of the items, while the remaining

20 percent of the value would come from 80 percent of the items."
    Ibid.,71.

73. Milsum, John H., *Health, Stress and Illness: A Systems
    Approach,*(NewYork: Praeger, c1984), vii.

74. Gwendolyn Puryear Keita and Joseph J. Hurrell, Jr., eds.,
    *Introduction to Job Stress in a Changing Workforce: Investigating
    Gender, Diversity and Family Issues,* (Washington, DC: American
    Psychological Association, 1994), xiii.

75. *"Medical-Surgical Psychiatry: Treating Psychiatric Aspects of
    Physical Disorders,* " Troy L. Thompson II, ed., Series: *New
    Directions for Mental Health Services,* H. Richard Lamb, ed., (San
    Francisco: Jossey-Bass Publishers), Number 57, Spring 1993.

76. Sheldon Cohen, Ronald C. Kessler, and Lynn Underwood Gordon,
    eds, *Preface to Measuring Stress: A Guide for Health and Social
    Scientists,* (New York: Oxford University Press, 1995), 15,129.

77. *WHO Expert Committee on Rehabilitation after Cardiovascular
    Diseases with Special Emphasis on Developing Countries,* (WHO
    Technical Report Series: 831), 1.

78. Wolff, Harold G., *Stress and Disease,* 2nd ed. Revised and edited by
    Stewart Wolf and Helen Goodell (Springfield, IL: Charles C.
    Thomas, 1968), 209-213.

79. Cary L. Cooper, *Executive Families Under Stress: How Male and
    Female Managers Can Keep Their Pressures Out of Their Homes,*
    (Englewood Cliffs, NJ: Prentice-Hall, Inc., 1981), 155.

80. See, for example, Ben C. Fletcher, *Work, Stress, Disease and Life
    Expectancy,* (New York: John Wiley & Sons, 1991).

81. For further information, see Mark S. Schwart, *Biofeedback: A
    Practitioner's Guide,* 2nd ed., (New York, The Guilford Press, c1995).

82. Dr. Herbert Benson, *The Relaxation Response,* (New York: Avon
    Books, 1976), 27.

83. Ibid., 141-155.

84. Ronald Kotulak, "'Doom Clock' Moved Back 4 Minutes," (*Chicago
    Tribune,* March 7, 1990) 1,6:6 and Steve Johnson, "Doomsday
    Clock Ticks Backward Thanks to Peacetime," (*Chicago Tribune,*

November 27,1991) 2C, 1:2.

85. Edward Zuckerman, *The Day After World War III*, (New York: Viking Press, 1984).

86. Malcolm Booker, *Nuclear War: Present and Future Dangers*, (Sydney: Left Book Club Cooperative, Ltd., 1993).

87. Amy E. Smithson, "Dateline Washington: Clinton Fumbles the CWC [Chemical Weapons Convention]," (*Foreign Policy*, Summer 1995, no.99), 168-182.

88. Robert Wright, "Be Very Afraid: Nukes, Nerve Gas and Anthrax Spores," (*The New Republic*, May 1, 1995, vol. 212, no.18), 19.

89. Alvin and Heidi Toffler, *War & Anti-War: Survival at the Dawn of the 21st Century*, (Boston: Little, Brown & Co., 1993), 13-14.

90. Jack Kidd, *The Strategic Cooperation Initiative or the Star Light Strategy*, (Charlottesville, VA: Three Presidents Publishing Company, 1988), 4-5, 106.

91. Doug Henwood, *The State of the U.S.A. Atlas: The Changing Face of American Life in Maps and Graphics*, (New York: Simon & Schuster, Inc., 1994), 68.

92. Ibid., 69.

93. Ibid.

94. Ibid., 68.

95. Swami Prabhupada, *Bhagavad-gita*, 3.21.

96. Tina Rosenberg, "Overcoming the Legacies of Dictatorship" (*Foreign Affairs*, May-June1995, vol.74, no.3),134ff.

97. Helen Fein, ed., *Genocide Watch*, (New York: Yale University Press, 1992), 32-37.

98. Tzvetan Todorov, *The Conquest of America: The Question of the Other*, (New York: Harper and Row, 1984).

99. Paul Elkins, Mayer Hillman and Robert Hutchison, eds., *The Gaia Atlas of Green Economics*, (New York: Anchor Books, 1992), 156.

100. Mary H. Cooper, "Arms Sales: Should the U.S. Cut its Weapons Exports?", (*CQ Researcher*, December 9,1994, vol. 4, no. 46), 1083ff.

101. David Corn and Jefferson Morley, "Up in Arms. (Global Military Spending)," (*The Nation*, January 30, 1988, vol.246, no.4), 114.

102. John W. Wright, ed., *The Universal Almanac*, (Kansas City: Andrews and McHeel, 1994), 311.

103. Robert Famighetti et al., eds., *The World Almanac & Book of Facts 1995*, (Mahwah, NJ: World Almanac Books, Funk & Wagnalls Corporation, 1994).

104. Jon Naar, *Design for a Livable Planet*, (New York: Harper & Row, Publishers, 1990), 10.

105. Famighetti, et al., *World Almanac*, 310, 312.

106. Gil G. Noam and Sophie Borst, "Children, Youth, and Suicide: Developmental Perspectives," in *New Directions for Child Development* (San Francisco: Jossey Bass Publishers, Summer 1994), 8.

107. See Famighetti, et al., *World Almanac*, 53, and *Statistical Abstract of the United States: 1994* (Washington, DC: Government Printing Office, 1994), 138.

108. Linda Wolfe, *The Cosmo Report* (New York: Arbor House, 1981), 45, 272, 293.

109. Keita and Hurrell, *Job Stress in a Changing Workforce* (Washington, DC: American Psychological Association, 1994), xiii.

110. Richard Douthwaite, "The Growth Illusion," in *Buying America Back*, eds. Jonathan Greenberg and William Kistler (Tulsa: Council Oak Books, 1992), 93.

111. O. W. Markley and Willis W. Harman, eds., *Changing Images of Man* (New York: Pergamon Press, 1982), 6.

112. Herman Kahn and Barry Bruce-Briggs, *Things To Come* (New York: Macmillan Company, 1972), 210.

113. Anthony J. McMichael, *Planetary Overload: Global Environment Change and the Health of the Human Species*, (Cambridge: Cambridge University Press, 1993), 217.

114. Ibid., 218.

115. Ibid., 219.

116. Ibid., 218-219.

117. See, for example, Frances Moore Lappé and Joseph Collins, *World Hunger: Twelve Myths* (New York: Grove Press, Inc., 1986), 13.

118. Ibid.
119. Terry O'Neill and Karin L. Swisher, eds., *Economics in America: Opposing Viewpoints*, (San Diego: Greenhaven Press, Inc., 1992), 98-99.
120. *The Higher Taste: A Guide to Gourmet Vegetarian Cooking and a Karma-Free Diet* (Los Angeles: Bhaktivedanta Book Trust, 1993), 14.
121. Aaron M. Altschul, *Proteins: Their Chemistry and Politics*, (New York: Basic Books, 1965), 264.
122. *The Higher Taste*, 19.
123. Ibid., 14.
124. Ibid., 19.
125. Ibid., 14.
126. Ibid., 2.
127. Ibid., 6.
128. Ibid., 4.
129. Ibid., 5.
130. Ibid., 5.
131. Ibid., 7.
132. Ibid., 7-8.
133. Ibid., 9.
134. Ibid., 31.
135. Ibid., 32.
136. Ibid., 44.
137. Ibid., 23.
138. Ibid., 27.
139. Ibid., 26.
140. John Robbins, *Diet for a New America* (Walpole, NH: Stillpoint Publishing, 1987), 137.
141. Ibid., 136.
142. Swami Prabhupada, *Bhagavad-gita*, 17.8-10.
143. Judith Mackay, *The State of Health Atlas* (New York: Simon & Schuster, 1993), 52.
144. Ibid., 112.
145. Wright, ed., *The Universal Almanac*, 382.

146. Ibid., 53.
147. Ibid., 112.
148. Mark A. Siegel, Nancy R. Jacobs, and Patricia von Brook, eds., *Abortion: An Eternal Social and Moral Issue* (Wylie, TX: Information Plus, 1990), 77.
149. Laurence H. Tribe, *Abortion: The Clash of Absolutes* (New York: W. W. Norton & Company, 1990), 56.
150. Wright, ed., *Universal Almanac*, 216.
151. Siegel, Jacobs, and von Brook, eds., *Abortion*, 58.
152. Tribe, *Abortion*, 55-71.
153 .Michael Wolff, Peter Rutten, and Albert F. Bayers III, *Where We Stand: Can America Make It in the Global Race for Wealth, Health, and Happiness?* (New York: Bantam Books, 1992), 233.
154. Viqi Wagner and Karin L. Swisher, *The Family in America* (San Diego: Greenhaven Press, Inc., 1992), 38.
155. Wolff, Rutten, and Bayers, *Where We Stand*, 237.
156. Ibid., 251-254.
157. U. S. Bureau of the Census, *Statistical Abstract of the United States: 1993* (113th edition) (Washington, DC: Government Printing Office, 1993), 133.
158. Emilie Buchwald, Pamela R. Fletcher, and Martha Roth, eds., *Transforming a Rape Culture*, (Minneapolis: Milkweed Editions, 1993), 7-8.
159. Suzanne Somers, *Wednesday's Children: Adult Survivors of Abuse Speak Out* (New York: G. P. Putnam's Sons, 1992), 310.
160. Ed Magnuson, "Crawling with Bugs," (*Time*, April 20, 1987, vol. 129, no. 16), 14-18, 22-24.
161. Wilson Bryan Key, *Subliminal Seduction: Ad Media's Manipulation of a Not So Innocent America*, (Englewood Cliffs, NJ: Prentice-Hall, 1973).
162. Larry Collins, "Mind Control: The Top-Secret Weapons of the Future Are Here," (*Playboy*, January,1990, vol. 37, no. 1 (ASAP Online Research Service)), 158ff.
163. Sheila Ostrander and Lynn Schroeder, *Psychic Discoveries Behind the Iron Curtain*, (Englewood Cliffs, NJ: Prentice-Hall, 1970), 291.

164. Ibid., 43.

165. Ibid., 104-105.

166. Ibid., 109-110.

167. Ibid., 115.

168. Ibid.

169. Ibid., 390.

170. Robert O. Becker and Gary Selden, *The Body Electric: Electromagnetism and the Foundation of Life*, (New York: William Morrow, 1985), 323.

171. Editors of Time-Life Books, *The Psychics*, (Alexandria, VA: Time-Life Books, 1992), 74-94.

172. David B. Barrett, ed., *World Christian Encyclopedia: A Comparative Study of Churches and Religions in the Modern World AD 1900-2000*, (New York: Oxford University Press, 1982), 6.

173. Swami Prabhupada, *Bhagavad-gita*, 4.11.

174. Matt. 5.8.

175. Sehbanul Hind Hazrat Maulana Ahmed Saeed Dehlvi, *Hadees-E-Qudsi: Commands of Allah*, trans. Mohammed Hanif Khan, 3rd ed., (Delhi, India: Dini Book Depot, n.d.), 187-191.

176. *McGraw-Hill Encyclopedia of World Biography: An International Reference work in Twelve Volumes, Including an Index*, (New York: McGraw-Hill Book Co., 1973) s.v. "Zoraster", "Socrates", "Gautama Buddha", "Mohammed."

177. *The Encyclopedia Americana: International Edition: Complete in Thirty Volumes*, (Danbury CT: Grolier Incorporated, 1993), Vol. 3, pg. 696.

178. Duncan Howlett, *The Essenes and Christianity: An Interpretation of the Dead Sea Scrolls*, (New York, Harper & Brothers, 1957), 150-151. For a detailed discussion of the Sermon on the Mount, see Edmond Bordeaux Szekely, *The Essene Jesus: A Reevaluation from the Dead Sea Scrolls*, (n.p.: International Biogenic Society, 1977), 6-34.

179. John 14:12.

180. 1 John 4:16.

Index

About the Author

Swami Krishnapada was born John E. Favors in a Christian, God-fearing family. As a child evangelist he appeared regularly on television. As a young man he was a leader in Dr. Martin Luther King's civil rights movement. He became president of the student council group at Princeton University and was also chairman of the Third World Coalition. His main degree is in psychology; however, he has many accolades covering such fields as politics, African studies, and indology. He is also a scholar of International Law.

His Grace has held several governmental posts such as Assistant Coordinator for penal reform programs in the State of New Jersey, Office of the Public Defender. He has been the director of several drug abuse clinics in the U.S.A. and has served as a campaign manager for politicians.

Swami Krishnapada has been a special consultant for Educational Testing Services in the U.S.A. and gained international recognition as a representative of the Bhaktivedanta Book Trust, particularly for his outstanding work with the scholars of the then-communist countries.

He directly oversees projects in Washington, D.C., Detroit, and Pennsylvania (U.S.A.), West Africa, as well as South Africa. He is the director for the American Federation of Vaisnava Colleges and Schools, and His Grace is presently the only African-American Vaisnava Guru in the world.

In the United States, Swami Krishnapada is the founder-director of the Institute of Applied Spiritual Technology, director of the International Committee for Urban Spiritual Development, and one of the international co-ordinators of the 7th Pan African Congress. He is also a member of the Institute for Noetic Science, the Center for Defense Information, the

United Nations Association for America, the National Peace Institute Foundation, the Global Forum of Spiritual and Parliamentary Leaders on Human Survival and the World Future Society.

A specialist for international relations and conflict resolution, Swami Krishnapada constantly travels around the world and has become a spiritual consultant to many high ranking members of the United Nations, various celebrities, and several chiefs, kings and high court justices. In 1990 His Grace was coronated as a high chief in Warri, Nigeria in recognition of his outstanding work in Africa and the world. In 1994 and 1995, Swami Krishnapada met with President Mandela in South Africa where they shared their visions and strategies for world peace.

Along with encouraging the process of self-sufficiency through the development of schools, clinics, farm projects and cottage industries, His Grace finds time to conduct seminars on stress & time management, and other pertinent topics. He is also acknowledged as a valuable participant in the resolution of global conflict. His book *Leadership for an Age of Higher Consciousness: Administration from a Metaphysical Perspective* is a invaluable guide for those committed to transforming the world through their role as leaders.

ORDER FORM

Title	Price	QTY	Total
Leadership for an Age of Higher Consciousness: *Administration from a Metaphysical Perspective*	$23.00 + $5.00 s/h		
Spiritual Warrior: *Uncovering Spiritual Truths in Psychic Phenomena*	$12.95 + $3.00 s/h		
The Beggar: *Meditations and Prayers on the Supreme Lord*	$12.95 + $3.00 s/h		
Yearly Subscription to **Spiritual Warrior**: The *Quarterly Newsletter of the Institute for Applied Spiritual Technology*	$10.00		
	Subtotal:		
	MD Residents add 5% sales tax:		
(Please make checks payable to Hari-Nama Press)	**TOTAL:**		

☐ **Please send me a free catalog of books, audio and video tapes.**
☐ **Please add me to your mailing list.**

Name:
Address:
City, State, Zip:
Telephone *(Optional)*:

HARI-NAMA PRESS
P.O. Box 4133
Largo, MD 20775
Telephone/Facsimile:
(301) 390-0672